The Difference

ALSO BY JUDY MANN

*Mann for All Seasons: Wit and Wisdom from the
Washington Post's Judy Mann*

The Dífference

GROWING UP FEMALE IN AMERICA

JUDY MANN

WARNER BOOKS

A Time Warner Company

Warner Books, Inc., 1271 Avenue of the Americas, New York, NY 10020

W A Time Warner Company

Printed in the United States of America
First Printing: August 1994
10 9 8 7 6 5 4 3 2 1

Library of Congress Cataloging-in-Publication Data

Mann, Judy (Judy W.)
    The difference : growing up female in America / Judy Mann.
        p.   cm.
    Includes bibliographical references and index.
    ISBN 0-446-51707-0
    1. Girls—United States—Social conditions.   2. Teenage girls—
United States—Social conditions.   3. Feminism—United States.
I. Title
HQ798.M434   1994
305.42'0973—dc20   94-5191
                                                               CIP

Book design by Giorgetta Bell McRee

For my husband, Richard T. Starnes, and my sons, Devin Mann and Jeffrey Mann—who understand that true joy is found in relationships based on equality.

My daughter, Katherine Mann, inspired this book. She traveled with me on a journey of discovery, and she let me travel with her as she entered the dangerous years of adolescence. Katherine—with love, admiration, and profound gratitude for who you are, in a very special way this book is for you. Stay strong. Stay proud to be a woman.

CONTENTS

E.T. was dying and the audience sat in heartbroken silence.
Suddenly an anguished wail filled the theater.
It was Katherine.
She was three years old.
It was "the difference."

PREFACE

One day when I was having my hair cut, I looked into the mirror and saw, across the room, a hairdresser showing a mother how to braid her little girl's hair. The child hardly moved, but when she did, one of the women would remind her to be still.

By then, I was well along in my research for this book. I understood I was watching a lesson in enforced femininity. At the end of the session, the child looked exhausted and pained from the hair pulling. Her mother coaxed her into thanking the hairdresser, and it seemed a cruelty. I was looking into their family mirror and seeing yet another girl being bound to ancient beauty rituals that defined her value. The braids became a metaphor for binding her to old roles and passive behavior, to learning to wait. Once I might have shared in her mother's delight as she left with her perfectly coiffed child. But I felt sadness, for I knew that she had already been turned into a good little girl. She was only five years old.

Several months later, I was writing at the table in the kitchen of a farmhouse we own in the Shenandoah Valley. Mike, one of our neighbors, was talking with my husband. Mike's idea of heaven would be to have his son play professional baseball. I listened to him describe how he talked to his son when they watch a game together on television. When a superstar makes a mistake during a game, Mike uses it as a teaching moment for his son. "See," he says, "he's making about four million bucks a year. He made a mistake and his tongue isn't dragging the ground. Brooks Robinson was one of the greatest gloves the game ever knew and he once made four errors in one inning. It's over, it's gone, it's history. You get ready for the next ball. Every time you take the field, you say to yourself, 'I'm going to handle every chance that comes my way, and if I make an error, then I'll say I'm only going to make one error this game.' If you make a home run you come into the dugout and you celebrate for thirty seconds, and then that's over and you forget about that, too. This game will humble you in a heartbeat."

Mike went on to tell of a Little League game the night before when the coach, whose name was Richy, was riding a twelve-year-old named Chris who had caught a line drive and then dropped the ball. "The manager was bitching about the error. The kid got tears in his eyes. I went over and said, 'Chris, that ball was curving away from you,' and he said, 'Yeah.' I explained to him when you get a ball hit to right field, a line drive hit off a right-handed batter, the ball will tend to curve away from you toward the foul line, so when it hits the glove with all that spin, the ball wants to pop out because it's spinning. I said, 'Is that what happened?' And he said, 'Yeah.' I said, 'Don't worry about it, pal, 'cause it's happened to me a dozen times and I've seen it happen to a lot of other guys.' I patted him and said, 'Get 'em next time.' Then I went and got Richy, and I said, 'Chris is sitting over there with tears in his eyes. Those boys don't come out to be treated like that. If I hear any more talk about that error I'm going to kick your ass.'"

I loved that story, for I knew it was a story about boys learning to take risks, being comfortable with talk about velocity and angles, learning to shrug off error and persevere. It was a story of a grown man giving his son and other boys the best of what sports can offer. Yet, here too, the father was mirroring his life and his attitudes onto his son, giving him the skills he thinks are necessary for a boy to become a man.

These stories about braids and baseball go to the heart of what this book is about: the difference between how girls and boys are brought up in America. I have spent more than two years trying to learn the truth about this, to get beyond the politics of gender to what actually happens to girls that makes their experience so disastrously different from that of boys.

I undertook this quest when my own daughter was eleven and I realized that I did not know what I could do to make her adolescence less painful for her than adolescence was for me and for most other women I have known. We used to say that age is a radicalizing experience for women. So is having a daughter. My quest has been more personal than anything I've ever done. I now know that there are ways that adult women and men—fathers, mothers, teachers, and others who guide young people—can help girls remain strong and powerful. In the course of my research, I interviewed more than 200 people, ranging from parents and children to educators, teachers, and preeminent authorities in such fields as psychology, religion, anthropology, archaeology, education, human development, economics, biology, and gender. I began most of my interviews by explaining that I was trying to write a book for parents, so that they could gain access to the information that the experts have generated. The response of my interview subjects was invariably enthusiastic. Many understood that while their research has had an impact on their own field, it has not spread even to other academic research into gender and human behavior. Some of this is due to the nature of scholarship: Researchers speak in their own, often unfathomable, jargon. They publish in academic journals, not in the popular press.

I especially appreciate the help I received from Dr. Anne Petersen, vice president of the University of Minnesota, Judy Touchton and Donna Shavlik of the American Council on Education, Marsha Lakes Matyas of the American Society for the Advancement of Science, Leslie Wolfe and Bernice R. Sandler of the Center for Women Policy Studies, archaeologists and authors Michael and Kathleen Gear, Mary Hunt, director of the Women's Alliance for Theology, Ethics and Ritual,

Carol Hollenshead and Eleanor Linn and their colleagues at the University of Michigan's Center for the Education of Women and Center for Sex Equity in Schools, and June Million of the National Association of Elementary School Principals. I encountered a spirit of generosity with their time and their expertise that convinced me that they, too, felt it was necessary to create a bridge between the academic world and the world in which parents are trying to raise a generation of boys and girls that will get along better as adults than we have in the past. I hope this book will serve as that bridge.

I am also grateful to the parents, friends, young people, and children who shared their thoughts and provided so many of the anecdotal insights that ground research in reality. A very special thanks goes to my daughter, Katherine, and her friends, especially Julia and Jenny, who trusted me enough to speak candidly about what it is like to be an adolescent girl today. These are three terrific young women. I hope this book will help keep them that way.

It would have been impossible to write this book without the intellectual and emotional support and encouragement of my sons, Devin and Jeffrey, who have generously allowed me to write about their experiences growing up male in America. Their thoughts and adventures, the thousands of hours we have spent on various sports activities, the conversations we have had over more than two decades, have informed the content of this book beyond measure. I hope it will make some contribution to creating a culture that is kinder for boys and men—for the sons we treasure as much as our daughters.

I owe special thanks to Elisabeth Griffith, headmistress of the Madeira School, who not only permitted me access to the school and its faculty and students, but was generous enough to turn over to me her voluminous files on gender research and single-sex education. Jean S. Symmes, founder of Psychoeducational Resources in McLean, Virginia, made critically important suggestions that shaped the scope of this work and its outcome. She, too, lent me research papers from her files and books. Sara Fitzgerald, my editor at the *Washington Post* while I wrote this book, was supportive throughout this process. I am deeply grateful to Dr. Deborah Tannen, author of *You Just Don't Understand*, for her encouragement at the outset. Beyond moral and intellectual support, she introduced me to her agent, Suzanne Gluck of International Creative Management, who not only represented this book but helped chisel and focus the initial proposal and has provided editorial advice and inspiration along the whole way. Jamie Raab, my editor, has the priceless ability to tell a writer specifically what needs to be done. "Be ruthless," was her motto when it came to crystallizing huge amounts of research into digestible portions. If readers are satisfied, much of the credit goes to her determination to give them a book that will enlighten, and not overwhelm.

Finally my deepest gratitude goes to my husband, Richard T. Starnes, who was ruthless when I could not be. He read and reread the manuscript in all of its stages. More than anyone, he protected the reader from the unforgivable, impenetrable academic jargon that has done so much to keep the information in this book a closely held secret. He took over the cooking and marketing in our household so I could write. He gave two years of our life to this book because he believed in it, too. And that I will never forget.

The Difference

PART ONE

The Early Years

CHAPTER ONE

It's a Girl

I thought I knew all there was to know about babies.

I had been through the mother mill twice. I had two sons, one thirteen and one three years old, and I was living in a warm, fuzzy pink cloud where I believed the little week-old bundle who was nursing in my arms would be a pure, unalloyed pleasure.

Then she bit me.

It hurt. I yelped, "Ouch," and added, only slightly less loudly, "Don't do that." At that point, my week-old baby released her hold on my nipple and opened her mouth to begin what would become one of the longest and most heartbroken—and heartbreaking—wails I had ever heard. Tears poured out of her eyes and down her cheeks. Her hands shook and trembled and clenched themselves into tight little fists that she alternately held close to her chest and thrust against her cheeks. I tried to soothe her and quiet her down, but she was inconsolable. She wept for perhaps ten minutes. At first I thought the loudness of my outcry had frightened her. I had reacted to the bite without thinking, having been quite unprepared for the painful moment. But as I listened to her cry and tried vainly to get her to stop, I understood that what I was listening to was not fear. I had hurt my daughter's feelings and she promptly fell apart on me.

I knew a good bit about babies by then. I knew how to take care of children who had been injured. I knew the signs of concussion to watch for when a child had bumped his head. I knew when to take temperatures, when to call doctors in the middle of the night, and when to wait until morning. But nothing had prepared me for the nine pounds of raw anguish and despair that I was holding in my arms.

I had been nursing her on my bed, holding her in my arms with my back propped up against a pillow. Finally I got up and, cradling her against my shoulder, began walking around the room, singing to her. After what seemed forever, the wails subsided into gasps and then sniffs, then a couple more gasps and, at last, a deep sigh. By the time the episode ended, I was also in tears, and the two of us were quite a mess. It was an event that I never forgot. It affected me on the deepest levels of motherhood—I was now the mother of a girl—and thus it had profound effects on my daughter.

I understood right then that she was different from my two sons. She had depths of sensitivity that I had never seen in the boys. She could also express it, as she had just demonstrated. And the feeling of hurt, of being corrected loudly, the anguish of feeling emotionally disconnected from me was a feeling that I intuitively understood, which is why I ended up in tears, too. We had been experiencing the physical and emotional closeness that comes with nursing, one of the simplest but most satisfying forms of nurturing. Then, suddenly, we were literally broken apart by my pained and angry reaction. She was disconnected from me—and completely devastated. I had never seen anything like it.

This wasn't the only time that Katherine displayed her sensitivity in the first two or three years of her life. Urged on by two brothers, she learned to talk early. I remember several episodes that occurred after she learned to make sentences. In the first incident, I saw her reach for a cheese knife that had been left on a cocktail table. I was on the other side of the room, too far away to grab it before she did. "Don't touch that knife," I called out sharply. That triggered another uncontrollable deluge that echoed all the notes of the first freshet of despairing tears I had witnessed. I gathered her up in my arms and tried to tell her that I wasn't mad at her, that I did not want her to hurt herself. When she stopped wailing and sobbing long enough to blurt out her words, this is what she said: "But you hurt my feelings."

Katherine remembers to this day the time that she knocked her Smurf glass off the kitchen table and it ended up shattered on the floor. She started to climb down from her high chair to retrieve the wreckage. Again: "Don't touch that!" I called out from the sink across the room. She was already on edge because a treasured glass was demolished, and afraid she might get in trouble for making a mess. My sharp comment pushed her over the brink again, and the torrents let loose. When her weeping subsided enough for me to get through to her, I explained that I was afraid she would cut herself on the broken glass. She said: "You can put a Band-Aid on a cut. But you can't put a Band-Aid on hurt feelings." At three and a half years of age, that was a sophisticated and, yes, sensitive insight.

Katherine stamped her style on the family, just as every other member of the mix did. And we learned to respect it. By the time her older brother was sixteen he had taken on something of an avuncular role and had learned that a particularly loud or harsh comment to her always produced an emotional typhoon. There was Katherine and there were her feelings, and woe unto anyone who messed with them. They would end up feeling like the family villain. Sometimes her older brother would tease her about it: "Oh, we've got to be careful not to hurt Katherine's feelings!" She delighted in the attention, but this banter was doing two things: It made him highly conscious of this aspect of a girl's personality, and it underscored to her the validity of her reactions. Neither of the boys had ever spoken of having hurt feelings as toddlers. If they understood that they had hurt feelings, and surely they must have had them on occasion, they did not express them. Sons are different from daughters.

IS THERE A DOLL IN HER BRAIN?

Are girls born with some mysterious female sensitivity as part of their original equipment? If so, where does it come from? Is it a function of hormones and brain chemistry? Is it genetically encoded? Or is it imprinted in a much more subtle way, in some subliminal communication link between mother and daughter?

We live in a culture where the belief is widespread that there is a highly prized "math gene" that shows up in disproportionately high numbers of boys. There is no evidence that any such gene exists, of course. But as readily as we assume that boys are better in math than girls, we also assume that girls are more sensitive than boys. This assumption undergirds some of our most basic precepts about femininity. It colors our perceptions of girls and women throughout their lives. It tells us how to treat them. One must also wonder why there isn't some reciprocal mythology about the "sensitivity gene"? Is it because sensitivity is not valued enough to be worthy of its own gene? Or can it be because the men who dominate the scientific establishment in Western cultures suspect that sensitivity might indeed be a worthy quality, but fear that if they raise it to the level of a sex-linked characteristic that shows up disproportionately among women, they might diminish themselves? Would a male-dominated scientific machine feel comfortable in acknowledging that the males of the species do not enjoy the benefits of this highly prized quality known as sensitivity?

Science has found no evidence that girls receive some hormonal ration of sensitivity in utero, or that they come equipped with a gene that makes them sensitive, warm, caring people who prize relationships and closeness from the moment they are born. Yet if you talk to parents who have had both boys and girls, or if you listen to conversations between mothers of girls and mothers of boys, the conversation quickly turns to a perennial favorite: "the difference."

Clearly the difference between boys and girls reaches beyond obvious physical characteristics, and one wonders why the question has been so studiously ignored. That question is what this book is all about. It has led me on a two-year expedition that has taken me from the dim beginnings of the Paleolithic cultures that existed 20,000 years ago in Europe to the trendiest new thinking in gender and genetic research. It has been a fascinating quest, yielding answers to a question that is critically important to anyone raising children in America today.

"YOU WOMEN WANT TO BE LIKE MEN"

In the early decades of the modern feminist movement, discussions about "the difference" were deemed politically incorrect. The obvious reality that girls and boys behave differently had to be dealt with, of course, so it was taken hostage by those early feminists and stuffed into the closet in the national psyche where we keep troublesome realities that are seasonally out of fashion.

It was a natural enough reaction: A quarter of a century ago, mainstream feminism was advancing the politically correct proposition that men and women should strive to be equal partners politically and economically, as well as equal partners in their homes. The feminists who cherished that vision of equality were greeted by the entrenched establishment with all the venom that has greeted heretics since the beginning of time. Established institutions in Western culture reacted to what they deemed a major power grab by using an old and effective political weapon: the big lie. Distort what your opponent is saying, keep hammering away, and eventually people will believe you. In the United States, as well as Europe and Australia, hostile interests ranging from political parties and religions to the media distorted feminist militancy. Feminists, they claimed, wanted to be like men. The innocent terms "same" and "equal" were shamelessly corrupted. Women's struggle for equality was twisted into the proposition that women really wanted was to be "the same as men." This tortured, self-serving line was a direct descendant of the hoary Freudian dictum that penis envy seizes the female psyche around the age of three and never lets go.

The staying power of this anti-feminist big lie has been formidable. As recently as March 5, 1993, in a heated confrontation outside a Melbourne, Florida, abortion clinic, Operation Rescue leader Randall Terry shouted at Eleanor Smeal, head of the Fund for the Feminist Majority, that she was "going to burn in hell." Then, if that were not enough, he reached back for the long ball that is supposed to knock feminists out of the box. "Two, four, six, eight, ten," he started chanting, "Why do you women want to be men?"

The repercussions of this campaign of distortion have been profound and enduring. Feminists' perceptions of their children were at odds with the phony "same" argument. Some little girls were aggressive, but many more little boys were. Some little girls were adventurous crawlers, but boys were infinitely more so. And there seemed to be no getting around the fact that little girls spend more time playing with dolls than with footballs. You could buy every "unisex" toy stocked by Toys 'R' Us and come home with products that your toddler would pick up only once. We had a plastic lawn mower that my younger son loved to push around the backyard when he was three and four years old. We passed it down to my daughter when she was about three. She lost interest in lawn mowing at three as decisively as her older brothers did at thirteen. "Unisex" child rearing got to be very baffling, because we were attempting to ignore the obvious, trying to drive our own politically incorrect—but factually accurate—observations underground.

PLANES OF EQUALITY

The climate has changed. One of the most influential thinkers to emerge in the 1980s was Carol Gilligan, a psychologist and professor of education at Harvard University, who has spent much of her career examining the human development of girls and women. Her book, *In a Different Voice*, published in 1982, has had a profound impact on feminist thinking about everything from how we learn to how we set priorities in our daily lives. She argued that men and women do, indeed, think and operate differently, and that we reach moral and ethical decisions within two entirely different frameworks about what we believe to be important and what we believe to be right and wrong.

Nearly a decade later, another highly influential thinker from the unlikely field of linguistics emerged to argue that men and women are raised in two different cultures and, as a result, communicate in two very different styles. Deborah Tannen's best-selling book, *You Just Don't Understand*, examined one of our most important social activities—conversation—and found that men and women do, indeed, talk very differently, that we use conversation to different ends, and that these differences in styles can lead to terrible misunderstandings between men and women at home and at work.

Gilligan and Tannen work in very different disciplines and each has developed her own world-class body of research. They don't claim that the male hierarchical style is better or worse than the female style, which is more focused on connections. But they do say women are different in the way they operate, and with this reasoning they have struck a mighty blow. They have elevated the female style to a plane that is equal to the male style.

Being "the same as men" is not what we want.

We want our differences to be recognized as one of equal worth. We want to be weighed on honest scales.

We want to contend on that most cherished of masculine metaphors—a level playing field.

What they, as well as others of somewhat lesser celebrity, have done is to make it possible for us once again to talk about the obvious: Of course boys and girls are different, and no rational person wants them to be the "same." Vive la difference—but this time around we aren't going to settle for putting girls on pedestals. That's a grand, sentimental phrase, a chivalrous image that masks its true sexual perfidy, which is to isolate women, weaken them, and render them powerless.

It is possible that we are inching toward a period of detente in the gender wars. Perhaps common sense and a yearning for genuine progress in the relationships between men and women will prevail. But before this can occur, we must acknowledge the differences that do exist and understand how they develop. We must discard dogma about what is the "right" role of men and women, and replace it with a rational understanding of what it means to be a female and a male in our culture.

SEARCHING FOR ANSWERS

Millions of parents can't be wrong. So, as a practicing feminist and the mother of a daughter profoundly different from her brothers, I set out to find answers to some of these questions: Is sensitivity unique to girls? Do more girls than boys have it? Do boys have it at all? Do we reinforce it in girls by acculturation and myriad devices of gender socialization? Are those same techniques used to suppress sensitivity in boys?

Are boys and girls different because of biological forces rooted in tens of thousands of years of evolution? Or are they more similar to each other than we think, and have they, in fact, been separated by artificial and destructive ideas? Is it possible that these constructions have no basis in biology but are wholly grounded in our culture? Is our culture placing infants in boxes stamped "boys" and "girls" and then sealing them up, shipping them off into lives with no wiggle room, no chance to break out of the confines of gender that hamstring them physically, emotionally, and psychologically?

How does it happen? How are these lessons taught, by whom, and by what techniques—and why, after three decades of feminist fulmination, has so little changed? Yes, we can point to isolated victories. Some husbands change some diapers and some women become astronauts. But we can also point to the fact that one out of every six American women can expect to be raped in her lifetime. Rape is the ultimate form of male domination, but its genetic tags are evident from elementary school days on. Starting in kindergarten, girls are sexually harassed by males seeking to put females down, keep them in their place, restrict their movements and their aspirations. Bernice Resnick Sandler, a pioneering researcher on acquaintance rape, has found that 70 to 90 percent of women students at the college level have experienced some form of harassment from male students. It is one of the techniques used to keep girls in their place. It is one of the answers to the central question that launched this book: What do we do when we raise boys and girls that makes girls come out feeling second best? What do we do as a culture that leads to the Tailhook scandal, in which twenty-six women, including fourteen officers, were sexually assaulted by hundreds of drunken Navy aviators during a convention at a Las Vegas hotel? The Navy was tarnished by the failure of the old boy admirals to prosecute the guilty Top Guns. Once again, a respected and honored American institution paid a huge price for living in a culture that allows the systematic debasement of women.

WHAT HAPPENS TO GIRLS

If you look at the development of girls and women within a hierarchical power structure, what seems to happen to girls is this: They start full of enthusiasm, ready to climb. They start, as a matter of fact, with measurably more enthusiasm and aptitude than do little boys. They have a developmental edge over boys from birth, and they score higher on standardized tests at the beginning of their education than boys do. They are generally more mature and readier to learn. But then something happens. When they leave high school, their scores on standardized tests are lower than boys'. Their loss of self-esteem is far more profound than boys'. They are convinced that they have far fewer options about what they can do in life than boys feel they have. Somewhere along the trip up the ladder to adulthood, girls get their fingers stepped on and they quit climbing. Twenty-five years into the modern women's movement, our daughters are still getting shunted aside.

Where do they get derailed? How does it happen? What is going on in the development of our daughters that is dooming them to live the same scenarios we thought we had fought our way free of?

Where did we fall short? And more important, what do we need to do to secure the progress women have made, to make it a permanent building block, so that the struggle of our generation does not have to be repeated again and again by our daughters and granddaughters. Our daughters have more options than we had, and they are coming of age with better and more varied role models than we had. But these are footnotes in the travel guide they need. They are still coming of age in a foreign country, where the customs and currency are male. Males still map the terrain, and young women have to figure it out. The signals mothers try to send their daughters about the options they must demand are undermined by the subtle and not so subtle signals they get from school, from rock music, from traditional religions, from the books they read, the movies they see, the television programming they watch, and the political dialogue they hear.

In recent years, much of the anti-feminist drumbeat has been the attempt to regulate women's reproductive freedom. What are the anti-abortionists telling an eleven-year-old girl about her right to run her own life? A whole generation of girls has grown up listening to men debate abortion: It is a debate in which men are desperately fighting to maintain control over women. The hierarchies of the Catholic and Mormon churches made common cause with the fundamentalist Christians in a crusade to keep women in check, to protect the traditional place of males as heads of families. The impact of monotheistic religions that put a male god at the center of spiritual power, the role these religions have played in crippling women and girls, was one of the most disturbing revelations I had while researching this book. I am now convinced that women will never achieve equal standing in their cultures until they reform these spiritual enablers of male domination. Religions define cultures. Women and children must, therefore, be able to lay claim to a spiritual footing within the religions that is as empowering to them as it is to men. This has been the most overlooked area in women's efforts to achieve equality. It was probably the most important, for had we challenged these institutions more effectively, we would have struck at the heart and soul of the forces that sanctify the rule of men.

We have known for more than a decade that gender bias is rife in America's classrooms and that it has a damaging effect on girls. We know that boys interrupt and command the attention of teachers while girls raise their hands politely and wait—often in vain—to be called upon. Experts are now referring to this phenomenon as "air time." Day after day in classrooms all across the country, year after year after year, boys get substantially more air time than girls do, and millions of girls are left to feel muted, invisible, and less important.

Somewhere in adolescence, our daughters are silenced. They are overwhelmed and submerged, just as we were. They become uncomplaining and compliant. They learn to wait. Carol Gilligan and her associates describe how girls drive their perceptions of reality underground. The work of these researchers evokes a powerful image of a turbulent subterranean river in women's psyches while their surface behavior adapts to the social imperatives to "be nice" and not to be "rude" or "disruptive." Excerpts from interviews with girls that Gilligan and coauthor Lyn Mikel Brown included in *Meeting at the Crossroads* are heartbreaking. Gilligan's research at the Harvard Graduate School of Education provides compelling insights into the psychological assaults that end up crippling girls and women. But there is much that happens to girls and boys that biologists, psychologists, and other social scientists, as well as parents, educators, and children themselves do not understand. There are many cultural cripplers of girls and enablers of boys that remain to be dragged into the light and destroyed.

CULTURE OF VIOLENCE

All-pervasive cultural influences such as rap music trash women and celebrate male dominance over them. But how many adult women have listened to this music and found out what our daughters and sons are listening to? How many of us have had the energy at the end of a working day to vet the musical tastes of children? I am speaking of both boys and girls here for a very good reason: The recurring themes of violence against women in this music send a destructive message of permission to boys as well as a message of submission to girls. Consider the lyric from the rock group Guns 'N Roses in which they sing of murdering a former lover and then burying her in the backyard so they will not miss her. Should anyone be shocked that a fourteen-year-old boy who listens to sadistic lyrics about women turns into a fraternity house gang-bang rapist a few years later?

Violent themes against women are a Hollywood staple. Violence against women is the norm on many television shows and rental videos. Our daughters and sons still come of age listening to an obbligato of primitive violence directed against women. Would we tolerate this kind of culturally sanctioned violence against African-Americans? Hispanics? Asians?

Teenage girls today are more confused about sexual mores than ever before. The United States has the highest rate of teenage pregnancy in the top ten industrialized nations. Over one million American girls become pregnant each year. Half have abortions and half have children out of wedlock.

Girls still measure self-esteem by popularity and their ability to please boys, not by their grades and their prospects for living self-sufficiently. Many parents are confused about what messages to give young women about their sexuality. While women suffer the consequences of unwanted pregnancies, we have not figured out how to give our daughters the emotional muscle to control the sexual agenda. Far from it. What we are discovering instead is that girls have much less control over their sexual lives than we realized. With horror, we are finding out that our friends, our neighbors, our co-workers, and, yes, some of our own children are victims of sexual abuse and incest. We are learning that the experience of growing up female in this culture is far more dangerous than we ever suspected. We understand that rape is a crime of power. We know that it is a sexual crime of power. We have no idea how to stop it.

There is much that remains to be done before women and girls can feel safe in our culture, before they can feel they are as valued and

valuable to the society as men are. The undermining of girls and the
false empowering of boys at the expense of girls begins at a much
earlier age than previously thought. The process is completed by the
time they reach adulthood. For girls, much of their early adult life is
one of recovery, of getting back on their feet, of trying to become
whole again, of becoming comfortable with who they are and with
learning how to excercise personal and political power. What would
happen to girls if they were not robbed of their "selves"? If they were
raised to be independent, self-sufficient women? What would happen
if boys were raised to respect girls as equals, to listen to their voices,
and to value them as friends? No patriarchal culture has ever tried to
do this. Leslie Wolfe, the executive director of the Center for Women
Policy Studies in Washington, D.C., who has spent twenty years
studying the effects of gender bias against girls, makes the point that
"we haven't tried an egalitarian, androgynous way of educating and
raising boys and girls. Until we try that, we won't be able to say what
are the differences that are immutable. You don't know the effect of
testosterone poisoning until you learn better ways of dealing with it."

BOYS AND GIRLS

One point is beyond question, yet it has been largely ignored by
the feminist movement, which has had its resources drained by the
assaults on abortion rights. The point is this: We will never effectively change the way we raise girls unless we also change the way
we raise boys, and we will never alter the outcome for most girls
until we change the way boys think of girls. We have to give girls
strategies for dealing with boys and boys strategies for dealing with
girls that are grounded in mutual respect, not fear of humiliation.
And we have to appreciate in much greater measure the qualities we
associate with girls—the sensitivity and the relational skills that bind
a society together—and begin to de-emphasize the qualities we associate with boys, such as aggressiveness and violence, qualities that

are currently consuming our society in bloodshed and tearing it apart. Until we do this, until we weigh boys and girls on an equal scale, generations of children will repeat the patterns of adversarial relations between the sexes—a pattern firmly rooted in an imbalance of power between the sexes, a pattern that has gone on so long that it has been called the longest war. Generations of girls will be knocked off the ladder and disabled, repeating the histories of their mothers. Generations will repeat our struggle for equality, until we truly find out what happens to girls. Then we need to implement the profound social changes that are still necessary so that girls can climb the ladder to adulthood without being dislodged, without being silenced and submerged into a male culture. This would be the lasting legacy of the women's movement.

For parents who want to see a treaty ending the longest war, who believe little girls and boys can be raised to be friends, for parents who share the vision that there can be a new covenant between the sexes, Leslie Wolfe offers an image that could be our vision quest: "Our daughters stand on our shoulders. And they get to see so much farther. They are going to see the promised land."

Whether they will ever reach it is another question.

CHAPTER TWO

The Difference

Boy. Girl. Each word has a history. What we don't understand very well is how that history affects our children, how deeply ingrained our own ideas of what is appropriate female and male behavior have become, and how we stamp those beliefs on our babies from the moment we learn their gender. How we nurture children is profoundly affected by our most deeply imbedded attitudes about what girls and boys are supposed to be.

The attitudes and behavior we see in adult men and women are rooted in infancy, not in college, adolescence, or childhood. They start at the very beginning. By the time they are six months old, we give cultural nudges and winks to boys that guide them into our perceptions of what is masculine. And most assuredly, our notion of the masculine mystique does not include little boys or grown men wailing about hurt feelings. Such emotional outbursts are unmanly; they are strictly reserved for females.

Looking back on it, I realize that my daughter had entered a largely masculine environment: two full-time brothers, three visiting half-brothers, a father—my former husband—who covered professional sports for a living. Sports, with all its masculine metaphors, was very much a part of the environment. To be sure, Katherine brought something special into the family: She was a feminine person, someone who was much more like me than the others, someone whose feelings were an overt part of her presence, feelings that had to be paid attention to. Hers was from the beginning a style that was distinct from the male style. She was like me. The boys were not. We shared an emotional base in the family ensemble. Feelings are fragile, and they can readily be reduced to grace notes in a masculine score. So I welcomed her femaleness, her femininity, and encouraged it. It was nice to have company.

What I did not realize at the time—and did not fully realize until I began researching this book—was how deeply, fully, and permanently I was imbedding and reinforcing what I believed to be appropriate and desirable behavior for a girl. Would I have responded to the wailing of hurt feelings from a male infant? Would I have interpreted the wail the same way, as an expression of sadness and hurt feelings? Or would I have interpreted the wail as one of anger or frustration?

All over the world the vast majority of couples want their firstborn to be a boy. In some cultures—including India, where girls are expected to bring dowries into their marriages, and China, which limits families to one child—abortion of female fetuses is an accepted method of insuring firstborn sons. This is nothing new: Demographers have concluded that the higher incidence of male births recorded in the Middle Ages was probably due to widely practiced female infanticide. Infanticide is still practiced in India today, with hundreds and perhaps thousands of infant girls being killed. On February 14, 1993, a front-page story in the *Washington Post* gave a chilling account of an Indian farm laborer who, with the help of her mother-in-law, mashed poisonous oleander seeds into oil and forced it down her newborn daughter's throat. Her excuse: "There was a lot of bitterness in my heart toward the baby because the gods should have given me a son."

The morning I left for the hospital to give birth, my two sons stood in the driveway of our home in McLean, Virginia, and wished me all sorts of good things, and promised to come to the hospital after school to see the baby. As I clambered into the car, the last thing I heard from them was: "Make sure it's a boy." Five hours later, the doctor announced: "You have a little girl."

My daughter.

My first female child.

Who are you?

So there she was, Katherine Margaretta, bundled up on my chest and I was holding her, all eight pounds and twelve ounces, with a very long name. A little girl. What did this mean? I was not disappointed that she was not a boy. I was surprised. What I did not know at the time was how much joy she would bring into my life. Looking back on it, I now realize that little girls are so overwhelmed in this male culture that the story of little girls' lives is whispered, while the story of little boys' lives is shouted in books, movies, cartoons, songs. There is no female parallel to Huck Finn. What is clear to me now is that we do not celebrate the wonderfulness of little girls nearly as much as we should. Had I known what a terrific experience was ahead for us I would have been whooping with joy, instead of feeling fuzzy-headed and wondering what I was supposed to do.

WINNERS AND WINNERS

Dr. James H. Humphrey, a professor emeritus at the University of Maryland who has written extensively on human behavior and especially on stress in children and adults, makes the point that we actually greet boy babies with considerably more fanfare than girls: "It's A BOY!!!" Whereas the female infant is likely to be greeted with "a more suppressed announcement: 'You have a little girl.' " And, he writes, "expectations are likely to be much loftier for males: 'maybe he will grow up to be president.' I have yet to hear this said of a baby girl."[1]

Professor Humphrey offers another thought, which he admits is "wild speculation." In athletic competitions, we reward victory with ribbons: The winner gets a blue ribbon, the runner-up a red, and the person who comes in third gets a white ribbon. Blue ribbons are for winners, red is for second best. We dress baby boys in blue and decorate their rooms with blue. We dress girls in pink and emphasize pink in their rooms. Linking these conventions together has set Professor Humphrey to wondering whether we "automatically declare boy babies winners over girl babies at the outset, by garbing them in blue and by placing girls somewhere between second and third place—pink being a combination of red and white?"

"HE" OR "SHE"?

Gender still dictates destiny in most cultures. "The first thing people ask is 'Is it a boy or a girl?' " says Dr. Patricia Ortman, who chairs the department of human development at Mount Vernon College in Washington, D.C. "Then they think they know something about the child's temperament or personality or future. They use that one piece of information to determine for a long time how they interact with that child and how they interpret the child's signals.

"The way parents name their children is gender-based," she continued. "There's an interesting trend toward naming girls with boys' names, but it hasn't gone the other way at all. It's always been okay for girls to exhibit what would be considered male characteristics. A girl who likes the outdoors and likes to play boys' sports when she's pre-pubescent is called a tomboy. It's humored. Whereas if a boy acts in the least feminine way, people get terribly upset and basically demand that he be different, immediately. . . . Little boys are supposed to be men right away and little girls are supposed to be little girls until they are thirty."

We label infants by gender and then interpret their behavior accordingly. Ortman cites studies that show how people interpret the cries of infants differently based on their sex. If they believe the baby is a girl, they interpret its cry to be one of sadness, as I did with Katherine.

If they think the baby is a boy, they interpret the same cry as one of anger. People expect children to have different characteristics, so they interpret their behavior to fit their expectations, says Ortman. "Then they respond to the child as if their expectations were the truth, therein creating those same expectations in the child. The child begins to modify his or her behavior accordingly."

STRONGER SEX/WEAKER SEX

In a classic study done by J. Z. Rubin, F. J. Provenzano, and Z. Luria that was published in the *American Journal of Orthopsychiatry* in 1974, fifteen pairs of parents with sons and fifteen pairs of parents with daughters were interviewed twenty-four hours after their babies were born. The babies were equivalent on such measures as length, weight, and robustness. Yet when parents were asked to rate their babies, it became clear that they had already developed gender biases. Parents of sons were more likely to describe them as big than were parents of daughters, and to describe their sons as large-featured and attentive. Parents of daughters were more likely to describe them as fine-featured, softer, more delicate. In this study, fathers were more likely than mothers to arrive at these gender-based distinctions—and again, these were firmly fixed in their minds twenty-four hours after the child's birth.[2]

Studies of how we select toys for infants show that this, too, is rooted in our perceptions of what we deem appropriate for boys and girls. Researchers L. S. Sidorowiz and G. S. Lunney asked a group of college students to play with an infant who was introduced as either Johnny or Jenny. Slightly out of reach of the infant were three toys: a little football, a doll, and a teething ring. The adults were far more likely to hand Johnny the football and Jenny the doll. What makes this important is that these are the toys that these children will spend time with and develop competency with.[3]

Few of us project toddlers' toys in terms of competence later on.

We don't fast-forward from the nursery floor into the geometry class-room. My daughter got exposed to Legos—and loved playing with them—basically because they were already in the house and her brother was willing to share them. At the time, I had no idea that manipula-tives, as Legos and similar toys are called, are widely believed by educational experts to be critically important to the development of spatial skills among children. I saw a payoff one day last winter when she was instructing me how to play the "Sonic" video game on Sega. I remarked on the fabulous designs and colors and the depth I saw on the screen. "It's nothing fancy," she said. "It's mostly your basic shapes of squares and triangles and circles." What caught my attention was not only the comfort she felt with shapes, but the fact that she was undaunted by these rapidly moving, complex images.

Numerous researchers have discovered that fathers are significantly more rigid in their beliefs about what are appropriate toys and appro-priate behavior than are mothers. Child-development researcher Bev-erly Fagot found boys got more positive responses than girls for playing with blocks, and girls got more negative responses than boys for manipulating objects. Parents were likely to encourage their daughters to play with dolls, and to discourage their sons. Fathers, in particular, promoted what they believed were sex-appropriate activities and toys.[4] Other studies have come to the same conclusions, finding that fathers tend to encourage girls to play with such feminine toys.

Sharp and important differences emerge in the physical play of fathers and sons, versus fathers and daughters. Fathers typically come home from work and scoop up their sons, toss them in the air, get down on the floor and roughhouse with them, hold them upside down, play with their arms and legs, and encourage adventure and exploration when the infant starts crawling. Their play with little girls is not nearly so rough: Instead of tossing them in the air, most fathers will gather them into their laps. A colleague of mine who was born in a culture that does not require ritual tossing of male infants into the air tells the story of her American brother-in-law, who arrived at their home for the baptism of his three-month-old nephew, my friend's son. The brother-in-law scooped up the unsuspecting baby and tossed him in the air. It was the first time anyone had ever done this to the child;

by the time he landed in his uncle's arms, the infant was wailing in terror. Studies have shown that we even hold our sons and daughters differently, with boys pointed outward and girls inward, facing their parents' bodies.

We are protective of little girls; we orient boys toward the world of adventure.

Another study found that at seven weeks, parents encouraged their daughters to smile and vocalize more than their sons, suggesting that the tendency of adult women to smile more than men—to be pleasant, to make the atmosphere around them pleasing—is one of the earliest lessons little girls are taught.[5]

THE MALLEABLE BRAIN

Anne Petersen, vice president for research and dean of the graduate school at the University of Minnesota, is convinced that these play patterns may actually affect how the brain develops. In an interview, she told me that old notions about brain development being fixed at birth are incorrect. Brain research, which is probably the most explosive area of current medical investigation, is yielding exciting information about ways that the brain remaps itself to compensate for loss of limbs and loss of certain faculties following accidents and strokes. "It looks like the brain is very malleable," Petersen told me. "One place we see the effects is in language development. It is much more difficult to learn language post-puberty than pre-puberty. There is a lot of evidence for experience influencing how the brain is wired. I remember when I used to run, I'd read these articles about developing tertiary blood systems. There is evidence that if you need a particular capacity, the brain develops in that direction."

She stressed that because something is biologically influenced, it does not mean it is biologically fixed. As an example, she used sports performances. "Strength is related to testosterone. But if women don't train, if they never lift a finger to do anything, they are not using the potential they have. That's influenced not by hormones, but whether or not they exercise. People are very fond of saying women can't do this or that because they are not wired that way. We have data that suggests spatial ability is influenced by playing soccer. Playing soccer could develop the brain in ways that would make better spatial ability possible. But if women don't play soccer at all, you couldn't even test that."

The sports records that women have broken during the past twenty years are both benchmarks of tremendous progress and a source of important lessons. One of the biggest lessons is that biology should not constrain women. Their explosive success in sports such as running and swimming, where speed and endurance are easily measured, is blowing apart the argument that women "can't do this or that," that it is biologically impossible.

I asked Petersen what we are born with that affects gender, and her answer was surprisingly clear-cut and simple. "Different reproductive organs," she said. "And that is really the most important factor. There are these other differences in things that support the reproductive system, but it really looks like this is less important than people thought initially." Here she is talking in part about the reproductive hormones and work she has done that suggests raging hormones have much less impact on adolescents' voyage through puberty than was previously thought.

I told her about my infant daughter's reaction to being yelled at. And she said the whole area of feelings, who has them, and where they come from is still a matter of controversy. "This is an example of an area where we create more differences than exist. It may be that girls are more likely to be emotional than boys. What we do is if a girl is not emotional, she's sort of helped in that direction. If a boy is too emotional, it gets suppressed."

My daughter, she suggested, would probably be more on the emotional end, even relative to other females. Petersen believes that females may indeed "be wired to have more social sensitivity." But she also points to the environmental imperatives that lead to a difference in the emotionality of men and women. "A man can get by without being socially or interpersonally sensitive. A woman who lacks that quality is in deep trouble. She is much less likely to have a normal life."

While we encourage sensitivity and emotion in girls, we limit and confine it when it shows up in boys. Weeping, a natural demonstration of such emotions as sadness, anger, and pain, is discouraged in boys. We think of weeping as a female display, and boys who weep are promptly labeled sissies. Fathers are particularly intolerant of such displays in their sons. Homophobia causes them to confuse crying and sensitivity with sexual preference.

While I felt free to encourage my infant daughter to weep over hurt feelings, and indeed probably gave her a vocabulary to express her feelings with, we do not as a culture encourage similar behavior in little boys. When we discourage the little boy from weeping too much when he falls off a bike, or from weeping with separation anxiety when we take him for the first day of preschool, we are silencing his emotions and depriving him of any way to express what he is feeling. He has no chance to practice the language of emotions. And, as Petersen points out, there are serious consequences. "We see men use violence when they can't communicate."

A TALE OF TWO MOTHERS

On November 21, 1991, Cynthia Peters, an editor at the progressive South End Press in Boston, gave birth to her first child, a daughter, Zoe May. Cynthia is a committed feminist who has joined her life to Paul Kiefer, Zoe's father, rather than enter into a contractual marriage. She has been bemused at how Zoe's human audience has reacted to her in the first fourteen months of life. Cynthia and Paul do not dress Zoe in pink. "I like to dress her in bright colors because babies are more attracted to bright colors than pastels." So Zoe, with pale blond hair, blue eyes, and pink cheeks goes out into the world, offering not a clue as to her gender.

"A lot of people assume she's a boy right off the bat," said Cynthia.

"One grown man came right up to her and said, 'Hey, fella, put up your dukes.' Zoe was about six months old at this time. Talk about projecting your ideas of masculinity onto a baby! There are a lot of examples of people saying 'Hi, fellow,' 'Hi, buster,' or giving a mock punch to the shoulder and tousling Zoe's hair. A lot of times I don't say anything, but if they say how old is 'he,' and I say 'she' is six months old, their tone of voice changes completely. They get this mellifluous sound in their voices, the baby talk comes in, and they twist up their lips and eyes and whole face. I always wonder what Zoe must be thinking when they totally change personalities because they've discovered she is a girl."

Keenly attuned to issues of gender as Cynthia is, she has been shocked to find herself still transmitting gender messages to her daughter. "I always used to refer to her as my baby girl, my little girl, and hold her close to me. I hadn't even thought about that at all until I found that this friend of mine who has a son would hold him up in the air and say things like, 'Aren't you my big boy?' The way I hold Zoe was pulling her in and lowering her boundaries and keeping this continuity between her and me. With my friend it was separation and distancing. You are out there and big, you are separate from me. Just those four or five little words had so much meaning and difference. Both my friend and I are very much feminist-identified and politically committed to raising our kids in a gender-neutral way, and yet we both found ourselves with this rolling off our tongues."

Zoe has gender-neutral toys. She doesn't have any dolls, and she doesn't have any trucks either. She has shapes and puzzles and books. When she was about fourteen months old, her mother took her to a science museum. They went with Cynthia's friend, Terri Goldberg, and her son, Micah. Cynthia and Terri met in birthing class. "He went around the museum making truck noises," said Cynthia. "He's the same age as Zoe, but she didn't have any idea how to make truck noises. I do feel there are diffferences between Zoe and boys, and I don't know where it is coming from."

Zoe, says Cynthia, is very careful. She never falls off the bed. She never trips over the threshold at their front door, while a little boy who frequently visits them trips constantly. He has far more experience falling than Zoe does. Cynthia and her sister Susan used to coach a soccer team of ten-year-old girls. "What we had to do was teach these girls it was okay to fall down and get dirty, and at the beginning of practice we had them roll around in the dirt to get dirty and get it over with. Girls hate this, but boys learn from their experience that it's okay. Zoe and this other kid have totally different life experiences with falling down, and where they got that from, I have no idea."

Terri Goldberg and her husband, Steve, have strived to raise Micah in ways that do not promote negative forms of male behavior. But she does not believe they are raising him in a gender-neutral environment. For example, she too has noticed the difference in the way she and Cynthia talk to their babies, and Terri thinks they would talk to Micah differently if he were a little girl. She also acknowledges that she and her husband don't try to make him look gender-neutral. "We don't dress him in frilly things although some of his clothes I would put on a girl," says Terri. "We don't put him into pink. I'm sure if he were a girl I would dress him differently. We've been letting his hair grow out and as it gets longer, more people on the street say, 'Isn't she cute!' and we are quick to correct them and say, 'No, this is a boy.' "

Zoe and Micah. At fourteen months, they are as different as the words their mothers use to describe them. Cynthia's baby is careful, little, she holds her close. Zoe moves thoughtfully. Terri could be describing a different species: Micah is large, not dainty, very aggressive, not cautious, tripping and falling constantly, fearless. While Zoe's attire gives no clue that she is a girl, no such high-risk outfit was put on Micah. It's okay for a girl to be mistaken for a boy, but Steve had no tolerance for any outfit that might lead people to mistake Micah for a girl. Despite their parents' determination to avoid gender stereotyping, both babies have fallen into predictable patterns. And they are as different from each other as they can be.

CHAPTER THREE

Nature, Nurture, and Genes

Women have public conversations, and we have private conversations among ourselves. Over the years, friends and I have had a repeated private conversation that usually ends on the same unfulfilled note that recurring dreams do. The theme of our conversation is this: Girls are different from boys, boys are different from girls, but we don't quite know why, and we are not sure whether it's even something we ought to be discussing publicly.

Girls are different from boys. We see differences in the way they crawl, how they begin their first explorations. Like Zoe's and Micah's parents, we can see it in the way they play. My daughter spent many of her toddler hours wandering around the house clutching stuffed animals. On occasion she would assemble them in the living room, in an early form of caretaking. My younger son collected toy cars and fire engines, and his favorite indoor play consisted of pushing these vehicles around on the carpet and making automotive and fire engine noises. His father used to take him for walks in a field of dahlias next to our house, and his first real word was "flower." But we didn't buy him flowers. We bought him Legos, trucks, cars, and toy fire engines, which he called firecars, and adored. It was a pattern that perpetuated itself: We discovered he liked these kinds of toys, so we bought them for him. Like parents since time began, we gave no thought to how these toys would affect his development or his thinking about himself. If my daughter was busy learning the art of caretaking with her stuffed animals, my sons were equally busy learning internal combustion noises, having adventures, and making machines do their bidding. Thus, when boys are given Lego sets at three and four and little girls are given dolls, boys are practicing construction and visualization skills, while girls are cuddling. Girls' activities are passive, they have nothing visible to show for it in the end, no big, colorful blocks of Legos that they have assembled.

Anyone who visits an elementary school will notice the differences in the way the children act: Boys call out in classrooms much more often than girls do. Boys have a harder time sitting still; they rush out of the classroom at recess, while girls linger behind and perhaps help the teacher with cleaning the blackboard.

These patterns are reflected in high school and college, and still later on, when we see men and women at work and in adult social situations. But where does it come from? When, or perhaps more to the point, where does it start? Is biology really destiny, or is it just an excuse dredged up by a culture to justify its dismissive, shelter-them-until-they-smother treatment of women? And if that is true—if biology is the chief myth maker in the gender wars—then what is really going on? What is the truth about differences between boys and girls and what is the truth about their similarities? What is the impact on children of the attitudes and expectations of adults who are rearing each new generation of children according to their own myths and half-truths?

BIOLOGY AS DESTINY:
IS THERE A TRUCK IN HIS BRAIN?

Researchers in every field that I interviewed repeatedly made the point that the range of difference among children within the sexes is vastly greater than the range of differences between the sexes. Whether we were looking at math ability, spatial skills, verbal ability, physical size, or measures of empathy and sensitivity—and yes, even aggressive behavior—the range within each sex was always much broader than the one between the sexes. Moreover, the differences that exist that appear to be linked to gender—such as better verbal skills in girls—are quite small. Thus, we might find a very small percentage of boys scoring higher at the highest levels of mathematics than girls, and a slightly higher percentage of girls scoring higher in empathy evaluations than boys. But the differences will be negligible. What portion, if any, can be traced to biology is at the core of the nature versus nurture debate that is still going on today.

Like Anne Petersen, most scientists say that the biggest differences between males and females is in their reproductive systems. Men tend to be taller and to weigh more than women, and men tend to have greater upper body strength. Researchers agree that there are clear biological causes for these physical differences and they are undeniably sex-linked. After that, however, the debate begins over what really are the differences, and what causes them.

Anne Fausto-Sterling is a Brown University biologist who wrote *Myths of Gender: Biological Theories About Women and Men*. The book is a one-woman demolition derby that junks most of the studies that purport to show that sex differences are rooted in biology. Small differences in visual-spatial skills, she argues, are due to thousands of environmental differences in the way boys and girls are raised—from playing with blocks and construction toys to shooting balls into a soccer goal—that are known to promote the development of these particular skills.

"Do we then even require the hypothesis of biologically based differences to explain our observations?" she asked. "I think not, although

I remain open to the idea that some small fraction of an already tiny sex-related difference could result from hormonal differences between male and female."[1]

For most gender differences, the argument that biology is destiny simply doesn't hold up. What is most devastating to the argument, however, is this: The differences are shrinking. The gap in visual-spatial skills has nearly vanished as girls have been encouraged to take higher-level math courses in high school. The surest predictor for how well someone will do on math Scholastic Aptitude Tests is not gender but what level of advanced math the student has taken. The more math girls take, the better they do on math standardized tests. What is different today from the 1960s and 1970s is that girls are being encouraged by guidance counselors, teachers, and parents to take algebra II and solid geometry. Only in pre-calculus and calculus courses are there significantly more boys than girls in the classes. Moreover, the difference between boys' and girls' verbal skills has also shrunk, with boys catching up to girls in verbal portions of recent Scholastic Aptitude Tests. The erosion of these gaps suggest that school environments and what skills they teach both sexes have far more to do with how well students do than genes, hormones, or male and female brains.

These changes are documented facts, not woolly-minded theories concocted to advance a socio-political agenda regulating the balance of power between the sexes. And they are proving difficult for the girls-can't-do-math bitter-enders to swallow.

ON THE TRAIL OF THE STEREOTYPES

In 1974 two psychologists—Eleanor Macoby and Carol Nagy Jacklin—published the most exhaustive analysis of studies on sex differences that had ever been done. To this day their book, *The Psychology of Sex Differences*, remains the foundation for any serious discussion of the large and growing body of research that our obsession with sex differences has generated. Macoby and Jacklin concluded that there was no solid scientific research to substantiate such widely held beliefs as: Girls are more social than boys; they have lower self-esteem; they are better at rote learning and simple repetitive tasks (a claim once widely popularized by no less an authority than the sainted Dr. Benjamin Spock); boys are more analytical than girls; boys are more affected by environment, while girls are more affected by heredity; and so forth. The jury was still out, they concluded, on whether there were differences in levels of physical activity, competitiveness, fear, and dominance, or whether girls were more compliant and nurturing than boys. They concluded that there were some sex differences favoring girls in verbal ability, and boys in math and spatial visualization (remember, this book came out in 1974, before high school girls were urged to enroll in higher-math courses, as well as in shop and mechanical drawing courses.) They also concluded that there was enough good research to back up the statement that boys are more aggressive than girls.

Taken as a whole, this makes for a very small area of difference between the two sexes. And even that has come under attack. Anne Fausto-Sterling challenged the validity of the few existing studies that purported to show a biological basis for boys' greater levels of aggression. Fausto-Sterling was deeply troubled because all the studies involved children under five, which meant they had had five years of social conditioning. Further, researchers all knew the sex of the child under observation, which meant they could project their own expectations about gender behavior onto the child they were evaluating, rendering their conclusions immediately suspect. As an antidote, she cited the work of anthropologist Carol Ember, who studied a community in Kenya and found an interesting correlation between the work that boys and girls were assigned and their levels of aggression. Boys assigned small amounts of feminine work such as child care, housework, hauling firewood and water—which are jobs assigned to women in most tribal cultures—were less aggressive than the average males. Fausto-Sterling concluded that the question of how aggression develops is complex and the product of numerous causes that interact with each other, including the way adults react differently to babies based on their different genitalia.

TESTOSTERONE: THE HOSTILE HORMONE?

Male violence and aggression is frequently blamed on testoterone, one of a group of chemically interrelated hormones known as androgens, which make their first mischievous appearance when the fetus is in its sixth week of gestation. Until that point, the embryo that has a pair of X chromosomes and will become a female, and the embryo with one X and one Y chromosome, which will become a male, are virtually identical. Both embryos have gonads, with an outer portion and an inner portion. Both have a set of female (Mullerian) and male (Wolffian) reproductive ducts. During the sixth week, however, genetic information on the Y chromosome initiates a series of changes that differentiate the male development from the female. Embryonic testes appear in the male and begin producing testosterone. This stimulates a growth spurt in the male reproductive system. Simultaneously another hormone appears that causes the female duct system in the male-to-be embryo to degenerate. In the female embryo, the ovary begins to develop in about the twelfth week and is fully formed three months before birth, along with a lifetime supply of about 400,000 eggs. The Mullerian ducts develop while the Wolffian ducts disappear; thus, in normal development the male embryo ends up with only the male reproductive system and the female ends up with only the female system. But their origins are identical: The labioscrotal swelling that appears before differentiation begins turns into the labia in females and the scrotum in males. The genital tubercle becomes the clitoris in females and the penis in males.

What is the standard against which to measure the other sex? The embryos that carry the XX chromosome pair naturally develop along female lines without the secretion of any additional hormones. It is the male embryos that secrete testosterone and a Mullerian inhibiting substance that differentiate themselves from normal development; in this process, it is clear that they become "the other." Statistically this produces a female advantage: She is more likely to survive to full term and be born healthy, and she is likely to be skeletally and behaviorally more advanced than males at birth. Boys are slightly longer and heavier at birth. They are far more susceptible to sex-linked disabilities such as color blindness and hemophilia. Most studies seeking significant differences in such things as touch, smell, frequency of smiles, visual recognition, and activity levels have found no clear, consistent, and sustainable patterns in early infancy.

GIRLS WHO PREFER TRUCKS

What I have described is the normal development of male and female fetuses. But things can go wrong, and from these developmental anomalies have come some of the most revealing findings about what has the most influence on the gender we end up with.

Some of the best evidence that androgen exposure in utero may account for significant behavioral differences between boys and girls has been developed by Sheri Berenbaum, an associate professor of psychology at the Chicago Medical School, who has been studying a group of girls who were born with congenital adrenal hyperplasia (CAH). Because of a genetic disorder that causes an enzymatic defect, these girls were all exposed to high levels of androgens in the prenatal and early postnatal period, and they were born with masculinized genitalia. Their conditions ranged from enlarged clitorises to fused labia that look like a scrotum. All of the girls had had surgical corrections for their masculinized genitalia and were being raised as girls. What makes this research so valuable is that these girls were compared with a control group of their sisters. At the time I spoke with Berenbaum, none of the girls had reached puberty.

"This is the best experiment of nature that we can have," Berenbaum said. "What I have found is that for toy play, girls with congenital adrenal hyperplasia have a much greater preference for boys' toys and boys' activities than do their sisters." They also play with girls' toys less than their sisters do. She cautioned that because they were born with a masculinized appearance it is possible their parents may treat them differently from their sisters, and that this results in different behavior. However, when their parents were asked whether they thought the girls who were extremely masculinized played a great deal more with boys' toys, the answer was no. Thus, their perceptions of girls' play preference was not affected by the degree of genital masculinization. Berenbaum also found that the parents believed they were encouraging their daughters "to act as a girl should."

Toy preference was measured by the amount of time the girls spent playing with various toys in a play area. Boys' toys included a plane, cars, fire engines, blocks, and Lincoln logs. Girls toys included dolls, kitchen supplies, a toy phone, crayons, and paper. Neutral toys were books, board games, and a puzzle. The results support the argument that there is a connection between uterine hormone exposure and masculine toy choices.

"The differences are quite large between these hormone-exposed girls and their sisters," Berenbaum told me. "And it is stable across time. The most parsimonious explanation is that hormones act on the developing brain to affect some process that influences toy selection. The question is: What is that process? I don't think there is a part of the brain that says boys play with trucks. My guess is that it has something to do with the reward value of motion."

For the most part, these girls studied by Berenbaum seem quite well-adjusted. They look like normal girls. The question is what happens at puberty when it is not as cool to be playing with boys' toys. Cross-sex behavior is tolerated in childhood, and much less tolerated among other children in adolescence. Many CAH girls marry, and some have children, Berenbaum said, although they have lower fertility than girls who do not have the disorder. "We don't know whether they are more likely to be lesbians," she said.

"They do have more interest in sports, blocks, Lincoln logs, trucks, and airplanes. We haven't found any difference in their activity level. We have also looked at rough play such as wrestling. These girls don't seem to engage in that more often," than their sisters. Rough play, she noted, is more a part of the socializing process than it is a manifestation of aggression. "You see boys 'killing' each other and they are giggling hysterically."

These CAH girls also show a much higher level of competence in spatial ability than their sisters. Berenbaum's findings support conclusions reached a decade ago by Susan Resnick, a psychologist at the National Institute on Aging, who has also studied CAH girls.

While noting that girls today often play with Legos, Berenbaum does not believe there is any evidence that random toy play or choice of toys is going to wipe out innate sex differences in spacial ability. She noted that other researchers, including Nora Newcomb at Temple University in Philadelphia, are coming up with similar results. "Newcomb's data would suggest that if there is a relationship, it's the reverse: Kids with high spatial abilities choose toys that facilitate that. It remains to be seen whether sex differences in spatial abilities will disappear. But I wouldn't put money on that."

Instead she puts forth the proposition that she first heard advanced years ago by Carol Nagy Jacklin, whose work with Macoby laid the groundwork for much of today's debate. "She said all the remedial education goes to boys. They're the ones with the reading and spelling problems. If girls don't have high spatial ability, why don't we put the money into remedial training of girls?" Intrinsically girls may not start out as well. Just changing the social environment in which girls are raised may not compensate. But we do know that it is possible to give girls remedial experiences that can help them catch up. We know, for example, that first-grade boys perform better when they are using blocks than girls do, but when girls are given the opportunity to learn how to play with blocks, they do as well as boys do.

Small biological differences are consistently reinforced by the environment. "If a child has a biological predisposition for things that move," says Berenbaum, "she will be interested in those and parents will soon stop buying dolls and instead buy things that move because those are the things she is interested in, and they make the differences bigger."

While the effect of extra exposure to androgens on girls produces masculinized genitalia and a masculinized preference in toys and in sports, extra androgen exposure in boys does not seem to make them any different from their brothers. "This," said Berenbaum, "is consistent with animal studies that show if you give males a lot more male hormones sometimes it makes them more masculine, sometimes it makes them less, and sometimes it does nothing at all."

How androgens affect behavior—the processes involved in the brain—is a mystery that is far from being solved. Berenbaum's work, however, has isolated them as prime suspects in the unfolding drama of what accounts for the differences between boys and girls in toy preferences, sports, and spatial abilities. While she agrees with other researchers that these differences are also reinforced by the environment, she validates the observations of millions of parents who have watched their sons and daughters choose a toy. "One of the things that's amazing to me," said Berenbaum, "is I'm a feminist. All of my friends are, and all of my friends with children who have created gender-neutral environments say their children go right to the sex-typed toys."

THE DEBATE

Ken Zucker, a psychologist who heads the Child and Adolescent Gender Identity Clinic at the Clarke Institute of Psychiatry in Toronto, cautions that terms such as "gender-neutral environment" are open to multiple interpretations. Zucker works with children who have profound gender-identity crises. His patients are young and adolescent boys who want to be girls and girls who want to be boys. "Some of the parents I see had the notion of wanting to raise children in nonsexist ways. Parents say it doesn't seem to work. But you don't know what they really did. A typical story might be that the mother was adamantly against the boy playing with guns and squirt guns and they'd censor cartoons with a lot of fantasy violence, but for a variety of complex reasons these boys start to cross-dress in their mother's clothes or they start wearing their sister's clothes. They start to play with

Barbie dolls. They become very female-identified. What prompts the referral is the boy starts saying he wants to become a girl. It's clearly not gender-neutral. It's the opposite of what the father and mother were trying to achieve. They didn't want the kid to end up super-macho, but the kid ends up as super-feminine, which they don't want either."

He makes the point that in all cultures that scientists have been able to get access to, there are differences in early play and toy selection that show up in preschool and early-school-age children. Boys affiliate with boys' toys and girls affiliate with girls' toys. These differences, he says, "are dramatic."

Dramatic they are, but where they come from is a source of spirited controversy. Zucker describes it this way: "There is a fundamental tension in the field that revolves around the relative weight of biological and psychosocial influences. On the one hand, you have people who are biological reductionists who say there are differences that are almost exclusively biologically determined. On the other hand, you have social constructionists or feminists who take the position that almost all of this is socially determined. Then there are the rest of us, who sit on fences. One of the tricks is to get a specific domain for analysis and then say how much is being contributed by biological forces and how much by psychosocial forces."

Zucker points out Berenbaum as one person who has been able to do this. He has looked at the long-term development of women with CAH and how they have matured into adulthood. "What is clear is that they are different from women who don't have that condition. They are not so different that one could clearly say that biology explains everything with them. There is a little bit of both.

"In adult sexuality, more of these women report bisexual fantasies than their sisters. They have less heterosexual experience and a lower rate of marriage. They remember themselves as being more boyish in girlhood."

Despite two decades of research and social prodding designed to modify stereotypes in children, boys and girls throughout the world still act very differently in terms of toys and play. Where the sex differences are much weaker, says Zucker, are in areas of cognitive ability. And it is I.Q. that is critical to determining a person's competence and abilities. "The differences in I.Q between boys and girls are almost nonexistent," he says. "It remains very intriguing why women are so under-represented in disciplines like mathematics and physics, but by and large, the average differences in the cognitive domain are relatively negligible."

AN AGGRESSIVE APPROACH TO AGGRESSION

Where Zucker does see a difference is in the area of aggression. The view he takes is that there is no question that boys are biologically predisposed to be more aggressive than girls. "If we look at the clinical referral patterns in childhood, we find that one of the most common reasons boys are referred clinically is because they are aggressive," and it has gotten them into trouble. "Most parents do not socialize their sons to be aggressive. They might socialize them to be rough and tumble and to engage in play-fighting with other boys, but I don't think we encourage kids to be violent." Boys who are overly aggressive, he said, come from families that have failed to set limits on children. "They don't come from normal families."

He agrees that the predisposition to aggression comes from hormones, but says the difference in physical size between men and women gives men a physical advantage that lends itself to making aggressive behavior efficacious. Zucker, like others, claims that we simply don't understand how testosterone affects levels of aggression. Having said that, he turns the controversy about aggression on its head: Instead of denying that boys have a predisposition to aggression, he proposes that parents and other adults concerned with raising boys should be aware that they may have this predisposition and then be prepared to take energetic socializing measures to channel it into appropriate behavior.

THE GENETIC IMPACT ON WHO WE BECOME

For decades, the debate about gender differences and what affects people's personalities and behavior revolved around a nature versus nurture controversy. But we are now discovering that genetics plays a far more critical role than previously believed. Studies in twins indicate that a person's temperament is determined at least in part by genetics. Provocative research that is coming out of studies of twins suggests that the personalities we are born with may affect the environmental stimuli that we receive, setting up a complicated interplay among biology, genetics, and environment.

All this is heavy going even for the experts. But it goes to the heart of what creates differences between boys and girls. Hormones play a role; so does environment. But the studies of twins point the way to an even more complicated variable: the estimated 50,000 to 100,000 human genes and what researchers are now calling "heritability." Identical twins have identical genes and they grow up to be pretty much mirror images of each other. Studies of identical twins separated at birth show striking similarities in how they turn out as adults. These studies have produced some of the strongest evidence ever developed that both intelligence and personality are heavily influenced by a person's genes.

NATURE VIA NURTURE

The Minnesota Study of Twins Reared Apart began on March 11, 1979, after Dr. Thomas J. Bouchard, a psychologist working at the University of Minnesota, read an article about the reunion of a pair of twins who had been separated at birth. He contacted them to see if they would cooperate in a study he wanted to do of their similarities and differences and their life experiences. They became known as "the two Jims." While the fact that they had the same first name was coincidental—they had been adopted by different families at four weeks of age—there was much more that they had in common that was eerie. When they were reunited thirty-nine years after birth, Jim Lewis and Jim Springer discovered that they lived within a hundred miles of each other in Ohio. They smoked the same brand of cigarettes, drove the same kind of car, held identical jobs, and had built mirror-image white wood benches around trees in their yards. Woodworking was the hobby of both. Both bit their nails and both had developed migraine headaches at the same age.

Bouchard swiftly realized that twins separated at birth could provide intriguing new clues to the mystery of what makes people who they are. His study grew from "the two Jims" into one involving more than 100 pairs of separated twins and triplets from the United States and the United Kingdom. Other reunited twins have come from Australia, Canada, China, New Zealand, Sweden, and West Germany.

What the researchers are trying to determine is just what percentage of a person's destiny is determined by genes and what percentage is determined by environmental influences. The results of their studies have given powerful ammunition to those who argue that genetics determine destiny. What they have concluded is that about 50 percent of our personality variables are heritable. Further, they conclude that personality differences are more influenced by genetific diversity than by environmental diversity. The genetic influence extends to such personality traits as authoritarianism, religiosity, and adherence to traditionalism. One of the few areas where environment seemed to be important to adult personality was in the realm of social closeness: Children brought up in families that were cohesive and relatively free of conflict were more likely to be normal adults. Those whose families encouraged personal growth also showed higher levels of emotional stability and normal patterns of behavior as adults.

The twins researchers do not know how genes affect behavior. But they are confident enough about their research to advance the proposition that about 70 percent of a person's general intelligence is affected by genes. They believe that genetic influences affect our personalities in ways that then affect the environments we surround ourselves with.

How or why the differences in human personalities evolved is unknown. But they are there, in every child, and they cause us to react to each child differently. Genes play a powerful role in triggering the chain of reactions that molds behavior.

Researchers have concluded that there is a genetic component to such mental illnesses as depression and schizophrenia. Genes have been blamed for criminal behavior. It's a dangerous line of reasoning, however. "My genes made me do it" may not yet stand up in court as a criminal defense akin to insanity. But every time we excuse some dreadful act on the part of boys and men on the grounds that "boys will be boys," we are in effect letting them cop a genetic plea.

BOYS WILL BE BOYS AND GIRLS WILL BE . . . ?

What is the truth about differences between boys and girls? We see from the biological perspective that testosterone determines sex and may have some influence on aggression, spatial skills, and a preference for toys that involve motion. These toys also provide and reinforce a sense of motion and power and energy, which may also explain part of their appeal. We know that biological events in the womb—specifically an overexposure to testosterone—can produce certain masculinized behavior in girls. We know from the study of twins reared apart that much of who we are in terms of personality traits and intelligence is determined genetically and in the womb. Obviously that applies to both boys and girls. And we know finally that every child who can be labeled "a boy" or "a girl" at birth begins at that moment to feel an environmental impact based on his or her gender, as the adult world closes in with a set of stereotypical expectations that are both rigid and constantly reinforced. Little girls are prompted to smile and cuddle; little boys are prompted to be tough and adventurous. We know that most researchers insist that the differences within a sex for the whole range of physiological traits are much greater than the overall differences between the two sexes. And yet we expect girls and women to be empathetic and caretaking, while we do not expect this in boys and are, indeed, surprised when we find it. We do expect aggression in boys, and are shocked when we find it in girls. Biology produces a difference in reproductive systems, and genetic traits influence temperament and personality; these, in turn, appear to affect the environment and how adults, siblings, and other children react to infants, toddlers, and preschoolers. What happens to girls and boys, then, is an interplay between the biological and genetic traits they are born with and the environmental influences, such as their parents' behavior, that they encounter from the moment of birth. And these adult behaviors are deeply affected by our own understanding of gender rules and the learning experiences we give our children. By the sixth year, the male and the female child are usually very different human beings, who have had very different experiences from the moment they opened their eyes.

CHAPTER FOUR

Learning the Rules of Gender

A pattern creeps in that creates two very different experiences from infancy on: Boys' lives expand, girls' lives are constrained, and both recognize the difference very early. Children use the word "boy" and "girl" by the age of two, and they will correctly identify themselves as well as others by sex. By four, they have a clear sense of themselves as boy or girl and are beginning to learn what is appropriate male and female behavior. They will correctly label the people they meet as boy or girl, man or woman. They are working hard to incorporate what they believe is appropriate into their own behavior; by the ages of four and five, they are insisting that other boys and girls behave in ways they deem appropriate to their gender. By five the gender lines are clearly drawn and children cross over at their own peril. While little boys and girls play happily together when they are infants and toddlers, by five they are segregating themselves into same-sex play groups.

Along the way, they have learned critical lessons about what it means to be male and what it means to be female. They know what toys are appropriate for boys and what are appropriate for girls. By the age of three, most children will select the gender-appropriate toy. Cornell University research psychologist Sandra Bem believes that while children use gender as an organizing principle for dealing with the world around them, they also learn from the world around them what it means to be male and female. Thus, as children are developing their sense of male and female they are also assimilating information about what are the desirable attributes of their gender and incorporating that information into their own behavior.[1]

FREEDOM ENVY

When my children were younger, we used to spend a week at the beach with a friend and her family. We had been next-door neighbors for fourteen years, and our children had grown up together. In August 1982, we rented a house on the Outer Banks of North Carolina. After breakfast one day, while people were still lounging around the dining and living areas, my daughter, who had just turned three, went into the bathroom and closed the door. Moments later she let loose a wail. I rushed into the bathroom, thinking she'd hurt herself. She was standing in front of the toilet, her pants down, and as soon as she saw me, she hollered at the top of her voice:

"I WANT A PENIS. I WANT A PENIS. JEFFREY HAS A PENIS AND I DON'T, AND I WANT A PENIS LIKE JEFFREY HAS."

A feminist mother's worst nightmare had come true. Sigmund Freud, the nemesis of modern women, had taken possession of my daughter's soul. And there I was, standing in the bathroom with the door open and a dozen friends and relatives within earshot while my daughter howled with the pain of penis envy.

I closed the bathroom door.

This time, there was no mistaking her emotions. Tears were spilling out of her eyes and down her cheeks, but she was not weeping out of sadness. She was furious. Her brother had something she didn't have.

I calmed her down by explaining that while boys have one penis, girls will eventually get two breasts and they will be able to feed their babies that way. She will have two of something her brother couldn't have, and she could put them to good use. She seemed satisfied with that, and I emerged from the bathroom feeling as if I'd successfully negotiated one of the critical psychological hurdles presented to the mothers of girls. But without thinking about it, I'd also given her a strong signal about what her future as a girl would be: She would have babies and take care of them.

The concept of penis envy was hatched out by Sigmund Freud on the basis of no evidence whatsoever. It is a notion that has so permeated our culture that it pops up in everything from movie dialogue to our most casual conversations. Freud believed that little girls blamed their mothers for the lack of a penis, and that this perception of missing a penis forever warped their personality development. If one thinks for a moment about the hugely repressed and circumscribed roles assigned to women during Freud's lifetime (1856–1939), there is no need to construct a harebrained theory to explain the depression and mental illnesses that drove women to seek his assistance. Yet, to this day, we still find widespread acceptance of the notion that girls envy boys because they have penises. It would make as much sense to assert that boys envy girls because they have breasts.

A little girl of Carol Travis and Carole Offir's acquaintance delivered a classic rebuttal to the penis envy theory that they recount in their book *The Longest War: Sex Differences in Perspective.* The little girl took a bath with a young male cousin and observed the difference in silence. When her mother was tucking her in bed later, she said softly: "Mommy, isn't it a blessing he doesn't have it on his face?"

The physical penis is not the object of envy. Far more likely, girls are envious of what it represents: freedom. Katherine, by age three, had plenty of reason to be envious of her brother's greater freedom. Four years older than his sister, he was able to venture farther out into the ocean and stray farther away on the sand. He could hazard farther out on the rocks with a crab net. She was forced to stay by my side or remain home. While she loved to play in the waves or sit on the sand and let the water rush up around her, she had to be accompanied by an adult. Her brother could go in the water alone, anytime he pleased.

Freud and his acolytes put a lot more stock in the importance of penises than my daughter did. She never mentioned wanting one again.

THE MEDIA: THE CULTURAL TOM-TOM BEGINS

Children typically spend hundreds of hours watching television cartoons and videos, all overwhelmingly populated by male heroes and male villains. Networks, goaded by research that shows girls would watch male cartoon heroes but boys would not watch female heroines, long since abandoned any pretense of offering girls heroic role models. So from the time girls understand that they are girls, they do not see themselves reflected as powerful or even important characters in the entertainment they are most likely to watch. The world they are learning about is depicted in male terms, and is principally populated by male figures of power, action, and authority. Males are the winners and losers in these dramas. Girls and women are relegated to roles where they squeak such banalities as "Help, Rodney! I'm stuck in quicksand!" In the world of kids' TV, women are all but invisible supporting players. It is the beginning of what Betty Friedan calls "symbolic annihilation."

A great deal of attention has been paid to cartoon violence. The nation's most respected researchers are now convinced that watching televised violence promotes violent behavior. Less attention has been paid to this point: The sexism in these cartoons is appalling. If we accept the findings that viewing violence promotes violence, we must recognize that viewing sexism promotes sexism. Some good may come of it if adults are there to use these sexist incidents as teaching tools so their children will not emulate it, but no realist can expect that to take place very often. The movement toward cultural literacy, in which adults and children learn to "read" the film media the way we learn to "read" symbolism in books, is in its infancy in this country. We have a long way to go before we are sophisticated consumers of television and films and are able to teach our children the dangers in the messages, and find alternative and more positive media experiences to expose them to.

Anyone who wonders why little boys behave condescendingly toward little girls need do no more than spend a weekend watching TV cartoons, as I did. In one episode of Hanna-Barbera's *Space Ghost*, for example, a young male space cadet named Blip is flying alongside a female space cadet and Space Ghost, who has just rescued them. The young man makes a joke about how "it is with women drivers." The young girl simpers, "Well, I like that!" They start to quibble, and Space Ghost concludes the episode by telling Blip that he's going to fly home "where it's quiet." The lesson could not be more clear: He is not going to address the bigoted remarks made by the young man or validate the young woman's efforts to defend herself. Space Ghost's need for quiet is more important to him than rebuking his sexist sidekick.

In another episode, Space Ghost has rescued these same characters from a ring of space slavers. The two young characters seek refuge in their space ship and the boy tells the young girl—who is his twin sister—to "stay here. I'll give Space Ghost a hand." On their way home, they have another dialogue that concludes with the male twin looking at the camera and saying derisively, "Ah, boy. Sisters!"

Space Ghost was followed by an episode of *Boomerang*, in which Matilda, a female gorilla, chases her true love, who doesn't return her affections. At the end, she goes off in pursuit of King Kong, and the ordinary gorilla is left behind, much to his relief. He turns to the camera with this observation: "Well, there goes the gorilla of my dreams. And what a nightmare she turned out to be."

I thought the next cartoon had some possibilities when I saw a female mouse directing a male mouse to take on the cat who was threatening them. But that was not to be. The female mouse's role was confined to inspiring the male mouse to heroics by planting big kisses on his cheek.

The only time real women are visible on these shows is during commercials, when they have starring roles in plugs for household cleaning products. "They never show any men using that stuff," my daughter pointed out to me, with considerable indignation. The message for little boys could not be clearer. They are symbolically absolved of any jobs that involve household cleaning. That's women's work. Always has been. Always will be.

COUNTERPOINT: BLENDING ROLES

The content of television cartoons reinforces images of girls as dependent and annoying. The commercials portray women as house-cleaning agents, and little more. When parents replicate these messages in the home by what they say and how they divide work, they amplify them. But parents can provide counter-programming to their children by how they divide housework and how they share, and by the kinds of remarks they make about gender. A genuine domestic partnership can give a priceless example to a family's children about what men and women can do, and can be. The power of positive influences on how very small children develop their ideas of appropriate roles and jobs for men and women can be illustrated by the following story.

Chris and Susan Koch own a television company that produces a series about inventors that is among the Discovery Channel's hits. At home, Chris does the cooking. A few years ago Jonah, his teenage son from his first marriage, was visiting them and Chris informed the family that he was going away on a business trip. Chris and Susan's three-year-old daughter, Haley, had this reaction: "Daddy's going away, so I guess Jonah will have to do the cooking."

In my family, my husband does most of the cooking and marketing and at least half of the rest of the domestic chores, including cleaning up the kitchen in the mornings. Is he some mousy reincarnation of Mr. Milquetoast? Hardly. He is also a weekend farmer who enjoys roughhousing with fractious 600-pound calves, a sometime airplane pilot, a fine writer, and, yes, an exciting lover. Sharing household tasks does not, ipso facto, un-man a husband. Any man who can drive a car or pilot a plane can also learn to run a vacuum cleaner—and maintain his masculinity at the same time. In fact, my husband sums up his domestic chores with a phrase that comes straight out of the male ethos: "Fair is fair."

This blending of roles has a powerful impact on children. Youngsters who see fathers cooking and cleaning and mothers earning a paycheck and buying their own cars are acutely aware that the rest of the world is one huge dichotomy. I learned how important these parental examples are when I did a column about housework that ended by requesting readers to call in their suggestions for how to equalize the burden. We gave a number where they could leave recorded messages. Within three days, we had received more than 200 phone calls. Both men and women underscored one outstanding point: Men who shared the burden of household chores with their wives had fathers who had done the same thing. If the old adage holds that men can foresee what women will look like by looking at their prospective mother-in-law, then it is equally true that women can foresee how a man will react toward housework by looking at the behavior of a prospective father-in-law. I learned from the tremendous response to that column just how sore a subject housework is in many households, and the lengths couples have gone to in order to strike a fair balance. Boys and girls learn their first lessons about housework by watching their parents.

My daughter, for example, a keen observer of how the world turns, is quick to speak up if she thinks the women in the house are being saddled with more than their share of domestic chores. She has also announced that she intends to marry a househusband when she grows up. At the age of thirteen, she had not only absorbed the lessons her stepfather and I have offered in our domestic partnership, she had already given some thought to how she plans to blend the professional and personal components of her adult life. While she sees housework as an androgynous occupation, however, few little boys who will someday grow to be husbands and fathers do.

FEAR OF HOUSEWORK, FEAR OF GIRLS' WORK

Raphaela Best, a reading specialist, has done pioneering research into how boys and girls are socialized by gender. She found that by the first grade boys already had a deeply imbedded abhorrence of housework. "The boys declared independence from housework vocally as well as in their behavior," she wrote. "On one occasion, for example, the first-grade boys made it known that they would never cook or sew or do any other housekeeping chore under any circumstances, even if they starved to death or had to throw away their torn clothing or go without clothes."[2] A desperate stand, indeed, and one that powerfully illustrates just how negatively boys regard girls and what they deem women's work by a shockingly early age.

Girls resent what happens. They see the unfairness and it makes them angry. I saw how schools reinforce these gender rules during an incident that occurred the summer after my daughter's sixth-grade year. She and her girlfriend Lisa hosted a party at our house. My daughter informed me it was to be a "mixed" party. There were five boys and five girls. Most of them had been together since kindergarten. The party went from six until ten o'clock, and the family room was littered with the detritus of pre-adolescent merry-making. At ten o'clock, one of the boys' mothers came and picked up all of the boys to take them to their homes. They left by the family-room door, and the mother, whose name is Linda, left by the front door after visiting a few minutes with me. As I closed the front door, I called down to the girls in the family room to see if they'd had a good time.

"Yeah," said my daughter, "but as usual the boys left and we're stuck cleaning everything up."

I told the girls to run outside and see if they could stop the boys' getaway car. Linda was more than supportive. The boys came in and helped clean up and then left again. You could tell it was a novel experience for them.

The girls had triumphed. But it was clear from my daughter's tone, and the phrase she used—"as usual"—that the boys had gotten away with not cleaning up in school for a long time. And I wondered how many more triumphs these little girls would enjoy.

While the debate rages on indecisively about the impact of biology on the development of masculine and feminine traits, no one argues that biology is responsible for stamping bigotry into the brains of little boys. Yet between birth and their fifth and sixth years, male children receive thousands of messages instructing them what boys are supposed to do and be, and what girls are supposed to do and be. In the grand scheme of categorizing by gender, boys have lodged girls firmly in their place as the negative reference points of what boys don't ever want to be. For those first five years, children have been bombarded with messages from television, books, toys, siblings, and parents that reinforce gender straitjackets for girls and promote high adventures for boys.

True, many parents who are concerned about these message may try to counter them with role modeling at home, as the Kochs have done. But their efforts are often undermined by those people on whom they are most dependent: the women and men who staff day-care centers and preschools or who provide care for infants and toddlers in their own homes. These underpaid, undervalued, and usually undertrained people are the adults with whom millions of youngsters spend most of their time during the day. We mislabel them as child-care givers but, in truth, research in early-childhood development tells us that these women and men are giving our children their earliest foundations for learning. They are their teachers, as well as their caregivers. Yet, in all likelihood, they give little thought to how they reinforce stereotypical gender roles in their young charges through toys, books, and play patterns.

WHO'S RAISING ARIZONA?

Keep these overwhelming (and under-reported) facts in mind: Half of all mothers of American infants return to the workforce. Almost two-thirds of American children under the age of four are cared for by a day-care provider or in a center. Most parents prefer small family-based care for their infants. Some can afford in-home care, but there is a woeful shortage of Americans who are willing to work as nannies, and the 1990 immigration law made it virtually impossible to hire aliens legally.

Federal regulations categorize child care as unskilled labor. Child-care workers are among the poorest paid in the labor force—another sign of where we put relationship skills in our scale of values. Child-care workers average $5.35 an hour, less than the average wage for people who muck out kennels or park cars for a living. The U.S. Department of Labor's *Dictionary of Occupational Training*, which is used in immigration law to determine whether there is an available labor pool of American workers to do a job, describes a requirement of between one and three months' training for child-care workers. The same rule book cites between six months and a year as the training required for workers who roll cigars.

Surely this is still another telling indication of the value we place on the people who care for our children in their most impressionable years. Yet, increasingly, these are the people who are responsible for raising our children. In 1989 the U.S. Census Bureau reported that more than half of all three- to five-year-olds attended preschool. While preschool centers vary enormously in quality, many are plagued by high turnover in staff and overcrowding. There is little in this picture to suggest that the preschool environment is any less hazardous to the gender health of millions of children than the rest of our society is.

MAPPING BIAS ON A CLEAN SLATE

"The thing we have to start thinking about is the fact that in the beginning children are born bias-free, and their biases and stereotypes are formed because of their interaction with their environment and the people in their world and the media," says Sandra Gellert, a children's advocate on the staff of the Children's Foundation in Washington, D.C. Gellert is one of the few experts who have looked at how gender biases are planted and cultivated in the fertile minds of children who are in child care.

Only recently have experts realized that these biases affect children from the day they are born—not from the day they start school—and the biases and stereotypes that are transmitted are based on the environments in which the caregivers grew up. "If we are to begin helping children to appreciate differences and to accept one another as equals, we have to start with the caregivers," says Gellert. "They are the primary role models."

The first step in attacking destructive stereotyping in child care is to show caregivers that they, like the rest of us, have biases. That done, we must try to get them to make a commitment not to pass these ancient cripplers on to the children in their charge.

Gellert never tells caregivers to throw out books that portray women as nurses, mothers, and teachers, and men as policemen, firemen, and adventurers. "They become learning tools in the other direction. You can point out the things that are stereotypical and have other books that show women who are wearing pants and climbing phone poles and men who are nurses in hospitals—books that show men can make good caregivers."

What Gellert and her colleagues have tried to do is to show caregivers that they have a responsibility to make sure these opportunities are equally available to boys and girls, and that both are encouraged equally.

It's an approach that works, Gellert says. "I think children are very open, and I think adults who make a conscious effort find that children are very willing and ready to be fair and accept everyone for who they are." She urged providers and parents who are experiencing a difference of opinion on gender training to talk it out and to avoid sending confusing signals to children.

SELECTING CARE

How can parents find a preschool that gives boys and girls equal opportunities? First, go and watch how the children sit in circles, advises Fern Marx, a research associate at the Wellesley College Center for Research on Women. "Are all the little girls grouped immediately around the teacher with the little boys far back? How are children given air time? How are they reprimanded? Do all the children dress up, and cook, and work with Erector sets? I would look at whether there is a conscious effort that every child, boy and girl, develop large-motor skills and that they all go out and play on big equipment, that this is not optional. I would watch to see if girls who are more verbal are also rewarded for nonverbal skills." She suggested that parents look at the books provided, and check out whether all children are playing with pre-science toys. She said parents should note whether boys are encouraged to develop verbal and social skills. Look, too, she suggested, at how boys are taught to resolve conflicts. Is peaceful negotiation stressed or is aggressive power play tolerated? "You look at how they cooperate. Little girls tend to come into the setting more socialized. The problem is that when girls are so well socialized, their special needs can be overlooked. Little boys tend to be the ones with speech defects. Little girls, with their politeness, seem to hide these things more.

"It isn't just girls, it is all children who are shortchanged when we keep perpetuating these miseries," she says. "Some people will say, 'You mean I can't dress my daughter in frilly clothes?' That isn't the point at all. It is saying that to be a whole human being all parts of us have to have a chance to develop, both our masculine and our feminine nature."

This idea has yet to win a toehold, let alone permanent acceptance into our consensus of what we want boys and girls to be. Although the *Heart Start* report issued by the National Center for Clinical Infant Programs in 1993 made a series of recommendations for training child-care workers in child development, nowhere did it even suggest training them in gender-neutral child care.[3] What this says is that the ruinous way we socialize children into rigid and often adversarial gender roles is not even on the radar screen of the most influential child-care advocates in this country. From the earliest days onward, schools devote more energy to boys. Boys get more time and attention from their teachers; they are rewarded for interrupting and speaking out, for boisterous behavior. Girls are reprimanded, silenced, and put down. The educational limelight is still shining on the needs of boys, while girls remain in the shadows. They are bit players in the classroom, just as they are in the Saturday morning cartoons. Silently the past is re-creating itself.

THE PRICE OF PREJUDICE

Perhaps the most damning indictment of the way America raises its children is to be found in our divorce statistics. Half of all American marriages end in divorce. Most marriage counselors have learned to start trying to put failed marriages back together by helping couples reestablish failed communications. Deborah Tannen tells of going on radio talk shows while she was promoting *You Just Don't Understand*, and having male callers tell her that her book had saved their marriages. Using a metaphor that Kate Millett developed in *Sexual Politics*, published in 1969, Tannen advanced the idea that men and women are socialized in two separate cultures, and that much of our differences and misunderstandings arise out of the fact that we don't understand what the other sex is talking about.

This dialogue of the deaf is directly linked to the way we bring up children. It is in the play of infants and toddlers that the first patterns setting boys apart from girls emerge. Girls play in small groups— dressing and undressing dolls, having tea parties, or coloring together while they chat away. Boys immediately fall into rougher, competitive play, with the goal of finding out who is strongest, fastest, biggest, toughest. How unrealistic of us to think that after twenty years or so of this sort of reinforcement that two such dissimilar people should marry and expect to be able to talk to each other, much less live happily ever after.

Alcoholism, battering, adultery, and abandonment often show up as reasons for divorce. But the underlying causes behind these events rarely surface. All too often the seething hostilities that explode into violence and divorce can be traced to gender roles learned in childhood, and to the misunderstandings and failed communications that occur years later when one party seeks to change the other. A favorite line among men who feel neglected because their wives are working outside the home is to call them selfish. A childish taunt? Of course. But I have seen that spear hurled with deadly effectiveness. For women raised since infancy to nurture others, the attack goes right to the core of their identity. Housework is probably the most important battlefield in which these gender roles collide, and no wonder. Wives and mothers who work outside the home still shoulder the vast majority of work inside the home, while husbands repeat patterns of avoidance learned in their earliest childhoods. What institution could withstand that kind of stress?

Marian Wright Edelman, founder of the Children's Defense Fund, made the point in *The Measure of Our Success*, her moving "letter to my children and yours."

"Many husbands," she wrote, "are happier to share their wives' added income than the housework and childcare."

It's an Archie Bunker cliché, but true. How many arguments have started with exhausted wives coming home from work only to go into the kitchen and see a pile of dishes in the sink, while their husbands sit in the living room watching TV? Nobody keeps records on matters such as this. But I know from conversations with people in all sorts of professions all over the country, as well as the conversations I had with callers who responded to my column, that who does the housework—and who doesn't do it—is probably the most contentious part of contemporary marriages. More than a dozen callers said it had broken up their first marriages. Pop psychologists talk about sexual maladjustment as the leading cause of failed marriages, but don't believe it. Many a bedtime I've-got-a-headache excuse has its origins in a kitchen still littered with unwashed breakfast dishes. Who wants to make love to a parasite?

While we may understand this from our own experiences, what we don't understand is how very early this behavior is imbedded in women and in men. If our spouses don't see dust, as a friend of mine said of her former husband, it's nothing new. That pattern was imprinted by the first grade, when sewing and dusting were already scorned as girls' work, and the girls who did this work were scorned as well. Boys had already learned their most fundamental gender lesson by then: Boys do exciting things with their lives, girls do scut work.

CHAPTER FIVE

Redesigning Children

The Women's Center of Northern Virginia—an organization that deals in such ugly realities as incest, beaten women, and men abandoning wives and children—holds a conference every March that is attended by hundreds of women from the Washington area. It is a meeting where the sisterhood hears lectures on strategy from some of the shrewdest and best informed women in the country. If there were a war college dedicated to teaching tactics in women's battle for survival, this would be it.

The 1992 conference was highlighted by a workshop on gender led by Shirley Fletcher, a Bethesda, Maryland, management consultant. Fletcher set the stage by saying that boys and girls were brought up in a power dynamic in which boys were taught to be dominant and girls were taught to be subservient. She said she wanted us to ponder how we learned to think about men and women, and to bear in mind that these messages were communicated to both men and women as we grew up.

Then we broke up into groups of ten, and we put our chairs in circles around an easel that held a large tablet of paper. At the top of the first piece of paper it said:

GIRLS ARE:

This is what my group wrote down:

sugar and spice
quiet
lady
clean
sweet
princess
smart
helpful
considerate/caring
leader not flamboyant
capable
loving and kind
responsible
loyal
peacemaker
strong in family
modest outside

The next page said BOYS ARE: and this is what we wrote:

snake/snails & puppydog tails
necessary
tough
sometimes weak/sensitive
self-directed
they will know mechanical things
aggressive
active
more fun

don't cry
attention-getting
allowed to be naughty more
can't control hormones
irresponsible/troublemakers

Next we were instructed to write down words we associated with boys when they reached puberty: "initiate, selfish, compete, good with hands, developmentally slower," we wrote. We found a set of mixed messages about sex: "respect girls/go as far as you can; go for it; don't get trapped; conquest; freedom; no responsibility."

For girls at puberty, we jotted down these thoughts: "responsible for our own sexuality; pretty/thin; not too smart; not too rough; prepare for future; study hard."

And finally we flipped the page to WOMEN AS ADULTS: and these are the words that came to us:

conscientious
reliable
versatile
caretaking/caregiving
moral
soft
patient
don't challenge
you can't change the system/comply/submit
boring
not smart
teacher/nurses
smarter but don't let men know

For MEN AS ADULTS: we listed the following:

men are children
their career is who they are
breadwinner

intelligent
good around the house
good at mechanics/math
tender/caring
stronger physically than women

Looking at these lists, I realize that neither is a profile of somebody who is interesting, accomplished, or well developed—emotionally, intellectually, or physically. At the time, though, what impressed us was not how one-dimensional men were as adults, but how limited women were. Don't challenge, be patient—this was a formula for creating doormats. There were no similar limits for men. When Fletcher asked for our reactions to the dead-end scenarios we had written for women, the women in the room shouted out their reactions. They were angry, sad; they felt powerless, repressed. Yet as they talked they began asserting their own strengths: "What I grapple with," said one, "is men can do one thing at a time, and I'm always doing four things at a time." Another spoke of the difference between her first-born daughter and second-born son: "By twelve she could run the house. She was integrated." Her son, she said, was not doing nearly so well.

"Boys now understand that girls are as smart and as athletically competitive as they are," said a mother of two sons. "I expect my sons to pitch in and to take responsibility for cleaning up." Another woman had a related thought: During adolescence, her sons could not organize their lives. "It was either all girls or all sex," she said. "By college they were more together. Boys bloom later. But my daughter had it all together all along."

Within an hour, we had seen how messages given to women limited us, cut us off from who we really were, and robbed us of the competence that was part of our heritage.

Most of those in my group were professional women. Yet our list for women's characteristics was painfully traditional. Old tapes were still spinning in our heads. As Fletcher had warned us, the gender socialization we went through had imprinted invisible codes on those tapes that produced the sounds in our lives to this day. Yet all of us knew the tapes were full of false notes: Those tapes found discord where we saw synthesis and harmony, weakness where we saw strength. "Women tend to be more vocal and emotional," said one member of the group, "but then we're supposed to cut off our emotions." "Women want to resolve issues," said another, pointing out a trait she clearly found highly desirable. Angry notes crept into the discussion, and it built to a loud volume with many women talking, voicing their strengths, voicing the lives they lead not with the hesitation of someone looking at a piece of music for the first time, but with the confidence of professionals who are playing a score they are finally able to read. One woman talked about the new understanding of how women learn differently from men, how they are capable of thinking in complex patterns rather than simple linear lines—and we talked about how women are able to manage two agendas, home and work, simultaneously during each day. "I think women are terrific," said one.

The music came together and this is what we heard: To read the score of women's lives is to understand that we have expanded into many roles. We aren't quietly playing scales or dabbling in a lone octave. We are all over the huge range of chords that life offers us. We are playing many pieces, singing many songs and using lots of different instruments to make the music we want to make. We play our music in private and in public. We want it to be heard. We play softly when we think that's what the mood takes and loudly when that fits, too. We have many voices, many rooms, and we are inside all of them.

THE INTEGRATED FEMALE

We had trouble at first reading this in the adult lives of women. Our list in fact contained not a single attribute or characteristic that was relevant to the score of our real lives. One mother had no trouble at all spotting the synthesis and harmony in her twelve-year-old daughter. At twelve—the age is important because that is when many girls begin to undergo a radical disintegration of personality—her daughter was "integrated." This is the word many adult women now use when they talk about their efforts to blend their work interests with their family. This concept of integration captures the characteristics that management experts say are so necessary in today's and tomorrow's workplace: integrated thinking—the capacity to loop various tasks and business or technical goals into a coherent unit, the capacity to nurture teamwork and cooperation rather than isolation and destructive competition. This integrated mind or integrated personality—a person who can connect laterally and accommodate several different agendas simultaneously—is a critical component of women's ways of knowing, of doing business. It is a quality—the quality of intuition—that a girl of twelve has. It is one of the female strengths that feminist management experts were the first to identify. It is one of our strengths that we can play to, when we start changing our tapes.

CLEANING OUT THE ATTIC

Psychoanalysts use the simplistic image of our minds as attics in which we have stored all sorts of memories, pleasant and unpleasant. When a child leaves home to go to college, for example, the event triggers a rush of bad memories of earlier separations. Similarly, our minds are a storehouse of expectations of what boys and girls ought to be, and ought to become. In order to redesign children, we need to modernize our inventory. Old notions need to be discarded, new ones need to be stocked. It is going to take a deliberate effort and commitment—a spring cleaning of the mind that can produce a fresh start.

Before we can do that, however, we need to reach a deeper understanding of the ways in which we think of boys and girls differently—and the impact it has on children. Dr. Bernice Sandler, a senior associate with the Washington-based Center for Women Policy Studies, has spent the better part of two decades studying how women and men act toward each other. She makes a point so obvious that no one bothers to put it in words, much less think about it.

"You think of boys and girls' futures differently."

She began our interview by telling a story about how she had recently seen a child's T-shirt for sale that said: "Future President." And she said she had wondered if anyone would buy it for a little girl. When she sees a likely moppet in the supermarket, she has been known to remark: "This could be the first woman president." When she says it, however, most people respond either, "No way," or doubtfully, "Well, yes, she could be." She rarely encounters an enthusiastic, "You betcha!"

While some parents do a passably good job of providing gender-neutral toys for their children, we have not begun to explore our unconscious expectations about male and female roles. Deep in our psychic memories lurks a vast repository of images and fantasies that we project onto our children. This kaleidoscope of expectations contains a treasure trove of possibilities for boys, but only a meager handful for girls. What will little boys do when they grow up? How will they earn a living? What will they be? The menu we proffer to them is limitless. Not so for girls. Their choices are sparse. It takes a conscious effort to project girls into a science lab, a boardroom, a courtroom, the front office of a car dealership. We see them sweating in delivery rooms often enough, but rarely do we visualize them presiding as surgeon-in-chief over an open-heart operating team.

Until I began researching this book, for example, I never visualized my daughter as a scientist. Nor did she. As firmly feminist as her upbringing has been, Katherine still cannot escape the stereotypes into which women are cast in classrooms and outside-the-home experiences, as well as in girls' parents' own rigidly masculinized and feminized expectations.

Girls who are most likely to become scientists are those whose parents are scientists. A realistic sense of what is possible is critical to girls' visions of their future. I saw dramatic evidence of this one summer day when my daughter was twelve. I was on the back deck and she sat down to join me for a chat that meandered around to her future. "I'm going to be a writer when I grow up," she declared. I suggested that it was a little early to be limiting her options. "Why not?" she countered. "All of my parents are writers."

It's true; her mother, father, and stepfather are all writers. To her, writing is something that she can reasonably aspire to. She is surrounded by books, she loves to read, she sees her mother and stepfather working at word processors every day. She has spent hours with me in my office at the *Washington Post* and is as comfortable in a newsroom as any well-adjusted person can be. She has a clear idea of what writing is all about, and she is not intimidated by it. And the truth is, I can see her as a writer much more easily than I can see her in a science lab. But this is a reflection of my own lack of experience in science and my own sense of unease around equipment that I don't know how to use. Call it Bunsen-burner phobia; I can remember to this day my discomfort and awkwardness when a science teacher pointed toward a Bunsen burner and told me to light it. I can understand a child who doesn't like science. I didn't either. But this is what substance-abuse experts call enabling behavior: If I project this attitude onto my daughter—that it's okay to blow off science—I'm giving her permission to do it, and thereby limiting her career options. I am restricting her future with my own doubts.

My sons and I have never had an "I hate science" discussion. Somehow they have gotten the message that learning about science is not optional. They know they are expected to learn it, and thus it becomes a part of their career menu. My middle son talks about becoming a marine biologist, and I can see him being one. But it takes a conscious effort to develop in my own mind a vision of my daughter as a scientist. It is as if I am designing a female scientist from scratch. And this is true despite the fact that I have met distinguished women scientists. I have told my daughter about Gertrude Elion, the Nobel Prize–winning scientist at Welcome-Burroughs whose work led to the development of AZT, one of the few drugs effective in treating AIDS. I have learned that if I talk about science in the cold, unfeeling language of technology I get nowhere, either in my own mind or in Katherine's. But if I connect what she is studying in biology—cell structure, for example—to research on how drugs can attack disease, I can help her stay interested, and the tremendous career potential in science and medicine may open up to her. But for that to happen, I have to change the tapes in my own head about what girls can be.

I have to do the same kind of spring cleaning about what boys can become. I see vivid examples of how boys' nurturing traits are driven underground in the environment in which they grow up, but when the moment is opportune and a boy feels safe showing a kind and sensitive side of himself, these qualities emerge again. When my middle son was twelve, he went to a picnic that my husband gave for his staff on a farm. It was a day-long family affair with volleyball and other games, swimming, fishing in a pond, and frequent sightings of the resident herd of cattle. The son and daughter-in-law of the newspaper's owner were also there, with their son Eamonn, who was about three. Bonnie, his mother, was well along in her second pregnancy and this was August in Virginia—hot and sticky, in other words. Eamonn was out of sorts, and Bonnie out of steam. My son went over to talk with Eamonn, and the next thing I knew the two of them were headed off hand in hand toward the pond. Later on they were headed to the pool, and still later on over to see the cows and then back to the pond and over to the barbecue for food and drinks. For much of the afternoon, Jeff, completely on his own volition, took care of a transformed Eamonn—to Bonnie's eternal gratitude and to my surprise. Jeff was not only a willing nurturer, but he was very good at it, and he had undertaken this mission all on his own. That day there were no other boys his age around, no one to exert peer pressure or to tease him for being kind to a little child. The quality he showed was caring.

REDESIGNING CHILDREN

To replace the old tapes, we need to develop a different way of looking at boys and girls, to expect the quality of caring, for example, as much in boys as we expect it in girls. We need to redesign children in our own minds, not based on appearance and traditional stereotypes of how they ought to behave, but with a new framework, and a new set of qualities we value. In redesigning children, we need to think about content and character. "Beauty is only skin deep" is the old saying. Perhaps we might finally start believing this and developing cultural standards of worth that reflect a deeper set of values about what we want to see in boys and girls.

If we were to begin thinking about the traits we want to see in young children, Dorothy Rich's "megaskills" are a good foundation to build on. Rich, founder of the Home and School Institute in Washington, D.C., calls these skills children's "inner engines of learning." Here they are, with Rich's definitions:

Confidence: feeling able to do it
Motivation: wanting to do it
Effort: being willing to work hard
Responsibility: doing what's right
Initiative: moving into action
Perseverance: completing what you start
Caring: showing concern for others
Teamwork: working with others
Common sense: using good judgment
Problem solving: putting what you know and what you can do into action[1]

None of these qualities is startlingly original, nor do they carry masculine or feminine coding. They all are qualities that we can encourage in boys and girls with equal enthusiasm. The words are particularly useful in trying to construct what we want in a young child precisely because they are gender-neutral. Patience is a synonym for perseverance. Patience often shows up as a trait associated with girls, and almost never shows up on the list for little boys. Patience is associated with waiting in women, with limitations. "Be patient. He'll call." Perseverance is associated with getting the job done—in men. Patience is laden with doughy, disabling gender implications, while perseverance is neutral.

Using the "megaskills" skeleton, I'd flesh out the attributes I'd want to see in a young child with these from the girl's list that we drew up during the workshop: "clean, smart, helpful, loyal, peacemaker, strong in family, loving and kind." From the boy's list, I'd graft onto the skeleton "self-directed," which I think adds a dimension of independence to the megaskill of motivation, and then I would include "sensitive, competitive, active."

Some other traits that were not on either list but seem to me, at least, to be more important than "lady" or "princess," are curiosity, the ability to be attentive, a sense of fairness and a sense of humor. I did not choose "aggressive" from the boy's list or "don't cry," nor did I pick "modesty" or "quiet" from the girl's list. "Sensitive," which interestingly enough came from the boy's list, to me means encouraging the young child to feel his feelings, whether it means permitting a little girl to get angry or letting a little boy weep with pain or sadness. A young child should be encouraged to be assertive and should be given the verbal tools to assert what she wants. That is one way of channeling willfulness and impulsiveness into assertiveness, instead of aggression. Drawing from what we know about the strengths of the female leadership style, I would add to the young child a sense of voice and a sense of being integrated within his family and interconnected to the world around him. The child who sees herself or himself as a lone warrior or the Lone Ranger, who is selfish and narcissistic, will not flourish.

Here, then, are some basic traits that our newly designed young children might share:

caring
confident
common sense
motivated
initiative
perseverance
honesty
teamwork
problem solving

responsibility
effort
loyal
assertive
attentive
family oriented
clean
sensitive
loving and kind
smart
peacemaker
sense of humor
sense of fairness
curious
self-directed
competitive
active
verbal
integrated

If we can think of our male children as being kind and nurturing to each other or to a younger sibling, we should also be thinking of our female children as being strong. Our young child should be at ease with his or her body and its abilities, she should possess a sense of joy in the energy and motion she produces, and an awareness of her physical power. We need to give opportunities to girls to express energy, to enjoy being in motion, to run and to explore the world around them. We need to talk to them about women athletes and their accomplishments and to build in girls a sense of physical competence. My daughter, for example, has a terrific throwing arm. I love watching her throw the ball to the dog, for she does it overhand and it hums. I let her know that I admire this.

Mariah Burton Nelson, a former professional basketball player, makes the point that people have a deep-seated belief that boys and girls are different sorts of people, and they set up different sets of expectations for their physical competence. "Lower expectations lead to inferior performance and, perhaps most damaging, to a belief on the part of both girls and boys that boys are naturally superior athletes," she writes.[2]

A little girl raised to feel good about her body and its energy and power will grow up feeling comfortable with the idea of her own strength. She will also feel less vulnerable to physical attack.

Not long ago, my husband and daughter and I were in the kitchen while he was fixing dinner. My son's seventy-pound Siberian husky was there, too, demanding attention. On a lark, my husband reached down and picked him up in his arms and held him up to his chest. The dog loved it and licked my husband's face with great enthusiasm. Not long after that, my daughter and I were in the kitchen fixing dinner. She reached over and picked up the dog in her arms, just as my husband had done.

I was impressed, but to my consternation I heard myself start to say: "Be careful, don't hurt yourself." I was about to use the voice of Clarissa Pinkola Estes's "too-good mother," the mother whom she describes in *Women Who Run with the Wolves*. Her too-good mother is someone "who cannot help herself; she is what she is. Yet if we merge with the too-good mother for too long, our lives and our gifts for expression fall into the shadow, and we become scant instead of strong."

Instead of the treacherous "Be careful, dear" I was about to utter, I put what I've been thinking about for this book into action. "You're really strong," I said to my daughter. "Look at you: Power-Woman. I'm impressed!" She beamed, and the dog, Magnum, licked her face.

One way we can encourage a sense of physical power in girls is to dress them in clothes that encourage movement and adventure. Typically we dress our boys in shirts and pants or shorts. Many of us still put dresses on our little girls, clothing that both constrains their movements and makes them vulnerable to the taunts of little boys on playgrounds. "I see London, I see France, I see so-and-so's underpants" is one of the earliest and most memorable lessons that little boys administer to little girls, to keep them off the swings and other playground equipment that involve motion, and in their place. Boys don't have to worry about their underwear showing or their dresses being pulled up. A girl wearing pants has much more freedom than a girl in a dress.

"When schools have dress codes, it means girls wear skirts and boys wear pants," says Bernice Sandler. "Try climbing a jungle gym in a skirt." More important, she observed, "You treat a kid in a sweatsuit very differently from a kid in a dress."

I don't think I'm dwelling overly long on the image of bodily strength and power in our redesigned young child. It is a critical new dimension for toddlers who will grow up to be women. One thing that parents can do is to envision their daughters as athletes and participate with them in such sports as tennis, swimming, rowing, or whatever is appropriate to the child's age and interests. This may require a bold initiative from mothers who were raised at a time when physical illiteracy, as Nelson calls it, was equated with femininity. Encouraging daughters to become athletes will help secure for them the same opportunities male athletes have: Sports are supposed to develop character and muscles; they are good for a person's health, and they are a source of prestige.

Physical strength has important repercussions on a girl's or woman's sense of her ability to defend herself, which in turn has significant implications on a woman's ability to go where she wants to go and do what she wants to do. A woman who has developed some talent in martial arts, for example, and who has successfully defended herself against attack, has overcome crippling feminine conditioning. Such a person will feel no need to rush into a romantic alliance because she thinks she needs a bodyguard to protect her from sexual harassment in junior high school or rape in college. "A world in which women were not physically intimidated by men would be a different world indeed," writes Nelson, and is she ever right.

Having said that, Nelson goes to the core of the problem: "I can imagine a woman, even an athletic one, being reluctant to inflict harm. Since childhood, women have been taught to be gentle and kind." And they have also been taught to be weak and submissive, instead of strong and powerful. If, instead, both little boys and little girls were raised with praise for their physical strength, stamina and bodily power, that would be one more playing field that would be leveled between the sexes. The female infant who grips our finger can be big and strong, and she can smile, too.

IN THE MIND OF THE BEHOLDER

Bernice Sandler has a grandson who loves pushing a ball with his foot. His parents say, " 'Look, he's going to be a soccer player.' When little girls do this, parents say, 'Look, she's pushing a ball.' There is no future attached to it," she says. One thing we can do to erase the old stereotypes about boys and girls is to think of what girls do in terms of their future and to talk to them about how their childhood interests relate to future careers. A girl who shows artistic promise, for example, has a wealth of career possibilities in relatively new fields of computer game design. For that, she must be technically literate, and parents can start early on discussing such careers with children.

"Most parents try to be fair, and I don't think they realize that they really do treat boys and girls differently," says Sandler. She cited a study in which a group of children were all given the same problem to solve. When all children had finished, the observers were asked whether the child had accomplished the task through luck or by skill. "Mostly, they said for boys it was skill, and they describe the same behavior for girls as luck. I recently read a cross-cultural study of brilliantly gifted girls and boys in mathematics, and the results were the same. The parents of the boys described the boy as very smart, very talented, very gifted, those kinds of words. The parents of girls say, 'She works very hard.' You could see that this would have an impact on self-esteem. These parents are already devaluing the girls' achievements. 'She works very hard' isn't nearly as good as 'He's very smart, very gifted, very talented.' " If, as parents, we think about complimenting boys more often for working hard and girls more frequently for their talent, we can raise boys and girls who think of themselves as talented, hard-working achievers. And any successful adult knows that it is a combination of talent and hard work (plus luck) that brings results.

We tolerate bad behavior in boys that we would never tolerate in little girls. When two little boys are fighting with each other in the supermarket line, we ignore it and often let it go on far longer than we should. We'd break two little girls up at the first sign of physical hostility. If we intervened quickly to stop little boys from using aggression in these everyday situations, we would be teaching them a valuable lesson: overt, physical assaults are not the way to resolve disputes. This is a lesson they can take into manhood.

Boys use girls as negative reference points, and parents are co-conspirators in this deeply embedded social libel. This, too, is something we need to change, and we can do it by correcting bad behavior when we see it in boys. For example, boys learn to tease girls at a very early age, and most adults condone it. "Girls do not have the same kind of need to put down the boys or to define themselves that way," says Sandler. "They are much more likely to define themselves by their behavior or their appearance."

Boys and men feel free to make comments such as: "Oh, you throw a ball like a girl." "You are crying like a girl." All of those male put-downs are quite acceptable, says Sandler. "Boys are learning that it's not as good to be a girl."

Sadly, girls are learning this, too. And as they move from early childhood into elementary school, these lessons will be driven home to both of them in the classroom, hallway, and playground with the same steady drumbeat they've always heard.

PART TWO

Educating Our Children—
Echoes from the Past,
Remedies for the Future

CHAPTER SIX

The Myth of Equal Education

Over the years I have written a number of columns about research that shows that boys and girls are treated differently in our classrooms. But what I did not realize until I started this book was the degree and extent to which this takes place, nor did I realize how clearly girls understand what is happening to them.

Some classroom sexism is subtle, but it is constant and pervasive. Some of it is so blatant, so ruthlessly destructive of our daughters' ambitions, that it ought to be indicted as malicious wounding. From the first years of elementary school through college and graduate schools, girls receive destructively different treatments in their classrooms. Girls know it, boys know it—and parents ought to know it as well. Our sons are at the center of the whole educational process, while our daughters are sitting on the sidelines—still waiting their turn, after all these years.

Among the pioneering researchers who have been sounding alarms about this have been David and Myra Sadker, both professors of education at American University in Washington, D.C. Myra is the author of *Sexism in Schools and Society*, a landmark work published in 1973. The Sadkers have been calling attention to sexism in the classroom for two decades now—long enough, one would think, for educators to have dispatched it once and for all. It's a good thing we haven't been holding our breath.

Blame for this continued crippling of girls in our schools must be shared by the Reagan administration. The great communicator's doorstep is by now littered with the detritus of many other scandals and failed policies. But while Reagan's followers were looting the savings and loan industry, his dreary ideologues were looting the futures of girls. They did it with a concerted, vicious, and unrelenting attack on a tiny federal program buried in the Department of Education.

The Women's Educational Equity Act (WEEA) program was the only federal program that promoted equal education for girls by raising gender issues among educators. It funded pilot programs to combat discrimination against girls and developed training manuals for parents, teachers, and school administrators. It was singled out as a hotbed of radical feminists by the Heritage Foundation and its henchmen in the seedier "new right" organizations that flourished around Reagan; WEEA was among the first targets of the Reagan administration's fierce backlash against the gains women made in the 1970s. Leslie Wolfe, a career civil servant who was WEEA's director, was backed by numerous liberal and moderate members of Congress in her courageous battle to preserve the program, but in the end WEEA's budget was gutted, its programs abolished, and Wolfe was forced to resign.

The result of the right wing's crude assault was that there was virtually no federal leadership for promoting educational equity. There would be no federal funds for retraining programs to redress unequal treatment in the classrooms. The subject simply fell off the radar screen. Even when President Bush misrepresented himself as the "education president," he never made the connection—at least not publicly—between the disparate classroom experience of boys and girls and how that ultimately wrecks girls' professional aspirations and capabilities.

The progress women had made in reforming the educational system was put into a state of suspended animation: People knew what had to be done to improve the classrooms for women, to give them adequate teacher attention and constructive feedback, but the will to do it, the leadership for reform, had vanished utterly.

Like so much sexism, classroom sexism is both insidious and ruinous. Even teachers who are committed to running honest classrooms are stunned when they see videotapes of the biased practices they are following. The Sadkers continue to be struck by how subtle these biases are, how unintentional they usually are, and how often the teachers themselves have no idea that they are responding differently to boys than they are to girls. "It goes undetected because we're living in a sea of bias," David Sadker once told me. They and other researchers investigating sexism in the classroom have found that males get more attention from teachers, they get more precise and challenging feedback, they get far more "air time" during classroom discussions, they interrupt more, they call out answers far more frequently than girls do, and girls are far more likely to be reprimanded for calling out answers than boys are. Boys are more likely to be praised for good work, and criticized and forced to produce better answers, and they are more likely to receive remedial help and be directed into special learning classes earlier than girls are.

The Sadkers were able to measure the disproportionate amount of attention that boys demand. In both elementary and secondary schools boys are eight times as likely as girls to call out and demand attention. Boys are called on from two to twelve times more often than girls in any class period, no matter the ratio of boys to girls or the sex of the instructor. The Sadkers concluded that boys are being trained to be assertive and girls to be passive.

Patterns of boys hogging classroom time, as well as equipment, are repeated throughout elementary school, high school, college, and graduate school. The same patterns have been found in the United States, Great Britain, and Australia.

The lesson is catastrophically clear: In classrooms, girls learn to be quiet.

To be passive.

To make do with less air time than boys get.

To get by with less feedback.

What they do not learn is how to accept criticism—since they don't get as much of it. From the lower grades on up, boys are more disruptive, and they get more attention from the teachers. In disciplining them, teachers give boys another learning experience that teaches them how to deal with criticism. Introducing an idea, taking ownership of it, and keeping it at the center of the class discussion is another experience that is largely denied to girls. Finally, girls do not get the experience of interrupting and taking over a conversation. Later, as adults, we see the results: One study found that 96 percent of the topics introduced by men were followed up in the course of conversation, while only 36 percent of topics introduced by women were developed further.[1] Men are much more frequently the ones to interrupt, and they interrupt women much more frequently than they interrupt other men. Men dominate professional meetings through interruption. Another way they gain verbal ascendancy is by answering questions not addressed to them—a way of seizing control of a meeting or conversation. Women, once interrupted, typically do not try to regain the floor.

TEACHERS' ATTENTION

The single most valuable resource in a classroom is the teacher's attention. If one group gets a disproportionately large share of that resource, it stands to reason that this group will have the most profitable educational experience. It came as no surprise to researchers that girls test as equal with or better than boys when they enter elementary school and yet fall behind at the end of high school. Such tests as the National Assessments of Educational Progress and the Scholastic Aptitude Tests uniformly document this retrogression. Small wonder. Given twelve years of such a thoroughly unequal educational experience—which gets progressively worse for girls as they leave elementary school and go through high school—it is remarkable that girls do as well as they do.

The Sadkers, Bernice Sandler, and other investigators have found that patterns established in elementary school and reinforced in high school persist in college. With one difference: They get worse. Since even fewer students actually participate in college classroom discussions, the cheating of women students becomes even more egregious. While a quarter of the children in elementary school classes did not interact with their teachers at all, the Sadkers found that this proportion doubled in college and university classes. Male students received significantly more attention. Another study found that college women speak two and a half times less often than their male classmates. In a review of the findings on women's experience in college that they did for the Association of American Colleges, Sandler and her colleague, Roberta Hall, found that professors are more likely to remember men's names, more likely to call on them in class and listen to their answers. Professors felt freer to interrupt women students and ask them less challenging questions.[2]

That is the bad news about what happens to girls who go to school full of hope and expectations about what they will learn, who they will meet, and what they can do—only to be diminished and sidelined in the classroom and, as we have seen, teased and harassed on the playground. The good news is that this can be fixed. Perhaps the most exciting aspect of the Sadkers' work is that by retraining teachers they have been able to promote equitable treatment of boys and girls in the classroom. By showing teachers videos of what they are doing wrong, the Sadkers alert them to the biases lurking in their classrooms. Having done that, they then teach them techniques for making sure that boys and girls participate equally. Simple techniques—such as "wait time," in which teachers wait a few seconds for both boys and girls to raise their hands, or alternating from boy to girl in selecting who will answer a question—promote greater participation of both groups. These routines help ensure that both boys and girls get access to the attention of teachers, and they create better teaching and learning environments overall. Boys who might have called out before learn to take turns. The Sadkers and other researchers are trying to get across one of the most fundamentally important lessons for parents, teachers, and children to learn: Equity in teaching promotes excellence.

THE FASTEST MOUTH GETS THE AIR TIME

Catherine G. Krupnick, director of the Harvard-Danforth Center Video Lab, led a research team that spent a year reviewing videotapes of twenty-four instructors at Harvard College. She observed a pattern that is familiar to all of us who have been in classrooms. A few people begin to dominate the classroom at the start of a class hour, asking questions, answering them, and becoming so engaged in running the discussion that the rest of the students drop out of the conversation. The pattern repeats itself day after day, and the less verbal students become more and more disconnected from the class. It is not the students who have the most thoughtful minds who run the class, but the ones with the fastest mouths.[3]

Krupnick concluded, as have others who have watched this pattern in classes, that instructors have to take a much firmer hand than they currently do in managing classrooms so that each student has an opportunity to talk. She suggests that teachers become close observers of their own classrooms—that they keep notes on who participates and how, have videos made, and ask colleagues to sit in and observe what goes on. Among steps teachers can take to encourage participation by everyone is to hold everyone responsible for each assignment, to call on all students—not just those who raise their hands—and to listen for interruptions and take pains to discourage them. United Nations Ambassador Madeleine Albright combated the interruption problem in her classes in the Georgetown School of Foreign Service with the opposite approach. She told me that she taught her women students to interrupt.

BOYS AGAINST GIRLS

Children segregate themselves by sex in school very early and they maintain an absolute minimum of cross-sex contact until they reach high school. Researchers who have studied this phenomenon believe that it has much deeper impact than commonly believed: The separation of the sexes contributes to stereotypes by reinforcing certain types of behavior in children and by labeling certain activities "masculine" or "feminine."

Researchers Marlaine E. Lockheed and Susan S. Klein believe that patterns of inequitable behavior we see in adult groups have their roots in elementary school. They reviewed eighteen studies of how students behaved in school situations, ranging from preschool through kindergarten and the eighth grade, and found a pervasive pattern of same-sex segregation in everything from selection of play partners and work partners, to seating patterns in cafeterias, to students' contacts with each other. Again the intensity of peer pressure showed up—and it showed up early. A study of preschoolers found that boys who had contacts with girls were criticized by other boys. They found that the children initiated the segregation and teachers rarely interfered. It was also evident that whatever contact boys and girls did have was characterized by a lack of cooperation and by male dominance.[4]

EYEWITNESS REPORTS

Do boys and girls understand what is going on in the classroom? Indeed they do.

The University of Michigan runs a summer science program for girls who are between the eighth and ninth grades. Carol Hollenshead, who runs the university's Center for the Education of Women, asked the girls to write brief comments describing their experiences in school.

Many were acutely conscious of sexist teachers they had had in regular school. They were also keenly aware of whether their teachers had encouraged them, and were immensely appreciative. Some told of their own efforts to overcome sexism. These girls didn't pull any punches, and some of what they wrote about how teachers behave is downright shocking.

"I have a science teacher who is all for Women in Science. He always supports whatever I do, and he even works for the Women in Science.

"On the other hand, I have a U.S. History teacher who is sexist and advertises it."

"This perverted teacher said to this girl, 'This class should be easy for you since you probably screwed every boy in this class.' He also wrote 'I love you' in my sister's notebook."

"I had a science teacher once who would ignore you, not call on you, and generally pretend you were not there . . . especially if you were a girl. He would interrupt you in mid-sentence to try to prove you wrong with his own point even if you were right. I started a petition and got 100 signatures to the principal. He sure changed his train of thought about good teaching techniques."

"I had a science teacher last year who very often would not call on me, even if I was the only person in the class with my hand up!"

"In the sixth grade, I had a math teacher who refused to sign a recommendation for a pre-algebra course. He said, 'You, a girl in algebra. I don't think so.' I was persistent and prodded him and he eventually gave in."

Whether teachers call on boys eight times as often as they call on girls, whether they ask boys the tougher questions, whether they

tolerate unruly behavior on the part of boys while squelching it mercilessly in girls—they are treating boys and girls unequally. Boys,
who receive more and more teacher attention as they go through
the educational system, retain their voice. Girls, who receive ever-
diminishing amounts of attention from their teachers, lose theirs. Boys
gain confidence in their ability to do math and science, while girls'
confidence erodes. Boys see a dazzling array of occupations and possibilities spread out before them as they proceed from grade to grade. Girls
find their options diminishing, their hopes dimming as they conclude
there are certain things they simply can't do. They conclude that forays
into the "masculine" fields of math and science aren't worth the social
cost, the perceived loss of femininity that goes with being smart. Boys
are being set up to be independent; girls are being set up to be
dependent.

ASIA: HARD WORK FOSTERS EQUALITY

Girls in Asian cultures undergo a far more egalitarian educational
experience than do American girls. While much attention has been
given to the better performance of Asian students as a whole over
American youngsters, we have not looked at this through the lens of
gender. But the fact is that in a major cross-cultural study girls in
Asian cultures did far better in math than American boys did. They
are being raised in cultures that stress the connection between hard
work, homework, and good teaching techniques that expect achievement from all youngsters, as opposed to a culture that clings to myths
about innate ability and math genes. These cultures expect their young
women and young men to develop mastery over certain core subjects,
including math. Japanese students, for example, have to pass a rigorous
exam to enter college. A student who declares a liberal arts major but
who fails to pass the math exam will not be admitted.

Shin-Ying Lee is a researcher at the Center for Human Growth and
Development at the University of Michigan. A native of Taiwan, she

has spent twelve years researching the differences in achievement that are found among Chinese, Japanese, and American children. Part of the team led by the University of Michigan's Harold W. Stevenson, she and her associates have been trying to find out why American children do so poorly compared to these other children, particularly in mathematics and science.

Asian children are the focus of ongoing communication between teachers and parents, with both emphasizing good study habits and expecting all children to master the material. Parents, particularly the mothers, are closely involved with their children's homework. They are expected to provide help. This home culture is a sharp contrast to the exchange that typically occurs in American homes when a child and his parents meet at the end of the day: "What did you do in school today?" The usual response: "Nothing."

Sex differences do not receive nearly the attention that they do in the American culture when children are young. They are not nearly as pervasive in terms of toys, clothing, and activities. Shin-Ying Lee tells this story about her mother, who picked out a pair of pink overalls for the son Shin-Ying was expecting. "I said, 'I'm having a boy.' She said, 'What does it matter? It's a nice color for a baby.' "

Shin-Ying visited a university professor at his home in China. A child of about three or four appeared in the room, its head totally shaved. "I said, 'Is this your grandson?' And he said, 'No, it's my granddaughter.' And he explained that when it was hot, it was best for the child not to have any hair. There is this feeling there that they are all children. We place a bigger emphasis on gender than Asian countries do, from very early on." By contrast, she said, the Asian cultures she has studied tend to start emphasizing these gender differences in adolescence and ascribe great weight to them in later careers.

Americans stress innate ability. Asians stress hard work. "We asked mothers at what age do you think you can predict how well your child will do on the S.A.T.s. American parents say, 'By the first or second grade.' Asian parents say, 'I won't know until high school. There are so many factors. How hard he works, the help I can give him.' If parents believe it is all innate, they are not going to do much intervention." Such as hiring tutors or spending time going over homework. Teachers will react similarly.

"You don't find ability grouping in Asian classes. In Asia, they set up a track so that if you work on it, every child can learn it. And it doesn't matter if you are a boy or a girl."

Americans put more stock in getting children motivated to learn than do Asians. "Asian students are taught to go back and check their work. It's habit. Later on, they internalize those habits and they become part of an attitude." This attitude breeds success. "If you don't do well, and you attribute this to ability, there is no hope," says Shin-Ying. "But if you attribute it to work, then you can always work harder." And she emphasizes another point: "It all starts in elementary school. In high school it is too late to start working on study habits."

More than half of the schools in Japan are single-sex schools, she says, and that promotes a school atmosphere in which boys and girls pay attention to the work, as opposed to the opposite sex. Japanese parents do not expect their children to start dating until after they have gotten into college. Shin-Ying noted that the percentage of Asian high school students who also hold jobs is very low. Both students and parents make school their top priority. The researchers asked children in Beijing and Chicago a wonderful question—which parents might want to ask their children: "Let's say there is a wizard who will let you make a wish about anything you want. What would you wish?" Chinese children—in overwhelming numbers—gave answers that centered on education, such as being able to improve a grade or get into the university of their choice. American children made wishes about money and material goods. Fewer than 10 percent said anything about school.

The Stevenson team conducted a series of studies on the attitudes, beliefs, and achievements of American children and their mothers, and their counterparts in Japan and Taiwan. They looked at the core subjects of reading and mathematics. The children were tested in kindergarten, and in grades one and five. There were several striking findings about how parental attitudes can affect performance.[5]

Mothers in all three countries think girls are better at reading than boys are, and this belief begins in kindergarten. It was particularly pronounced among Japanese mothers, although the performance on the achievement tests do not bear this notion out. But the researchers were able to establish an important correlation between what the mothers believed and how well their daughters and sons would actually perform. Girls whose mothers believed that girls were better readers received significantly higher reading scores than those whose mothers thought boys were equally able at reading.

Mothers in all three cultures believed that boys were better at math than girls are, as early as kindergarten. These beliefs—that girls are better at reading and boys are better in math—appeared in the mothers before their children had any formal instruction.

More Japanese boys than girls thought girls were better than boys in math. This, in a deeply patriarchal culture that is far behind America in the progress of its women, is an arresting piece of data. American children, more than any other group in the studies, say that girls and boys are equally talented in math. But by the fifth grade 17 percent of the boys think boys are better and only 10 percent think girls are better. In Japan, meanwhile, 39 percent of the fifth-grade boys think girls are better than boys in math. Between the first and fifth grades Japanese boys had developed a high regard for girls' math ability. This attitude can emerge in an educational climate in which all children are expected to learn, and in which both boys and girls are taught that effort and hard work—which transcends gender—produce achievement. Boys, however, were better at certain visual-spatial skills than girls in all three cultures, to a remarkable consistency. The researchers concluded that even though the skills of the Japanese and Chinese teachers had pushed the Asian children far ahead of the Americans, they had not entirely eliminated gender differences.

These cross-cultural studies can teach us a great deal about how to improve the education of boys and girls. There is much here for parents to ponder about their own involvement with their children's schooling and their own attitudes about the difference between boys' and girls' capabilities. Many of the research findings—especially about teaching techniques—parallel findings of American educators who are concerned about why girls drop out of math and science. Researchers who are investigating how girls learn are telling educators that girls, and probably most boys, learn better through interactive teaching methods and collaborative group efforts, rather than the lecture method. The Asian schools produce a supportive learning environment with a lot of teacher feedback. Teachers recognize that children learn in different ways, and they provide a variety of drills and exercises, small-group work, and individual tutoring. Mistakes are treated as opportunities for teaching, rather than a failure by the student to provide the "right answer." These are all aspects of the collaborative teaching techniques that American reformers are urging educators to adopt in order to develop a better learning environment for girls. It is not that girls cannot compete: It is that girls are more comfortable learning in a collegial rather than a hierarchical environment. In the Asian classroom, the teacher is the guide to learning, rather than the dispenser of knowledge. What is clear from this look at how Chinese and Japanese children are learning is that these techniques benefit both boys and girls. They do better than our children do. Their parents and teachers believe that children will succeed if they work hard. The children believe this, too. They practice what Americans preach: Work hard and you can do it. In Asia, they have learned the lesson that girls' advocates are trying to teach here: Equity breeds excellence. These studies are powerful weapons in the arsenal of those who argue that culture, attitudes, and expectations provide an environment in which children can turn hard work into success, while other cultures that devalue intellectual accomplishment and let girls off the hook get what they ask for.

Nowhere is this more evident than in the anxiety-ridden relationship most American parents and their daughters have with science and math.

CHAPTER SEVEN

The Masculine Mystique

One evening, toward the end of my daughter's sixth-grade year, she announced that she needed help with her math homework. This was my response: "Sweetie, see if Dick (my husband) can help you. I'm in the middle of cooking dinner, and besides, I can't do math."

In one fateful exchange, I had told her that her stepfather was more competent to help her at math than I was, that I was cooking dinner—translated as men do math and women cook—and to top it off, that it was okay not to be able to do math since I had just publicly announced that I couldn't do it, with no apparent shame or remorse.

"That conversation," biologist Marsha Lakes Matyas told me, "goes on every night in millions of households." At the time I interviewed her, Matyas was directing the project on Women in Science of the American Association for the Advancement of Science (AAAS).

Without realizing it, I was modeling the worst possible set of attitudes and behavior toward math for my daughter. And I was typical of mothers and female teachers—the very people who have the best chance to break the chain of math and science anxiety that keeps women out of the best-paying jobs.

"It's okay for a girl to get by not knowing as much about math and science," says Matyas. "You'd never hear someone at a cocktail party say, 'I'm illiterate,' but it's okay to say, 'I can't do math.' That's a social norm we'd better change or we will be in terrible trouble."

The National Science Foundation has estimated that there will be a 700,000-person shortfall of scientists and engineers by the year 2010. The Department of Education has estimated that between 1990 and 2000, there will be at least 25 million new jobs created. One out of four of them will be technical positions. This portrait of the future workforce underscores an important fact: Anyone who wants to compete on an equal footing for the jobs of the future will have to be comfortable with technology. Anyone who is not, who parrots such defeatist phrases as "I hate math" or "I can't do science," might as well write off 25 percent of the employment opportunities. Morever, at least one major study of job offers to college graduates found that those who majored in the demanding math, science, and engineering fields commanded top dollar and received 45 percent of the job offers.[1] Clifford Adelman, who directs the U.S. Department of Education's ongoing study of the high school class of 1972, found that women who took at least eight credits of college math earn an average of 16 percent more than men with comparable educations. Math pays off.

THE LAST REDOUBT

The notion that girls can't do science or math is deeply rooted in families. We can trace this crippler all the way back to Aristotle and the Greeks' exclusion of women from the schools of medicine. The belief that women were the intellectual inferiors of men has been maddeningly persistent across time, and nowhere has it taken hold with greater force than in the hard disciplines of math and science. To this day, researchers are finding that by the time they are in the third grade, girls identify math as a masculine endeavor, and as early as first grade they have identified the physical sciences as a masculine field.

Indeed, science has proven to be one of the most politicized of all of the disciplines that have examined questions of differences between men and women, with conservative scientists marshaling evidence to support biological arguments of male superiority and liberal scientists arguing that environmental influences create the differences. With the field of science as political as it is, and as historically dominated by men as it has been, it is no wonder that it remains one of the last intellectual redoubts for women to storm. That people trained in science—our doctors, for example—are among our most highly paid professionals no doubt adds to its luster, and the desire of men to maintain science as a male preserve. Entitling girls to work in science, making them feel that it is their domain as well, probably comes as close to a cultural transplant operation as any change we will need to make. To transform the image of science, not reproduce it in yet another generation, we will need to transform it in the minds of teachers, parents, and our children. This is no small task. But the payoff in our collective knowledge ought to be enormous when we engage the minds of all of our brightest people, not just half of them, in the search for cures for diseases, for ways to better manage our environment, for clues into the unfolding mysteries of the universe.

The filtering out of women from these high-paying jobs and challenging careers begins in high school, when women elect fewer math and science courses than men do. Men enter college better prepared in math and science than women. At the University of Michigan, 76 percent of the women who entered in the fall of 1989 had four years of high school math while 90 percent of the men did. Women who concentrate in science are more likely than men to choose biology or medicine, while men are three times more likely to choose math or pure science. The percentage of women receiving degrees in math and science has steadily increased over the past twenty years, but they have made much greater strides in math than in physics, because the number of men majoring in math has plummeted from 17,117 in 1970 to 8,333 in 1989. Thus, in 1989, 7,106 women received almost half of the degrees awarded in math at the bachelor level and only 15 percent, or 642, of the physics degrees. That's not very many women physicists to help us discover the secrets of the universe or to be role models for daughters who might want to be scientists. The female avoidance of math and science is perpetuated for yet another generation.[2]

Researchers have identified a number of reasons why girls steer clear of math and science. Girls quickly identify these interests as masculine, an idea reinforced by the lack of women science teachers and role models, as well as textbooks that present problems in the context of boys' experiences rather than girls'. Parents frequently don't expect their daughters to do as well as their sons in math and science, and teachers have similar biases, which show up as early as the first grade. This lower expectation has no basis in fact: Girls' grades are similar to boys and they are often better in science and mathematics. But teachers who expect less of girls get less. Counselors still do not encourage girls to pursue math and science all the way through high school. Yet we know that once a child gets off the math and science track it is almost impossible to get back on.

High school math is called the "critical filter" for continuing into math and science in college. It has been called the gatekeeper to chemistry. Yet by the eighth grade half of our boys and half of our girls have assimilated the notion that math is for boys, and not for girls. By junior high school, boys are more confident in their math abilities than girls are, and they believe it is more useful than do girls.

TOYS, SPORTS, AND SCIENCE

Matyas is convinced that girls fall behind in science very quickly for two reasons: Teachers expect less of them, and girls do not do the kinds of extracurricular activities in their free time that boys do—activities that hone science skills. It is a double whammy that goes a long way toward explaining why girls begin to feel alienated or at least disengaged from science. Throughout the elementary school years, most girls are engaged in sedentary play while boys continue to play with the energy and motion toys that engaged them as toddlers. Girls usually have fewer opportunities to manipulate equipment or to build things—model planes and racing cars. A walk down the aisle of a toy store tells the story: The girls' aisles are filled with dolls, toy animals, toy jewelry, and makeup kits. The boys' aisles are filled with science and construction toys, chemical sets, and trains—toys that emphasize motion and things they can do. Parents don't shop on the boys' aisles for their daughters, and the packaging is not designed to appeal to girls. As a result, parents direct their daughters away from science toys.

Throughout the elementary years, boys' achievement-oriented toys become increasingly more complicated, and often the boys are beginning to build them with considerable sophistication and skill. They also have chums who share their interests, help them with projects, and are there to validate these activities as important and manly. Often their fathers work on such projects with them, teaching them new skills, engaging them in ever more complicated levels of construction. "Boys grow up with a cohort of friends who do the same activities," Matyas says. "They do model rockets together. They have a chemistry set. They do soap box derby racing; you learn beginning physics doing that. They carve cars out of wood; you are building something that works, using tools, using spatial skills to envision this block of wood becoming a car. This is traditionally not what girls do."

Boys are involved with balls and bats, which they use as levers, and although there has been some change in girls' involvement in sports, their experiences are significantly different than boys'. "The kinds of things boys do leave them with more points of reference for the traditional ways science is taught," says Matyas. Boys' interest in professional sports gives them an opportunity to work with numbers and become comfortable with them, as they converse with their fathers and friends about batting averages, won/lost percentages, earned run averages. Over the years I've listened to my sons in countless hours of these conversations. I've never heard my daughter discuss these points at all. By the ages of thirteen to seventeen, young women are significantly less likely than young men to read science books and articles, to watch science shows on TV or go to science lectures, to talk science with friends and do science projects or have scientific hobbies. Yet these are the activities that nurture a child's initial interest in science into a career.

THE INVISIBLE GIRL

Textbooks, the way science is taught, and the examples given continue to favor boys' interests and relate to their activities and ways of learning over that of girls. And this makes a difference. Research has shown that girls are far more likely to answer "I don't know" when problems are posed using contexts that are familiar to boys and unfamiliar to girls. Women continue to be under-represented in the illustrations in science textbooks, the contributions of women scientists are not acknowledged, and the pictures of children doing experiments send a subtle but ancient message: "Girls and minorities are doing the watching," Matyas says. "Boys are doing the experiment." Anyone doubting this need only look at an eighth-grade student's textbook, as I did. The first illustration showed the girl taking notes, and the boy doing the work.

CHILDREN ARE WHAT WE THINK

Jacquelynne Eccles, a professor of psychology at the University of Michigan, has identified parents' expectations of their children as critical to the subjects their children excel in and what courses they choose to take. She has determined that parents' belief that math is important and their confidence in a daughter's math abilities is even more important in a girl's decision to pursue an elective math class than her grades. Children's attitudes about their abilities are more influenced by their parents' attitudes than their own performance.

Parents can encourage and stimulate their children to pursue math or they can subtly undermine their children's confidence. And parents who bring stereotypes into the echo chambers get them right back.

Eccles's research, spanning a decade, has one resounding message to pound home to parents: Children are what we think.

But what we think about our sons and our daughters are two very different things. A British study by D. C. Entwisle and D. P. Baker found that parents have lower expectations for their daughters in math than they do for their sons as early as the first grade.[3] Parents were overly optimistic about their boys' abilities and overly pessimistic about their daughters' shortcomings.

Eccles's team conducted studies in twelve different school districts in Michigan. The first study was done on 1,000 families with sixth- and seventh-graders, and it followed them all the way through high school. The second study has looked at 600 families with children in kindergarten, first, third, and sixth grades. Researchers obtained objective measures of students' abilities, such as standardized test scores, grades, and teachers' evaluations of their abilities and interests. Parents' expectations and the experiences they provided their children were compared to these objective measures.

What the researchers were trying to find out was whether parents who thought boys were better than girls at math and sports ended up distorting their view of their child's performance, Eccles explained to me. "If they had a boy child, did they think he was better than he actually was? And if they had a girl, did they distort to the extent that she was not as good as the objective indicators would suggest? In general, that's what we found they do."

This is how it works, she says: "If I believe that a girl is not going to do as well, then I am likely to believe she is not as talented as her grades would suggest. And it is that latter belief that is the important one. They know that their daughter is in the 98th percentile on performance. But they explain that by focusing on her hard work rather than her talent. It's very subtle, but it has the impact of undermining her own confidence in her talent. She starts to believe she is doing well because she is a hard worker rather than because 'I am good at this.'

"If the parents believe the stereotype, they say to the girl, 'It's because you're working hard.' And to the boy they say, 'You are working hard and you are talented.' Over time, he will come away with more confidence in his ability."

This is reinforced because to the extent that parents hold these stereotypes, they will provide children with experiences that nurture them and enhance them. A child who is encouraged to play soccer in childhood will be better at it than someone starting in adolescence.

Eccles has some suggestions for parents:

• Give kids credit for talent when they have it.
• Every time you've got a daughter on the sports field and she comes off the field and you want to say, "You worked so hard," resist that temptation and say, "Gee, honey, you're great." Girls, she notes, "have the tendency to assume that if they work hard it must mean they don't have as much talent as everyone else."

Girls who were good in math but whose families place a premium on girls' being popular derive their self-esteem from other people's evaluation of their social skills rather than other people's evaluation of their math skills. Eccles suspects that these will be the girls in her studies who drop out of math classes. "It is not that they don't think well of their math abilities. It is that their math abilities are not as important to them." Boys, on the other hand, place more importance on math. "They are going to end up leaving high school with very different kinds of skills," says Eccles. "Girls have selected themselves out of some of the courses they will need to get into good colleges and to get a good job."

ECHO CHAMBERS

Math anxiety ambushes girls earlier than boys. It lasts longer for girls and has more enduring effects on their career prospects. But the truth is that math anxiety is like acne: It is a gender-neutral condition that creeps up on most adolescents, crippling their intellectual development just as surely as a chronic case of pimples cripples social development.

Mothers and fathers who hit the wall with geometry or algebra II are walking echo chambers. To this day, I am awe-struck when I hear someone say, "I just loved geometry." In ways we are not even aware of, in patterns of conversation and behavior, we radiate our discomfort and our anxieties from our generation into the minds of our children just as surely as if we were on a direct satellite feed. We are doing our children a tremendous disservice. In a world where math and science are critical skills, children who are mathematically illiterate will find themselves almost helpless. The youngster who drops out of the math pipeline is constricting her future more than ever before. Yet America's encounter with math continues to be a catastrophe. Students are emerging from high school with little competence to do basic problem solving needed on the job, and those who are heading off to college don't have the foundation for doing college-level math.

Half of the students who are in the math pipeline drop out each year, according to a 1991 report from the National Research Council. About 10 million youngsters are enrolled in high school math courses each year. In the 1988–1989 school year, there were about 900 doctorates awarded in mathematics. Only 45 percent of these went to American citizens. Only 97 were awarded to American women. To give this a little perspective: A person's odds of breeding a Kentucky Derby winner are one in about 40,000 each year. Your odds of having your high school math student go on to get his or her doctorate in math are one in 25,000.

THE NATIONAL MATH REPORT CARD

The National Assessment of Educational Progress (NAEP) started issuing report cards on how the educational system is performing in

1969. In 1990, the NAEP assessment of the math abilities of fourth-, eighth-, and twelfth-graders asked the states to volunteer for a state-by-state breakdown in which eighth-graders would be assessed. The Trial State Assessment Program, as it came to be known, has yielded the richest and most detailed veins of information about mathematics teaching and learning ever mined in the United States.

A similar survey was done in 1992, and that year it included fourth- as well as eighth-grade public school students in the forty-four states that chose to participate in the comparative survey.

It discovered some good news: Students in all three grades in both public and private schools had improved in average math proficiency since 1990. Eighth-graders showed significant increases in their proficiency. The disheartening news, however, was that just over 60 percent of the students in all three grades had achieved or exceeded a basic mastery of the skills and knowledge they should have. Only about 25 percent of students were performing at a proficient level or higher. Only 2 to 4 percent were performing at the advanced level.

How does this affect children's ability to function in the real world? Well, in 1990 a sample at all three grade levels was given a typical lunch menu to read, and then asked how much it would cost if they ordered soup of the day (70 cents), beefburger with fries ($2.70), and a cola (60 cents). Only 37 percent of the fourth-graders got the correct answer ($4.00), and only 66 percent of the eighth-graders got it. Nearly one-quarter of the high school seniors could not get out of a restaurant knowing how to add up a simple bill.

FINDING A CULPRIT

We know that American youngsters begin to feel anxious about math as they enter middle school. But there is something else at work here—one of those large, ugly truths that hit you as you look at the dozens of tables that measure how students are doing.

And that is television. The relationship between the number of hours children watch TV and their woeful lack of proficiency in mathematics is one of the most jarring statements to come out of the 1990 state-by-state assessment. At all three grade levels, fourth, eighth and twelfth, students who watched the most television were the least competent in math. Fully 25 percent of fourth-graders reported watching a mind-numbing six hours of television a day.

The most compelling evidence of the crippling math-television connection is this: The top ten states in math proficiency—North Dakota, Montana, Iowa, Nebraska, Minnesota, Wisconsin, New Hampshire, Wyoming, Idaho, and Oregon—are the same states that report the least time spent by students watching the tube. The parallel between the bottom ten states in math proficiency and the top ten states in television viewing proficiency is almost as absolute. There's no mystery to this: Subtract six hours from your productive day, and see what it does to your performance.

A child devoting five or six hours a day to television will be skimping on homework, and there is strong probability that the child will neglect the homework that he or she thinks will be the most difficult: math. In math, the correlation between homework and success radiates through the national assessment, particularly in the eighth and twelfth grades.

But I suspect there is another factor at work here. My daughter's seventh-grade math teacher, Vernon Williams, is a former Virginia state teacher of the year. His students routinely return home from state math contests with the top honors. "You have to be very aggressive with math," he told me during one of our conversations, but he did not see this trait as the exclusive province of males. "You'd be surprised. Some of the girls in my classes are very aggressive toward math."

The successful math student, he was saying, understands that she has entered into a contest: Will the math problem beat her, or will she beat it? For that psychological state of mind to flourish, the student needs energy and drive. She must be a person who thrives under the pressure of competition and the exhilaration of winning. A problem

solved is a contest won. I told this story to my husband, the enthusiastic former aviator, who nodded sagely and said: "Old-time pilots tell
beginners, 'You fly the airplane, or it's going to fly you.' "

This frame of mind is the exact opposite of the passive, reactive
couch potato whose brain functions principally as a receptor of electron-
ically generated images. Television addiction carries with it a whole
pathology that undermines learning: poor nutrition—snacking on
junk foods and swilling soft drinks while sitting in front of the tube;
laziness; time wasting; a focus on passivity and entertainment rather
than productivity and achievement. Studies abound that show that
TV-addicted students are less verbal and have trouble concentrating.
They are passive absorbers of shoddy entertainment—for more time
than most of them spend in a classroom. It follows, then, that the
passive style of learning will spill over into the classroom and color
the psychological state of mind they bring to a difficult subject. The
teacher may be introducing long division, but the student is reliving
last night's shoot 'em up.

What can parents do to offset the destructive influence of TV? The
solution I arrived at and put into effect at my house as a result of my
research for this book was a simple one: We turned off the TV on
school nights.

CLOSING THE GAP

The child who does best in math is likely to have parents who have
done graduate work, who monitor homework and curtail television
time, who are both in the home, and who are cultivated readers.

No surprise in that, but does this highly proficient math student
also have to be a boy?

Close analysis of the NAEP numbers shows that the difference
between the proficiency of girls and boys is really quite small. Given
the enormous educational and social advantages that boys have, it is

remarkable that girls come as close to boys' achievement levels as they do.

Much attention has been given to an American Association of University Women's study that attempts to relate the plunging self-esteem that overwhelms adolescent girls and their diminished performance in math and science. But the NAEP data does not support the conclusion that girls fall significantly behind boys in math.

The good news that was buried in that data and received almost no attention was this: Girls have caught up with boys in math except at the twelfth-grade level. At that point, 18 percent of the males were operating at or above the proficient level and only 14 percent of the girls were.

HOW CHILDREN LEARN

People versus things. Trucks versus dolls. Motion and distance versus closeness and caretaking. These behavioral traits that are learned and reinforced throughout infancy and childhood reveal themselves as important influences on the way children learn. Researchers Elizabeth Fennema and Penelope Peterson, who are in the School of Education at the University of Wisconsin at Madison have suggested that learning habits that involve working independently on high-level tasks may enable some children to do better in math and science. These learning behaviors involve choosing what task to do and persisting at it until it is accomplished. The more a child works or plays in this way, the more proficient she gets in these skills, and the better she will perform at tasks that require independent thinking and persistence. Fennema and Peterson note that traits of independent learning frequently show up in the backgrounds of outstanding mathematicians. And, of course, independence is precisely the quality that we promote in boys and discourage in girls. Young girls, Fennema and Peterson point out, are socialized to be dependent, and they receive more protection and more assistance in doing tasks from their parents and teachers. As a result of this social reinforcement, the researchers write, "when children enter school girls tend to be more dependent on others and boys tend to be more self-reliant."[4]

Once Fennema and Peterson established that independence is an important autonomous learning behavior, the next question they addressed was this: Why do some people become independent learners while others do not? This led them to explore the connection between learning and people's internal belief systems. They make the link between self-confidence and math competence this way: If you are confident that you can use and learn math, you will be inclined to take on a math task and persist at it until you have mastered it. If you think you can do something, you'll do it. The more competent you feel, the more willing you are to tackle difficult tasks; the more you do this, the more able you become.

If, however, you attribute failure to a lack of ability, or success to sheer luck, you are relinquishing control over what happens to your learning process. Fennema and Peterson cite studies that indicate that when it comes to mathematics, men attribute their success to their ability and effort, while women attribute their success to unstable, external factors over which they have no control. If you combine that style with the idea that women do not put as high a value on the need to learn math and science, you can see how the tenuous connections they feel toward these disciplines are easily severed.

THE MAD (MALE) SCIENTIST

One weekend afternoon I asked my daughter to draw a picture of a scientist. She sat down, pencil in hand, and sketched me a scientist. A while later, my son emerged from his room and I asked him to draw a scientist. He was suspicious of my motives, since he knew what I'd been working on; nevertheless, he complied. The two drew precisely the same figure. The styles were different, of course, but the scientist was essentially the same: A white male, alone in a lab, with a stethescope and a slightly mad look in his eyes. My son said, "I thought about drawing a woman, but you wanted me to draw a scientist, so I drew a typical scientist."

As early as kindergarten, girls who are asked to draw a picture of a scientist sketch a picture of a white man, wearing a white lab coat and glasses. He is mixing chemicals or experimenting on animals. He is working alone, often on something evil, and he looks either angry or insane. From kindergarten through college, boys and girls in industrialized nations throughout the world draw this amazingly consistent picture of what a scientist does and what he looks like. While both boys and girls portray scientists this way, there is a critical difference in the pictures. Both see scientists as men and science as masculine. For boys, this means it is something they can do. For girls, it means it is something they can't do. Science, for girls, violates the gender rules. And this is as true today as it was for the girls' mothers.

Research on why women do not pursue the lucrative, nontraditional careers that men do has repeatedly concluded that the single biggest factor that discourages them is the sex-role stereotyping of these occupations: Scientists are males, therefore females can't be scientists. This is a concept cheerfully known to behavioralists as sex-role congruency. It means what girls do and what boys do. These stereotypical beliefs are widely held throughout society, and they reverberate throughout girls' selections of classroom subjects and careers.

Fennema and Peterson, as well as others, believe that sex-role congruency is a major reason why girls disassociate themselves from math, just as it leads them to distance themselves from science. Girls get the idea that teachers don't expect them to do as well as the boys, and if they do, they are then seen as less feminine, and that makes them uncomfortable. Success in math is not valued, because girls think other people harbor negative views about how well they are doing. Fennema has found that these negative feelings about girls' achievement in math intensify between the sixth and eighth grades.

STARTING EARLY

Research has demonstrated that girls will not easily cross the line into "masculine" subjects. They must have a great deal of self-confidence and be supported by a network of family, advisers, teachers, and peers who share the conviction that math and science are appropriate and important for women as well as men. A girl whose mother is a scientist, for example, is far more likely to major in science in college than a girl whose mother is not. This underscores the importance of family influence and expectations in girls' developing a fluency and sense of entitlement in the world of science. For parents—particularly mothers, who may be illiterate in science—it points to the need for them to change their expectations of their daughters and to literally change their own thinking.

Parents don't have to be scientists, but we have to have the right attitude. We have to start inculcating a comfort with science in our children at a very young age. One way we can do that is to expose children, even at home, to experiments that are simple, easy to grasp, and fun.

One experiment Matyas describes, for example, involves stretching the opening of a balloon over the top of a soft-drink bottle. Then fill one bowl halfway with hot water and another bowl halfway with ice water. Holding the bottle upright, put it first in the bowl of hot water to see what happens. After a few minutes, put the bottle into the bowl of ice water. In the hot water bowl, of course, the ballon will expand. When put in the cold water, it will contract as the air gets cooler and the molecules slow down and stick together. "Four-year-olds can understand this," she says. So can mothers who weren't shown such science-can-be-fun experiments when they were four.

Matyas tells of teachers at a day-care center in Sweden explaining how electricity works, and what a conductor is and an insulator is, by taking nine-volt batteries and instructing the children to stick them to their tongues. "If the battery is still good, it will make your tongue tingle," she says. "Even if kids don't get all the science, the fact that they did it gives them points of reference for later on."

Girls' service organizations such as the Girl Scouts of America and Girls, Inc., have been at the forefront of efforts to help connect girls to the world of science and the career potential it holds for them. They quickly realized, however, that their programs are staffed by mothers who had the same science and math phobias inserted into their psyches most of us did. To help overcome this multi-generational science gap, the American Association for the Advancement of Science has developed training programs and a workshop manual for volunteers to help demystify science and give it a feeling of relevance to the lives of girls. The aim of their work has been to get girls to make a mess, make mistakes, try again, predict the outcome, find out why things happen, estimate, take risks, observe what is going on, ask questions, concentrate, explore, dig in, and get dirty.

SCIENCE CAN BE FUN

In the middle of her eighth-grade year, my daughter mentioned that she was going to have to do an experiment for science. By that time, I'd spent a good part of a year reading about the problems girls had with math and science and interviewing some of the leading researchers in the country about this. I knew very well the importance of having girls do the experiments and not avoid them. So as the weeks went by, I asked discreet questions about my daughter's experiment, such as: "Have you selected the experiment you are going to do yet?" The day before it was due, I discovered she had not.

I got the AAAS manual that Matyas helped develop for the Girl Scouts and took it into the living room. There I found an experiment that looked doable and rather dramatic. More to the point, we had all the supplies that you needed to conduct it: a bottle, paper towels, a match, and eggs. I suggested Katherine read about it. She sat down on the sofa and after a few minutes announced that this experiment would work.

She hard-boiled some eggs and peeled one of them. My husband

and I went into the kitchen to watch the experiment. She took a paper towel and lit one end of it and put it into the bottle. Then she placed the peeled egg atop the bottle opening. It began to jump up and down and then suddenly, with a great whooshing noise, it got sucked down into the glass bottle and settled with a plop on the bottom. What had happened? My daughter explained that the burning paper had heated the air in the jar and caused it to expand, so that it had to escape. That's why the egg jumped up and down. After the hot air escaped, the egg settled back down on the neck of the bottle and the air inside started cooling, contracting and creating a partial vacuum and sucking the egg into it. It was thrilling to see an experiment actually work. When Katherine conducted the experiment two days later in school, she got a B. That quarter she earned a B in her gifted and talented physical science course. As far as science experiments go, she has established a precedent of hands-on work and success, not avoidance and failure. And I have learned something I missed thirty-odd years ago: Science can be fun.

CHANGE THE SYSTEM, NOT THE GIRLS

To intervene effectively and change the direction of girls' thinking, say the experts, we have to change just about everything in the current educational system so that mental barriers never get erected in the first place.

"There are two different ways to go," says Marsha Matyas. "One is you can fix girls so they can work in the system; two, you can change the system. That's harder, but it's more effective in the long run."

She described a program in Minnesota in which talented junior high school students could take math courses in state universities. Not enough girls were qualifying and those who enrolled soon dropped out. The people administering the program first decided that the solution was "change the girls." Then they realized that the system— and by that they meant everything from the way junior high school classes were run to the way the qualifying tests were administered, and to whom—was designed for boys, not boys and girls. This insight led them to work with teachers to show them how to identify gifted and talented girls. "Teachers don't know how to do this," says Matyas. "Highly talented girls don't act like boys do." They then retested girls who were "near-qualifiers." That time they got a lot more qualified girls into the program. Then they looked at the classroom and found that when it is dominated numerically by boys, boys answer most of the questions. When most of the students were girls, there was a lot of cooperative learning. This cooperative learning program has subsequently been incorporated into the teaching design in junior high classrooms. "They made a program that's better for everybody," says Matyas. "The assumption was that there is something wrong with the program, not with the girls."

She cautions against simplistic answers to the complicated dynamics that keep girls from embracing math and science. Self-confidence is a part of the puzzle, but she draws a distinction between a girl having a legitimate belief in her ability and an artificially inflated sense of self-esteem. "We have to be careful about self-esteem and throwing that around a lot. Girls don't need artificial props. Self-esteem has to be built from actually doing stuff."

Fennema and others have demonstrated repeatedly that there is a high correlation between students' achievement in math and how their teachers treat them—with nonsexist teachers getting a higher performance out of girls in math and science. Recent intervention programs that exposed young women to positive female role models, as opposed to math-anxious mothers, have also been effective in nourishing continued interest in math. Researchers have found that a lone teacher can have a significant impact on girls' attitudes toward math by providing active encouragement to girls through role models, sincere praise for good work, and explicit advice regarding the value of math and its usefulness in high-paying careers.

THE INTELLECTUAL GIRAFFE

Researchers who have been concerned about girls dropping out of math have devised some clever strategies for breaking down the barriers and overcoming girls' math anxieties. In November 1992, the National Coalition of Girls' Schools sponsored a Symposium on Math and Science for Girls, which drew equity experts from around the country.[5] One of them was Dorothy Buerk, an associate professor in math education at Ithaca College, who led a workshop on Women's Metaphors for Math. She urged the assembled educators to have their students write about their feelings about math by using metaphors. Again, the underlying principle for this approach is connecting women and girls to the subject—and enabling the teachers to learn more about the individual students by reading and studying their metaphors. One student wrote: "For me, math is like an earthquake," for if you make one small mistake it "can ruin or tear down all of your work." Another said math was like quicksand.

The most disturbing metaphor Buerk ever got illustrates the power of this process in enabling a teacher to learn more about her students. This was what the student wrote:

"For me math is like an abusive parent. If you do not stay on guard, your parent will strike you when you least expect it. It's not rational and it's difficult to understand why things are the way they are. Parents and math are supposed to help you get through life, not screw you up and hinder you. I hide from the parent, yet it always seems to find me. And that sense that math is out to get me, no matter what I do."

Buerk shared with the workshop a protocol for stimulating students into thinking about metaphors for math. I followed it in an exercise with my daughter. I told her to pretend she was describing mathematics to someone. These are some of the questions, followed by Katherine's answers.

"If math was weather, what kind of weather would it be?" I asked.

"Winter," she said. "Because it can be harsh."

"If math was a food, what food would it be?"

"Carrots. You have to chew it. It would be hard."

"If math was a means of travel, what means would it be?"

"Walking. Because it takes a while and it's not very easy, and you get really tired out."

"If math was a color, what color would it be?"

"Red," came the unequivocal response. "When I think of the word math it's always in red letters."

"If math was a way to communicate, what way would it be?"

"Latin. Because it is so technical and because Latin is the basis for a bunch of languages, kind of like math. Like, if you know math you can do science and if you know Latin you can do Spanish."

"If math was an animal, what animal would it be?"

"A giraffe."

"A giraffe?"

"You know how people think math is intellectual? I thought of the most intellectual animal I could, and I thought of the giraffe."

"If math was a plant, what plant would it be?"

"A cactus. If you are stranded in a desert you can cut it open and get water. Math is like that. It can be helpful, but it also has all these thorns on it. Stuff you really don't want to do."

Science and math are hard disciplines that are perceived as cold, isolating, laden with rules and right and wrong answers, as masculine pursuits that are pointless and unrewarding for girls, and may even undermine their gender identity. But we know now that these subjects can be made more accessible and rewarding to girls when classroom teaching techniques make girls feel welcomed, when they are praised for good work, when they are made to feel valued and supported through the use of role models and with career guidance and encouragement. Researchers have urged teachers to de-emphasize the military and industrial uses of science, and to highlight instead the social benefits that science has produced. Intervention programs that portray the human and environmentally useful aspects of science expand girls' ideas of what science can be, and help overcome their perception that scientists have to be terribly smart and willing to work long hours and that science is a lonely, isolated, and indoor occupation. Among the tips that AAAS trainers give to teachers is that they refer to scientists as "her" or "they." Children don't generalize. When you say "he" they think of male, not male and female. "You do it in little bits at a time," says Matyas. "And it's the same with parents."

One important but neglected resource is girls' networks of friends—their groups—which look to be much more crucial to girls during the school years than they are to boys. Matyas envisions this dialogue: " 'I'll take calculus next year if you will.' If five of you say you will take calculus, that's a lot less intimidating. We are trying to get that started much earlier."

STUDY GANGS

The power of a group was documented by Uri Triesman, a professor at the University of California–Berkeley, who noticed that the Chinese students in his calculus courses consistently excelled while the black students had a steady pattern of failure. He spent eighteen months investigating how these two groups spent their time, and discovered two disparate patterns of socializing and studying. The Chinese combined the two, forming "study gangs" whose members critiqued each other's work, shared information, and created an atmosphere of healthy, friendly competition. Black students, on the other hand, worked alone, separating their academic and social lives. Triesman observed that this emphasis on self-reliance—a trait much prized in the dominant white male culture—was working to the disadvantage of black students, and he designed math workshops in which students studied together in an atmosphere in which they were expected to succeed. Study groups and support groups have proven to be so valuable in recruiting and retaining minority groups in nontraditional fields of study that advocates for girls at the Center for Sex Equity in Schools at the University of Michigan are urging schools to establish them in schools for girls who are enrolled in advanced math, science, and computer classes.

During their elementary school years, most children spend their days in the same classroom with the same group of children. They have the same teacher or teaching team. There is a reassuring constancy to their day, a reliable structure. Then just as they are about to hit puberty, they are also dispatched out of the cocoon of elementary school and into the cold, unfriendly halls of a new school, with six or seven different teachers, all of whom have different teaching styles, grading systems, homework demands, and project requirements. Despite the thrill they feel at growing up and going to junior high or middle school, for many children this is the transition to hell. And for years, study after study has shown that this is the period when the self-esteem of girls begins to plunge.

Educational strategies that take into account girls' core values of sharing and cooperation, as well as their need for close relationships with other girls, will produce a school environment that is more supportive of girls. Having other girls they know in their classes, particularly as they make the transition into junior high, is more important to girls' sense of security and confidence than we have realized. But we don't value girls' friendships as educational resources. Instead, many school systems move sixth graders into large middle schools, dislocating networks of friendships that girls have spent years building. Our daughters come home after the first day of middle or junior high school, utterly distraught because none of their friends are in any of their classes. We mothers are very reassuring: "Oh, don't worry about it," we say. "You'll make new friends in your classes in no time." They've been trying to tell us something, and we have not heard them. The social network for girls can form the nucleus of a peer support system that can give girls the courage to speak out, to raise their hands and risk an incorrect answer, that can help them steer a classroom discussion in a direction that will interest girls. To understand this, all you have to do is listen to a group of girls talk about ways boys act in their classes and the way teachers act. They reinforce each others' commentaries about boys and teachers with a steady stream of "I know's" or "Did you see the way he . . ." and "She always calls on the boys first." For girls in a classroom environment that favors boys from the outset, their female friends can provide the support systems that adult women have come to yearn for and depend on in hostile work environments. If we need the validation and support for our views and our voice at work, we should not be at all surprised that girls who are coexisting in classrooms with boys would feel the same need.

Mere tinkering with the system is not going to create the changes that will allow girls to cross over into a "masculine" world, just as they reach puberty, in a new school. The "masculine" worlds of math and science have to be made gender-neutral, and girls have to be made to feel welcomed and supported. Matyas and her colleagues emphasize that math and science have to be taught from the outset in ways that make them relevant to children. Stereotypical expectations and beliefs, the patterning and molding of children's lives begins, as we have seen, very early. It is critical for parents and teachers to root out their own beliefs about girls not being able to do math or science and to replace these myths with facts. Despite the discouragement, despite the unequal opportunities that girls get in their classrooms and in the minds of the adults raising them and teaching them, they do better academically than boys. Think what they could do if they had an equal shot.

CHAPTER EIGHT

Girls and the Single-Sex School

"It's the difference between breathing fresh air and smog. The sexism—smog—isn't there at a women's school."
  —Former Wellesley President Nannerl Keohane

There is one place within the academic spectrum where girls are getting better than an equal shot. At the academically demanding all-girls schools they are getting every shot. And these are the schools that have solved the mystery of how to keep girls enrolled in the highest levels of math and the most challenging fields of science.

I attended single-sex schools in the first through fifth grades and went to Barnard, the women's college that is affiliated with Columbia University. So did my mother and sister. Mother was a classmate of Margaret Mead's and frequently enlisted her as a role model of female achievement. Over the years I have written a number of columns extolling the virtues of single-sex colleges for girls. When I began working on this book, I knew that women's schools held important clues about how to instill confidence and a drive toward achievement in their students. What I did not realize was how much of what they have uncovered can be translated into public education in ways that benefit all our young people, not just the daughters of privilege.

An education at an academically demanding girls' school is the best education a girl can get. Evidence of this began surfacing in the late 1960s and 1970s, when researchers discovered that girls who went to all-girls schools did not suffer nearly as much from "fear of success"— the fear that professional achievement would leave them socially and emotionally isolated. Paradoxically, just as researchers were beginning to prove that single-sex schools work better for girls, we began drifting away from them and their numbers declined sharply through the 1970s and 1980s. This came about partly as a result of financial hard times but, ironically, all-girls schools were also casualties of the women's movement, which once campaigned against all forms of separateness as inherently unequal for women. Between 1960 and 1990, for example, the number of all-women colleges dropped from 298 to 94. The number of all-girls independent elementary and secondary schools dropped from 500 to 97 by 1993. The independent girls' schools that have survived have gone after their market share with all of the modern sales tools at their disposal: surveys, polls, and research into the accomplishments of their graduates. Their efforts have yielded an unprecedented amount of knowledge about how girls learn, how best to teach them, and how to instill in them the self-confidence people need in order to achieve. These schools are pointing the way toward how public education can be reformed so that girls can be educated to be all they can be. Far from being a dying breed, academically demanding girls' schools are on the cutting edge.

We have known for more than a decade that public schools short-change girls. In the March 1986 *Phi Delta Kappan*, Charol Shakeshaft, of Hofstra University's School of Education, provided an important insight into the core of the problem. Two recurring messages were coming out of research into girls' experiences in coeducational schools, she wrote. "First, what is good for males is not necessarily good for females. Second, if a choice must be made, the education establishment will base policy and instruction on that which is good for males."

Academically demanding girls' schools do precisely the opposite: They put what is best for girls at the center of every decision about how to run the school. What is good for girls is the constant and consistent measure of how to do things. The results could not be more telling.

Ask a fourth-grade student who is attending an all-girls school what her favorite subject is, and the chances are that she will tell you it is math. She will give you the same answer that the majority of boys give in the fourth grade. What's different between the experience of girls at these schools and girls attending large, public, coeducational schools is that they retain their interest and fondness for math all the way through their education. The National Coalition of Girls' Schools surveyed more than 500 fourth-grade students and found that 43 percent of them selected math as their preferred subject. English was second, with 29 percent. The coalition also surveyed more than 700 graduating seniors at its sixty member schools and found that 48 percent planned to pursue math, science, business, or engineering degrees in college. This is almost double the national average for girls.

The coalition represents schools from many different traditions and academic programs and philosophies. What the schools have in common is a deep commitment to the values of girls' schools and the advantages they can offer students. Coalition members want public educators to incorporate techniques they have developed for enabling girls to succeed—for they understand that this is the way to improve the social and economic standing of the vast majority of girls and women. They have the salary figures to make the case for the way they are educating girls. A survey of 1,200 alumnae of girls' schools done by the polling firm of Yankelovich Clancy Shulman found that their average personal income was $44,000—about $5,000 more than the mean annual income of men in 1990 and more than double the mean income for women with college degrees. Thus women who graduated from girls' high schools came far closer than other women to having incomes that approximated and, at times, exceeded that of men.

These women far outdistanced their peers in both academic and career achievements: 85 percent of them graduated from college and 52 percent pursued a graduate degree. This is an important finding:

An advanced degree has enormous impact on a woman's earning potential, and thus her economic autonomy. The mean income for women with college degrees was $20,376 in 1990; for women with master's degrees it was $31,368. For men, a master's degree increases their earnings by $6,156, or about 16 percent. For women, it increases their income by $10,992—more than 50 percent.

THE CONFIDENCE TO EXCEL

Girls' schools expect a lot from their students, and they give them the self-confidence to expect a lot of themselves. A measure of the girls' self-confidence came when they were asked whether a woman should be president of the United States: 92 percent of both fourth-graders and seniors responded with a resounding yes. Eighty-three percent of these graduating seniors said that if they had to do it again, they would choose to go to an all-girls school.

Girls' schools validate girls' learning style by teaching to their strengths. Whitney Ransome, the coalition's co-executive director, believes that the poor retention rates for women in math and science can be laid squarely at the doorstep of inhospitable teaching techniques and classroom environments that prevail in coeducational junior and senior high schools. Traditionally math and science have been taught in ways that demand a right or wrong answer within a limited period of time, and each student is on his own to get the answer. However, as we have seen, research on women's learning styles show that women learn better when they work together to solve a problem. "Many of the math and science strategies we see being used throughout our member schools value learning through cooperation and team exercises, realizing that there may be more than one right answer, and giving girls a lot of hands-on experience," says Ransome.

Girls are hungry for information that is relevant to their lives. Thus girls' schools use teaching strategies that relate math concepts to everyday uses, such as balancing checkbooks and managing homes. When teaching percentages, for example, teachers will have girls design the areas of a house, do architectural layouts, select building materials, and apply geometric concepts to such uses as wallpapering rooms. "Some of the things we are suggesting have applications for teaching boys as well as girls," says Ransome. "Some people assume that if you alter the teaching style, you are watering down the curriculum. Nothing could be further from the truth."

Role playing is another technique girls' schools use to make subjects relevant and exciting, and to illustrate why science and math are integral parts of students' lives. Girls' schools know, for example, that today's adolescents list safeguarding the environment as their top concern. When teaching about the effects of slash-and-burn policies on the tropical rain forest, teachers will set up situations in which girls take on the role of the various players who are affected by these events—the farmers, the predatory lumbermen, the scientists trying to protect the environment, the economists trying to figure out a substitute for the income from the rain forest.

Academically strong girls' schools provide their students with a steady show of role models, from headmistresses to the women who run the math and science departments and the women who coach their athletic teams. A survey sponsored by the Coalition of Girls' Boarding Schools (which merged into the National Coalition of Girls' Schools in October, 1991) found that at independent girls' schools—both boarding and day schools—85 percent of the faculty were women, while at coed independent schools only 36 percent of the faculty were women. When girls see women heading math departments, when they have women teaching them science, the message is very clear: Women can excel at math and science. Girls who attend academically demanding girls' schools are expected to take three to four years of math. Girls are expected to do well, and the achievement goals are set high. This environment encourages girls to take risks in challenging subjects, to blurt out the answers—as boys do.

"One of the things that is so important is the power of connection, the power of being linked with other girls and women," says Ransome.

"When you are the only girl in a science class or the only one in a law firm, it doesn't work. Women don't work well in isolation."

THE GRADUATES' ENDORSEMENT

Graduates say girls' secondary schools gave them a significant edge over their peers both in college and when they entered the workforce. They also say a single-sex education gave them a handle on better ways of coping with the conflicts between work and family. The Yankelovich survey found that they described themselves as independent, confident, successful, satisfied, and involved with their communities. The women felt that the single-sex environment helped them develop more self-confidence and a firmer sense of identity. Some comments that they offered were: "It gave me total freedom to be myself and to find my special talents without worrying about the whole boy/girl question." Another, who now teaches in public school, said: "I see a lot of girls not wanting to be smart because there are guys in the class. . . . I didn't have any of that."

NO FEAR OF SUCCESS

Elizabeth Tidball, a professor emerita of physiology at George Washington University, was the first to draw attention to the compelling link between women educated in an all-girls school and their future success. In surveys she conducted in the 1970s, she established that graduates of women's colleges were more than twice as likely as other women to be honored for their career accomplishments, even though the percentage of women who attend women's college is quite small.[1] More than 95 percent of American women who attend college choose coeducational institutions. Of the twenty-five colleges that produced the women who would earn the most doctorates, twenty-three were women's colleges. She and other researchers concluded that, without question, women's colleges produced a disproportionate share of women leaders, and this was particularly true for the so-called Seven Sisters—Barnard, Bryn Mawr, Mount Holyoke, Radcliffe, Smith, Vassar, and Wellesley. Research by the Women's College Coalition has found that graduates of single-sex women's colleges are six times more likely to sit on the boards of Fortune 500 companies than their counterparts from coeducational schools. The leadership training girls get at all-girls school was underscored in the 1992 election year when the Women's College Coalition found that 41 percent of the women who ran for the U.S. Senate were graduates of women's colleges, again a remarkable figure when one remembers that only 2 to 3 percent of women graduate from all-women schools.

But the most compelling evidence about the positive impact that single-sex education has for girls came from a study of Catholic schools in Chicago. Valerie E. Lee of the School of Education at the University of Michigan, and Anthony S. Bryk, of the Department of Education at the University of Chicago, used a random sample of 1,807 students in seventy-five Catholic high schools, forty-five of which were single-sex institutions. Far from being quaint anachronisms, they concluded, these single-sex institutions may assist adolescent academic development by providing children a place to learn without the distractions of the adolescent social agenda.

In a 1986 article in the *Journal of Educational Psychology*, Lee and Bryk reported that girls at all-girls schools showed a consistent and positive attitude toward school; they were more likely to associate with academically minded friends, and to express specific interests in both mathematics and English.[2] The girls did more homework, although boys in the single-sex schools did more homework than boys in coeducational schools. Boys in single-sex schools were much more likely to enroll in a larger number of mathematics and sciences courses than boys at coed schools. The girls in single-sex schools took more math courses than girls in coeducational schools.

The researchers examined the effects of single-sex schools on academic achievement in the sophomore and senior years. They concluded that there were no areas of achievement in which students at coeducational schools surpassed students at the single-sex schools in either year.

The benefits of single-sex education for boys showed up most significantly in their sophomore year and then tapered off by their senior year, although the benefits were clearly present.

For girls the pattern was dramatically different: The benefits of a single-sex education increased between their sophomore and senior years, and they achieved statistically significant gains in reading and science.

Lee and Bryk made another striking discovery: The girls in the single-sex schools had taken the same amount of coursework as the girls in the coeducational schools had taken, but they had done better. This points to the importance of the different classroom environment and type of instruction that girls in these single-sex schools had as the factors that made the critical difference in their superior performance. The gains these girls made were particularly large in science. Lee and Bryk estimated that the achievement in science that girls in single-sex schools made compared to girls in coeducational schools amounted to a year's worth of growth, or about 50 percent more than the amount typically learned during the last two years of high school.

The two researchers also found evidence that:

- Girls in single-sex schools had higher educational aspirations.
- They had a more positive self-concept.
- They harbored far fewer sex-role stereotypes than girls in the coed schools.

The researchers noted that boys in single-sex schools harbored more sex-role stereotypes in their sophomore year than did boys who attended coeducational schools, but this difference disappeared by the time the boys in boys' schools were in their senior year, leading Lee and Bryk to conclude that an all-male environment does not inevitably have to produce sexist attitudes.

BASTIONS OF SEXISM: PRESERVING THE OLD ORDER

Some academically demanding girls' schools have discovered valuable information about how to educate girls so that they strive for excellence. But Lee's research should not be taken as a blanket endorsement of single-sex schools or of private education over public education. As with public schools, some private single-sex schools can be good and some can be harmful. Subsequent research Lee did of classrooms in twenty-one private schools should serve as a warning sign to parents who are trying to sort out whether they want their sons and daughters to attend private school or public school. They should be aware that expensive private schools, particularly those that were once all-male schools, can be bastions of sexism.[3]

Unlike public schools, which must comply with federal civil rights and due process laws, independent schools are fiefdoms run by boards of trustees and headmasters or headmistresses. Lee and her colleagues suspect that many private schools are responding to the conservative bias of affluent parents. Far from being agents of positive change, some private schools may in fact be redoubts of the old order, perpetuating the male-centered educational tradition that has dominated learning for centuries. The exceptions they found were in Quaker schools, schools that had made a subtantial commitment to equity, and the academically demanding all-girls schools.

Chemistry classes were especially perilous. Two-thirds of all sexist incidents in the coed schools they visited occurred in chemistry classes. Since only one-fifth of their observation time was spent in chemistry class, chemistry was clearly the most sexist subject they observed. In one class taught by a woman, with fourteen boys and five girls, the teacher allowed the boys to talk without raising their hands and favored a few male star pupils, but she then reprimanded girls for talking without raising their hands. In another class, of nine boys and five girls, the male teacher actually threw a graduated cylinder full of water at a girl who had asked him a question about it.

Observers found other examples of sexist behavior in the English classes taught in boys' schools. Discussions and essays were read aloud that described men degrading women through the sex act or through lascivious preoccupation with women's bodies. One male English teacher instructed his students to include a woman's looks and "her measurements" in their descriptive writings. A cartoon of a bare-breasted woman adorned one classroom.

Private schools and single-sex schools are not necessarily the answer, and some may in fact be extremely perilous for girls—as well as for boys who come out of them with distorted attitudes about women. These schools and the research Lee conducted into them, however, have provided important insights into the process researchers are now calling "engenderment."

Lee's research teams observed eighty-six classrooms at seven girls' schools, seven boys' schools, and seven coeducational private schools. "The notion was if girls' schools are doing better, what is it that they are actually doing?" said Lee. In the course of their search, the teams began identifying both positive and negative forms of engenderment. And again, her findings should serve as a cautionary note to parents: Not all girls' schools are great for girls.

"GIRLS CAN'T TAKE IT"

What they found in one girls' school that described itself as providing a "super supportive environment" was what Lee described as "encouragement on dependence." At one classroom, for example, the teacher assigned a term paper to upper-level students and then told them she would be available for " 'major hand holding on this project.' There is the assumption you're going to need it. It wasn't in the best interests of the students," Lee told me in an interview. They found that girls' schools that came out of the finishing school tradition were the most likely to condone male-bashing and coddling of female students.

They found an aggressive teaching mode where students were challenged to defend their ideas and encouraged to comment on each others' ideas—but they found it only in boys' schools. "This led me to the kind of assumption I don't have total confidence in," she said. "There is the kind of feeling that girls can't take it. This is shortchanging girls a lot." For all her impressive research on how good girls' schools are for girls, Lee has at least one important caveat: Schools that coddle girls aren't doing them any favors. Coddling is another form of sexism—and it can show up in private or public schools.

Lee's research highlights ways in which sexism is perpetuated in schools, but it also points to ways that schools can end classroom sexism—such as promoting teaching techniques that blend the intellectually challenging "individualistic" style with the "relational" style identified by Carol Gilligan. They also looked for clues at schools they identified as exemplary. One was a coeducational school that was formed twenty years ago in the merger of a boys' school and a girls' school. The merger had been accompanied by the formation of a gender-equity committee that has remained active. Another school singled out for its low level of sexism was a two-centuries-old Quaker school, the only coed school they visited that was headed by a woman. Concerns about societal equity—including gender equity—suffused every aspect of school life. Clearly one way to reduce sexism is to provide more female teachers and principals.[4]

The traditional criticism of all-girls schools is that a single-sex environment is artificial, that it does not reflect the world girls will enter as adults. There are no boys, therefore the girls do not get the experience of learning how to relate to the opposite sex. They have no opportunity—so the argument goes—of discovering how boys operate and of acquiring the social skills they need to handle them. A mirror-image critique is often offered about all-boys schools. Boys are portrayed as benefiting from the "gentling" influence of girls in the classroom, while girls are more often portrayed as needing their boy-girl social skills as a vital tool to a successful life. But more than two-thirds of the 1,200 girls' school alumnae said that attending an all-girls secondary school did not hinder their ability to relate to men and did not prevent them from having a well-rounded, satisfactory social life.

Moreover, recent graduates of these schools are even more convinced than older graduates that the single-sex environment helps prepare them for the challenges contemporary women face. The Yankelovich survey of 604 women who graduated between 1955 and 1960 and 600 women who graduated between 1975 and 1980 found that the younger women believe that a girls' school experience is even more important than did women who came of age three decades ago.

"The most important gift parents can give their daughter is an inquisitive, well-trained mind," said Arlene Gibson, headmistress of Kent Place School in Summit, New Jersey, and president of the girls' school coalition when their survey of graduates was done. "We offer girls the tools to work with and their confidence levels soar. Our graduates believe they have unlimited possibilities and they expect to accomplish whatever they set their minds on."

Arlene Hogan, headmistress of the all-girls Hamlin School in San Francisco, said their survey showed a portrait of women who were confident, satisfied, and ready to handle whatever life threw at them. And she cut through to the ultimate question that lurks in the minds of all fathers and mothers who are sending their daughter off to school: "What more could a parent want for her daughter?"

Successful, ambitious, satisfied, independent, confident, and competent. What more could a mother want for her daughter—or for a son?

CHAPTER NINE

A Day at Madeira

I decided to find out what an academically demanding all-girls high school was really like. I wanted to know what the campus felt like, what happened in class and in the hallways. What do they do that is so good for girls?

The search took me to the Madeira School, a respected, academically demanding girls' school near Washington where many of the people who run our government send their daughters. The school was founded in 1906 by Lucy Madeira, a thirty-three-year-old Vassar graduate who had taught at the Sidwell Friends School in Washington before deciding to start her own school—with not a single student lined up. This was a woman who believed in taking healthy risks—and she set a tone that permeates the atmosphere of the school she founded to this day.

The school's mission is deceptively simple: to provide young women with a strong college preparatory education. Located on almost 400 acres of lush meadows and woods in Fairfax County, Virginia, Madeira draws students from about thirty states, thirty foreign countries, and from the extraordinarily diverse community of people who live in the

Washington area. About a quarter of its students receive some financial assistance. Madeira embraces an appreciation for tradition and manners, strong belief in the importance for girls of forming life-long friendships, and an understanding that a classical education is the mark of an accomplished woman. Routinely all of its seniors go on to college or specialized professional schools in the arts.

Athletics and outdoor activities are essential features of the school, an indication of an underlying educational philosophy that emphasizes both intellectual and physical development. At Madeira, there is a solid commitment to the belief that sports teach girls to take risks, to be aggressive, to work on teams, to learn to lose, and to think strategically. On the grounds are tennis courts, playing fields, riding trails, an amphitheater, an outdoor pool, and ropes and initiative courses of the type that are used in outdoor adventure programs that teach teamwork and develop people's inner resources. The importance Madeira places on sports in a girl's development was underscored when it built a 32,000-square-foot, state-of-the-art sports center that opened in 1992.

Heading Madeira is Dr. Elisabeth Griffith, an historian and author of *In Her Own Right,* the biography of Elizabeth Cady Stanton. Betsy, as she is known, is married and has a son and a daughter and two stepdaughters. Clearly, she provides the 300 girls who attend Madeira with a living example of how a woman can combine a demanding job with marriage, children, and stepchildren, as well as a role model of someone who has succeeded at the top of her academic field.

Madeira begins at the ninth grade. Fifty-five percent of the girls board and 45 percent are day students. My guide during my visit is Janelle Irick, a young woman who went to public school in Washington, D.C., until she transferred to Madeira at the beginning of the tenth grade. She is a boarding student. During the day, I find out a lot about Janelle: She has recently won a Carl Rowan Scholarship to attend college (named for the distinguished columnist who has raised millions of dollars in scholarship money for African-American youngsters) and she is president of the student body. The summer after she graduates, she will work as an intern at Boeing. She has chosen to go to Florida A & M for college. She has pondered the matter and concluded that she will get more support and intellectual challenge at a predominantly black school than she would at a predominantly white school.

Our first class is Latin III, with Mrs. Elizabeth Heimback, and we meet in the first floor of a small house on campus. It is a glorious day near the end of May and the doors and windows are open. The room has the fresh smell of the outdoors. Sunlight filters in. There are fifteen desks but only four girls in the class. They are dressed casually in shirts and shorts. Mrs. Heimback and I are the only ones wearing any makeup. We are sitting more or less in a semicircle and the class begins like a conversation. Heimback, a lively person who shifts effortlessly from English to Latin, starts the class by handing back a test and telling the girls that they all did well. She tells one that she loved her paraphrases of Cicero. She elaborates on some of the answers, explaining ways of improving them. Her style is relevant: The Latin term *campo vaccino* comes up, it means cow pasture, and Heimback wants to know words that derive from it. Vaccine, one girl answers. The small size of the class allows Heimback to give each student personal attention. The girls interrupt, talk often, volunteer the answers, and ask questions. We talk about Gaius Valerius Catullus, a lyric poet who lived circa 84 B.C. to 54 B.C. One student wants to know the female version of Valerius. Valeria, Heimback tells her, as in malaria. We learn that Catullus believed profoundly that big books are boring, so all of his poems have less than twenty lines.

"What's in his poems?" asks Heimback.

"Emotion," offers Janelle. "They are passionate."

"Right," says Heimback. "It is heavy stuff. Who was he passionate about? Claudia." A married woman, and that's just about all anyone knows about her. The girls are curious about the relationship, but they are not scandalized.

We find that Catullus described his beloved as *mea Lesbia*—and not *mea Claudia*. Heimback tells her students that Catullus admired Sappho, the fifth-century B.C. Greek poetess who lived on the island of Lesbos and who greatly influenced him. "Sappho attracted a group of intellectual, talented women to Lesbos. Maybe they were lesbian, maybe not," Heimback tells her four girls. "When Catullus calls her

Lesbia, it is an incredible compliment because it means she is fun to talk to. What makes her superior is her wit and charm." Heimback is teaching the girls about great women, not just great men. And she is obviously a great teacher of women.

No one in the class ever raises a hand. They speak up. They translate a poem together, with Heimback coaxing and encouraging. Torri Eubanks, a cute, round-faced boarding student, wants to know if Catullus and Claudia "ever had a relationship."

"All we know is what he put in the poetry," Heimback answers. "I think they did. Maybe it was all in his head. But older people were gossiping about them." She points out that Catullus was very young—he died when he was thirty—and so was Claudia, young lovers the subject of adult scorn.

"Does this ever happen today? And what does this say about older people?" asks Heimback.

She makes sure that each girl takes part. She teaches with drama and flair, using her voice, her hands, the blackboard to illustrate her points. When one girl used the wrong structure, Heimback turned it into a teaching opportunity. "I'm glad you said that. It's wrong." And she illustrated the correct structure on the board. During the last part of the class we are translating. "Nature renews itself, but humans die," Heimback recites the line they have just puzzled out: "Nature renews itself, but humans die. What does this have to do with love?" she asks.

Vallery: "We're going to die, so love me now."

Janelle: "What a loser line!"

Heimback: "Don't tell me you've never heard that!" The girls smile. It's a loser line, but it's been enough of a winner to have endured across the ages.

The class is interrupted when the bell rings. Before I leave, I talk with Heimback. This is what she said about teaching girls in a girls' school:

"They are able to be themselves. The things they are able to share are remarkable. Boys are anxious to cut each other off at the knees."

Heimback has also taught Latin to boys. She knows what she is talking about.

Janelle next takes me to Sophie Speidel, the director of counseling, with whom I will spend second period. We walk into her office, and find on the table a pamphlet telling children about death. Janelle whispers as she drops me off, "She's having a baby." Above Speidel's desk is a sign: "Pain is inevitable/Misery is optional." I can see from the books in her office that she is prepared to counsel girls on a world of worries. Some titles: *Fat Is a Feminist Issue, Beloved, Peer Counseling, Making Decisions, Children of Alcoholism,* and a video, *On Being Gay.*

Speidel, who has a master's degree in education from the University of Virginia, lives on campus. She has a dog that some of her quieter protégées like to walk. "It's a door opener and gets them feeling more comfortable around me."

Speidel went to the National Cathedral School for Girls in Washington, D.C., and she has worked in a public school. She offers some contrasts: "Probably one of the greatest things they get in an all-girls school is self-confidence. They don't worry about what they look like. They are not caught up with the competition with their peers. They can be openly affectionate with each other; they are more self-conscious in a coed environment. They have more chances to be involved in every aspect of the school. The kids here are really into activism. They are not afraid to stand up and say, 'We've got to do this for the environment, for animal rights.' They have a drive to be involved."

Speidel played lacrosse for four years at the University of Virginia. She had an athletic scholarship. She played U.S. Team Lacrosse for three years. She is a role model of the female scholar/athlete.

When students go to her for information about contraception and sexually transmitted diseases, she provides it. She counsels ninth-graders that when they choose to become sexually active, they need to get routine pelvic exams from a gynecologist. While the prevention of teenage pregnancies was once an overriding goal, today Speidel is equally concerned about protecting the girls from sexually transmitted diseases. "Recently they wanted me to provide condoms. At first they wanted condom machines and Betsy said no. They wanted a reason. She said if you are responsible enough to have sex, you are responsible enough to go to a drugstore and buy condoms yourself." Condoms are not distributed at Madeira. Students are well educated about eating disorders, however. "They watch each other closely for things like obsessive exercise. They won't let someone slip through the cracks," says Speidel. In an all-girls school—where girls' concerns do not have to compete with boys' for attention—girls receive potentially life-saving preventive education.

Janelle and I walk together to her photography class. The day has gotten warmer. Girls are wearing shorts and sandals. Few wear any makeup. The atmosphere is cheerful, full of "hellos," "heys," as girls pass each other in groups as they change classes. What is strikingly absent is the hand holding and hallway necking between classes that you see in public high schools. No one is preening for the opposite sex. The noise level is even different.

The doors and windows in the photo room are open. The teacher is Frank Lavelle, and he is wearing an apron that says "Function in Disaster, Finish in Style." It's Lucy Madeira's admonition, and the school's unofficial motto. He is young. He spends the first part of the period in a semi-darkened classroom displaying slides of pictures and asking the girls to analyze their artistic meaning.

A girl tells him she has lost her slides. His response is a lesson in personal accountability. There is no coddling. "Well, I'm not going to stop what I'm doing and look for them, if that's what you're asking," he tells her. "Or are you just giving me the bad news?" Later I will learn that one of the girls had sought his counsel about a social problem involving a date. I discover that Lavelle does something besides teach: He functions as a big brother for girls who are living away from home.

POWER VS. OPPROBRIUM

Patricia Wilson is the academic dean at Madeira. She also teaches women's history. She describes herself as having two personal daughters and 300 professional daughters. She and her colleagues see what happens to the girls at Madeira as well as their own daughters. These women—mothers of daughters who are also teaching girls—have collected astute insights into what happens to girls. "When does self-esteem fall apart?" asks Wilson. "It corresponds with puberty and goes beyond that to the ninth and tenth grades. Something happens to girls that tells them they just won't do."

She gives the students in her women's history class an exercise to do. "I tell them to think back to the seventh grade and describe the boy who at twelve is physically precocious. They say: 'leaders, macho, athlete'; sometimes they'll say 'bully, hunk.'

"Then when you ask them to think about that girl in the seventh grade who was physically developed, they say: 'fast, bimbo.' Maybe they say 'pathetic' or 'popular,' and by that they mean popular with the boys as they get breasts.

"The idea for boys is manhood and leadership. If you're a boy you get power with getting older. With the female you get opprobrium. There is nothing to do with leadership." If you do the same exercise and ask what the girls think about the boy who developed late, they use words like "nerd" and "fink." For the girl who was slow developing "you get a titter of laughter and then they'll say 'lonely.' It is couched in terms of relationships."

THE MISSING MODEL FOR GIRLS

"The model for integrating growing into womanhood with academics and achievement has not been made yet," said Wilson. "It saddens me that this is the generation brought up by feminist parents. What's changed here?" To hear Wilson tell it, not much. By high school, girls' self-esteem has dropped and they are coping with enormous physical changes that are taking place in very visible ways. Many are wearing braces and feel pressured to wear makeup. In public schools, all of this is being done under the watchful eyes of boys. At an all-girls school, they can make the transition from girl to young woman in a more protective and supportive environment. There are no boys staring at the girls. Moreover, the absence of boys enables girls to focus on academics.

In coed schools, says headmistress Griffith, there's a cost to being smart. Girls see that the boys concentrate their attention on girls who are pretty, not the ones who are smart. "There's a risk to being smart," she says. "Wherever girls got it, they've internalized it. I've always told my daughter that smart is better than pretty. Smart can lead to pretty." A smart woman can find the money and resources to improve her appearance. Pretty doesn't lead to smart.

Girls internalize an event much more than boys do. When girls get a bad grade, they blame themselves. When boys get a bad grade, they blame the teacher or the subject. Wilson said that if there was one thing that she could pick out that was different at Madeira than in coeducational classes, it is that girls find their voices. "These girls know how to take a position, and many have said to me they would not have done that in another environment. I think it is about risk taking. We need to show them that taking risks, especially interesting risks, is really seizing what's out there as a human being, the pleasure and power that comes with using their brains."

She gives an example of a girl who is having a problem and who comes to her for help. She asks the girl if she has talked to her adviser and gets this answer: "Well, no, not really, well, she is very nice but we don't connect." Then, says Wilson, "I say, 'You have a right to have an adviser you can connect with.' " The student may then say she doesn't want to hurt her current adviser's feelings or rock the boat. To which Wilson responds: "You are allowed to have needs that have to be met." In a large, co-ed system, that kind of child is not going to be heard, she tells me. But what Wilson is giving her in that conversation is a sense of entitlement.

TELLING THE TRUTH ABOUT MATH

Girls are required to take three years of math before they can graduate from Madeira. Most take four. The women who teach and lead at the school know what happens to girls with math, although they don't claim to know exactly why it happens.

Says Jean Habermehl, Madeira's admissions director, "We know girls like to discuss an issue. They don't do as well in multiple-choice tests that are timed. The concreteness of math is bothersome. But math doesn't have to be taught that way."

Wilson tells her students straightaway that girls who are satisfied with learning the grunt work of math and nothing more are removing themselves from the loop of good schools and good career possibilities. She tells them that a low level of work in math is unacceptable and intellectually lazy. For them to stop at that level, she tells them, is to put themselves "at risk for being a bimbo. I am telling them the truth. They hear I am not going to coddle them. They appreciate that."

REMEMBRANCE OF THINGS PAST

All morning I have been harboring a secret anxiety. It struck shortly after I arrived, when Jennifer Salopek, Madeira's public affairs director, handed me my schedule. After fifth period, it said: "Physics." I gulped but didn't say anything. I had succeeded in ducking physics when I was in high school and college, but apparently my good fortune would not last. I knew this was an important class to witness, since physics is the least attractive of all the sciences to girls. If girls' schools are succeeding in attracting girls to physics, they are doing something important. So why was I scared? Why was I having these feelings like I'd had in high school? Wilson walks with me to the physics class and she introduces me to the teacher, Clark Deveneau. He is young, casually dressed, with white shirt sleeves rolled up. He greets me with a hearty handshake, and this: "We are going to put you to work." And it hits me: a full-blown attack of science anxiety. Across the ages it came—from tenth-grade biology and my fateful encounter with the Bunsen burner to a sunny classroom at Madeira more than thirty years later. The only thing that is different is that my defenses are better, sharper, and quicker. I've had several decades of practice. Instantly I smile and say that I'd be happy to participate but I have to be free to take notes. Wilson and I sit down at desks and I am feeling like a fool. I am a grown woman on a mission of discovery, and the mere suggestion that I am going to have to do physics has created a physiological surge of panic: My throat is dry, I can feel my heart beating faster, my palms are moist, and I am making excuses about taking notes. I am totally annoyed with myself. I do something I know I can do: I count the number of girls in the class. Fifteen.

Deveneau begins. "I am worried about something and I am taking an informal poll. What is the maximum number of times you can say 'God Bless You' after someone sneezes?"

"Two," says one girl.

"One," says another.

"What on earth does this have to do with physics?" says a third.

Deveneau is filling a plastic container with water. He places it near another container but at a higher level. Water begins to flow through a thin, black tube in a steady stream from the first container into a receptacle on the top of the container below it. "If you had to think about it," Deveneau tells the class, "and you are going to have to think about it, what is going on here?"

Vallery, from Latin class, is the first to speak up. She wants to know if there is something more dense than water in the first container. "I don't know," says Deveneau. "What do you think?" The girls begin offering suggestions: "Lower it and see what happens." He lowers it. The flow continues. There are more suggestions. Girls are throwing out ideas and theories about why the water is flowing. They listen to the person who is talking and then build on what she has said if they think it's relevant. At one point Vallery offers a theory and another girl says: "That's what I just said."

"That's what I thought," says Vallery.

Wilson leans over to me and whispers: "No girl would have said that in a coed class if a boy had repeated her thought. It's ownership of an idea. She was claiming ownership of her idea."

As I watch, I realize the girls are solving the problem collectively and Deveneau is acting as a coach. "That's very much the mode here," Wilson tells me. "It is especially important in these areas," meaning physics, chemistry, mathematics. At one point we take a vote on what we think is going on. Each girl is given ample time to describe her thoughts about the experiment. Deveneau highlights the inexactitude of science and nature: "We think things work a certain way, but we can't pull it apart and be sure." He uses phrases such as "in your view" and "Let me ask you this." He uses powerful visual images of nuclei flying apart, and balancing acts between electrical forces and nuclear forces. But what he is also doing is involving the students in the class and giving each of them a stake in working with the concept.

At the end of the class, we break into small groups at small lab stations and do an experiment with M&Ms, as Deveneau moves from group to group. We start by spilling all of our M&Ms out of a cup onto the lab table; then we discard the ones with the M side showing. We put the remaining M&Ms back in the cup, shake it up, spill it out, and repeat the process until there are none left. Then we start the whole experiment over again, and find that the same thing happens in the way the M&Ms spill out and we discard them. The results are the same, even though there are fewer M&Ms. We have eaten some.

What we were doing was modeling radioactive decay. The unifying point to our two experiments was that there are certain processes in nature that you can't directly investigate, but you can tell something about them by looking at their large-scale behavior. Deveneau has taken the formidable and inapproachable and turned it into something I could understand.

Deveneau makes a final stop by our group, and I am feeling enough at ease to confess my initial reaction when I heard him tell me he was going to put me to work. "The physics pain," he says. "It's a well-known phenomenon."

But not in his class.

OVERCOMING MATH ANXIETY

I had not visited a math class, and math had been very much on my mind ever since physics class, for I had found out from Patricia Wilson that Deveneau was tutoring her daughter in math. Wilson's daughter was in the same accelerated public school math program as my daughter. Wilson was determined not to let her fall behind in math or get discouraged about her skills. I told her that my daughter was not going to take algebra I in eighth grade. She'd lost her confidence. And I couldn't see much merit in her going into another defeating year. "Don't let her fall behind," Wilson said forcefully.

So here it was again, the math dilemma: Do you keep pushing girls to continue in the challenging math tracks when they are not doing well, or do you let them take it at a slower pace, and eventually fall behind and drop out? Poor grades aren't going to do anything for a girl's self-confidence. But what comes first: the loss of confidence or the poor grades? How far can, or should, a parent push a child to excel in a difficult subject without becoming part of the destructive machinery that saps a child's confidence? I wanted to talk to a math teacher to get a better sense of how they coped with this dilemma at Madeira.

I met Mary Ann Clark, a ninth-grade math teacher who has a contagious warmth that makes you like her right away. We sit down to talk in her classroom. It has been a long day of reporting and taking notes for me. My right hand is hurting. But, oddly, I feel comfortable, as though I have come to the right place. I sense there are answers here.

She explained that her approach involves building girls' confidence in their math abilities. To do this, she establishes a relationship with each girl. "You set up a climate where it's fun. You use gimmicks— even songs—to try to hook them. I constantly have them repeat things like, 'Algebra is easy, geometry is easy.' " She has them work in groups and go to the board in twos. "You create a climate so they are comfortable. Your aim is to set a climate in which they can manage math. An atmosphere of caring is what there is at this school." Often on weekends, if the girls can find a block of time, she will go to Madeira to help them. "What you are saying is math is important, they can manage it, and we are not giving up here until they have mastered it to the level they want."

Clark says that girls bring a lot of preconceived ideas about math into the classroom, and a lot of it is pure misinformation. At the time I interviewed her, Mrs. Clark had taught high school math for seven years and in public coeducational schools as well as in a small private coed school that went through the eighth grade. I asked her what happens to derail seventh-grade girls and she said: "I don't know."

But she had some ideas: "The girls don't bring with them all of the experiences they've had. When I taught fourth grade, we'd go out and measure things like volume, the area of an oval, the tops of picnic tables and boxes. By high school geometry they had no memory of this." Boys were up and about, she says, so she sent them out to measure things and they remembered the experiences. Girls put their emphasis on developing a relationship with the teacher.

She has noticed something that girls do: They make up steps and invent their own processes for doing math—and often they are wrong. She has noticed that boys whom she has tutored do this, too. For example, children who have missed a few days of school due to illness when they were in fourth or fifth grade may never have learned how to work with decimals. They invent their own system—and make mistakes.

This insight into children inventing their own methods rather than asking questions seems particularly relevant to what puts girls off the math track in the seventh grade. By the seventh grade, the idea that math is masculine is deeply imbedded and girls have already lost their voices in the classroom. Girls are reluctant to do anything that will draw attention to themselves or their changing bodies. They do not want to be ridiculed or humiliated in the classroom or the hallway. When you think about it, you realize it would take a brave girl indeed to ask questions in her seventh-grade math class, to risk the laughter of the boys by exposing her shaky grasp of math. No. Far better to figure out the solution by yourself. Or flip a coin. It may not be the correct process, but you are spared from the laughter of boys.

GETTING HELP

I learn that in the past Mrs. Clark has tutored children who have
been in the seventh-grade math class my daughter is enrolled in. She
tells me that these classes move very rapidly, and if a child misses
anything, it is nearly impossible to catch up. I ask her if she would
tutor my daughter, and she said she would. That night I broach the
idea to Katherine. To my surprise, my daughter embraces the idea.

Mrs. Clark and Katherine hit it off superbly. They worked at the
dining room table. I could hear laughter. I would hear my daughter's
voice asking questions and Mrs. Clark's voice, kidding her, encouraging her, challenging her, praising her. She is a wonderful teacher.

Katherine barely passed math that year, but she did not fall any
further behind. During the last three weeks of her seventh-grade year,
she and Mrs. Clark embarked on a program of rebuilding my daughter's confidence in math. By the end of the school year, she was still
scheduled to go into the less-demanding math track that her seventh-
grade math teacher thought was appropriate.

One day I asked Katherine what some of her friends were going to
be taking. She mentioned the name of one who was going to be taking
algebra I. This was a child who had gone to the same elementary
school as Katherine and she had been a very good student. But so had
Katherine.

"Katherine," I said, "You are every bit as smart as she is, if not a
lot smarter. If she's going to take algebra, you can do it."

"I know," she said. "I don't know what's happened. Math used to
be my best subject."

I had an idea: "What would you say if I called Mrs. Clark and asked
her if she could coach you during the summer and then see if she
thinks you could handle algebra?"

"Fine," she said. "Call her." And that is what we did. By early
August, Mrs. Clark said Katherine was ready for algebra I. I called
the school and she went into the accelerated algebra class. Mrs. Clark
continued to tutor Katherine once a week during the school year. "She
never gets mad," Katherine told me. "If I get a bad grade, she never

says stuff like, 'Oh, I'm very displeased with you.' She says, 'Well, what can I do to help?' " And after Katherine started working with Mrs. Clark, I never heard her say that she couldn't do math again.

Has she gotten the message Dean Wilson tries to give her girls about the importance of math? I got my answer when Mattel introduced its Teen-Talk Barbie. This doll could say 270 things, and one of them was "Math class is tough." The AAUW went nuts: Mattel was serving up the old stereotypes about girls and math.

"Who cares, anyway?" said Katherine. "Everyone knows Barbie's a bimbo."

CHAPTER TEN

Reforming Schools for Girls

My day at Madeira provided eloquent arguments on behalf of single-sex girls' schools, but I was left with the question: How can Madeira's lessons be translated into public schools? How can public schools replicate the experience of academically strong girls' schools so that girls emerge feeling as confident, strong, and capable as boys do?

Well, for starters, public schools can make sure that assigned English readings offer women heroines and women authors, and that rite-of-passage stories so important to adolescents include girls as well as boys. Next, public schools should examine their science texts to make sure that girls are pictured doing experiments as often as boys are. Are their history books telling the history of men, wars, elections, and economic cycles, or are they depicting the history of an entire era, in which women played critical roles as pioneers, social reformers, inventors, and entrepreneurs? Young women need women of achievement as role models.

Public schools need to crunch their numbers and determine whether girls are doing as well in math and science courses as boys are. If they are not, public school administrators should consider segregated classes for both boys and girls. All of these fixes could be done quickly and cheaply—and almost certainly effectively.

Public schools can create a healthier atmosphere for girls by mandating teacher training about promoting equity in the classrooms. PTAs can pay for making videos of classrooms so teachers can see what they are doing. If the experience of educational researchers is any guide, even the most progressive teachers will be stunned at the gender bias they see in their own teaching. Are girls reinforced and supported in classes, or are they allowed to lapse into apathetic silence? Teachers can be taught to use simple techniques such as "wait time" and making boys and girls take turns to answer questions.

Public schools need to critique their own environment. What do girls and boys see when they enter the classroom? Pictures of women in outdated roles or pictures of women conducting a scientific experiment or directing a film or chairing a board meeting?

Public schools can incorporate the teaching techniques that top-flight girls' schools use, with heavy emphasis on collaboration, hands-on learning, and relevance, and cut down on the competitive style. "One of the things we do in math is to put four chairs together and the girls all correct their homework together," says Madeira's Betsy Griffith. She calls it "teaching on each other."

At the Emma Willard School, where Carol Gilligan has done her pioneering studies of how girls learn, one teacher changed the way she gave vocabulary tests—dividing the girls into groups to study vocabulary lists and to teach each other, and then giving them the test. Scores are averaged and the group score becomes the score of the individuals. Science teachers let students start working in pairs, and only when their confidence is strong do they move to individual work.

Paul Lamar, chair of the English division at the school, provides forums for students to state their points of view on controversial topics. Everyone is heard. Madeira provides forums for girls to talk about what is on their minds. Madeira has an issues book where students write down things that are bothering them and suggest solutions. Public schools can easily provide such avenues for making sure that girls' voices are heard.

Public schools need to pay more attention to the cultural and ethical atmosphere they are encouraging, or in some cases condoning. Girls' schools provide a model of respect and caring for other members of the school community that comes out of the emphasis that girls and women put on relationships. This, too, is something that public schools can work to foster in the classrooms and hallways. By emphasizing the validity of the female value system and its importance to the school community, public schools can offer a counterbalance to the machismo atmosphere that prevails—and too often creates a culture of violence—in public schools.

Public schools need to incorporate the findings of Gilligan and her associates in evaluating the school's atmosphere and how decisions are made on such matters as discipline. Is it very hierarchical, judgmental, and male? Or is discipline handled in a more open-ended manner, with an emphasis on justice? Is domination prized in classrooms, or is the mood one of tolerance and respect? This is probably the most important point of all, for it goes to the heart of the content of teaching, the style of teaching, and whose value systems are being perpetuated and honored.

Gilligan and her colleagues established in the Dodge Study, as their work at the Emma Willard School is known, that this sense of values, of what's important to girls, permeates every aspect of their learning experience. Their ethic of caring is the antithesis of the rigid male style that is obsessed with maintaining authority and discipline, no matter the cost to a child.

Lamar illustrated how this atmosphere of caring and mutual respect worked with the story of a girl who wrote a paper about a painful moment involving her brother. When she began to read it aloud, she broke down. Lydia, another student, went to her weeping classmate and asked if she could continue reading the paper aloud. It was, said Lamar, "one of the most human and authentic moments I've ever spent in a classroom."[1]

SINGLE SEX IN PUBLIC SCHOOLS

What cannot be translated to the public schools is the all-girls atmosphere and the benefits girls get when every decision is made with their welfare in mind. Perhaps the best way of providing that would be to offer single-sex environments within the framework of our public school system. It's an option worth considering, perhaps, but ironically the same law that has helped level the playing field in athletics for girls might be the biggest barrier to leveling the playing field in academics by providing girls with opportunities for separateness.

Title IX of the Education Amendments of 1972 bars discrimination on the basis of sex in any federally funded programs. The law rose out of the widely held perception that separate is not equal, a belief grounded in our sad history of racially segregated schools. In today's climate, separating students by gender in public schools runs counter to the powerful currents in social reform based on the idea that integration leads to equality and diversity leads to greater tolerance. Changing this deeply imbedded philosophy isn't going to be easy.

The courts have issued several ambiguous rulings in cases that have challenged the legality of running sex-segregated schools with public funds. Title IX does not directly forbid admission policies that segregate students by sex. It does not address admissions procedures at all. Title IX does forbid segregating by sex in programs that receive federal funds, once students are admitted to an institution. Thus, single-sex classrooms within a public elementary or secondary school are more clearly against the law than are separate admissions policies.

The Girls High School in Philadelphia survived a challenge to its sex segregation when the Third Circuit used a "separate but equal" analysis. The court found that Brown vs. Board of Education did not apply.

The court based its decision on findings that Central High (for boys) and Girls High were of equal quality and attendance was voluntary. It found that there was sufficient evidence to establish that legitimate educational goals could be served by single-sex schools in which young people could study better. Finally, the court did not find any evidence of anyone being harmed by the sex segregation, in contrast to the findings in Brown vs. Board of Education in which the court agreed that race segregation produced devastating psychological effects on black youngsters.[2]

The option of separating schools by race was foreclosed by the Brown vs. Board of Education decision, but the court has never spoken so forcefully on the matter of single-sex education, and there may be legal avenues that would allow communities to establish such schools. Certainly there is much evidence to support a claim that girls are not getting equal education in public schools. Are we to sacrifice the futures of girls to a legal standard designed to secure equal education for blacks—but which isn't doing it for girls? Does it not make more sense to revisit the issue and figure out how separate facilities or separate classes can be made to work so that both boys and girls get a top-flight education? What would be wrong with a magnet school for girls sharing a campus with a magnet school for boys, so that youngsters could take academic classes separately and perhaps share clubs and coed athletic teams—such as the swim team—and jointly sponsor school socials?

Another option could be to offer single-sex classes in math and science, and have the rest of the classes be mixed.

TESTING THE CLIMATE FOR GIRLS

Anne E. Bekebrede, headmistress of the MacDuffie School in Springfield, Massachusetts, has set forth ten criteria for picking out a school for girls. While her focus was private schools, her measurements can be generalized to all schools and can be helpful to parents who want to test how healthy the climate is at any schools, including colleges, their daughters are attending.[3] Distilled to their essence, here are her guidelines:

• Beware of schools where boys significantly outnumber girls. (This would be compounded if the school were a boarding school.)

• Parents should check on the ratio of females to males on the faculty. Women should be visible as department heads and administrators, bringing a feminine point of view to bear, and leading to greater equity in policies affecting boys and girls.

• What are the opportunities for girls to be student leaders?

• To what extent is the faculty engaged in ongoing discussions about the growing body of research on how schools shortchange girls—and, more important, what are they doing to repair their own environments?

• Is the faculty aware of the new research on how the intellectual and moral development of girls differs from that of boys? Are they assimilating this information into their teaching methods?

• Are girls' sports really getting their fair share of attention and resources? The message "comes through clearly about which group is important when the girls inherit the old gym and locker room and the boys get the new facilities," Bekebrede writes.

• Are there some facilities officially opened to all students that somehow become the special zones of males? Bekebrede notes that computer rooms can quickly become male preserves.

• Woodworking, shop, and mechanical drawing classes can enhance girls' comfort with science and disciplines that depend on spatial skills. Are girls encouraged to take these classes? Are girls taking the highest levels of math and science in proportions that reflect their presence in the student body?

• Does the school offer opportunities to boys and girls for service to others?

• Does the curriculum include one or more courses in women's studies? "Boys as much as girls should be encouraged to enroll in such classes," argues Bekebrede, "because equity in education ultimately depends on a widespread understanding of women in the past and where they are and should be in the world today."

A COMMITMENT TO EQUITY

Public schools and the communities they serve need to commit themselves to the proposition that all children deserve an equitable education and that sidelining girls into less demanding roles in school does them a lifelong disservice by tracking them into the low-paying end of the labor market.

Reform will not come about until teachers, administrators, and school boards, as well as parents and children, develop a much deeper and broader understanding about how schools continue to discriminate against girls. Teachers will have to become sophisticated enough about gender to spot discrimination in textbooks and then to lead classroom discussions about it. They will need to develop a teaching style that is a mixture of the individualistic and relational, drawing on the best of both styles, challenging both girls and boys to think, and enabling each to express their thoughts in a variety of ways. They will thus create a classroom atmosphere in which both boys and girls feel fully included.

Guidance counselors must be trained to encourage girls to pursue physics, chemistry, and the higher levels of math. They need to join forces with faculty members to make sure that career days feature women scientists and mathematicians, and that girls are encouraged to attend summer science programs and math enrichment programs that are offered at universities. Parents can support these efforts by lobbying to make sure that state universities offer these enrichment programs for girls. Many universities sponsor soccer and basketball camps during the summer. Surely math and science camps are just as worthwhile.

AGENTS OF CHANGE

Of course schools should not favor one gender over another. How dare they? Or, perhaps more to the point, why dare they? What earthly rationale can there be for favoring one style of learning over another? What equity, or practical good sense, is there in anointing one group of students as the norm and another group as "the other"?

Constipated careerist educators have no business prolonging "the longest war" by training boys to be sexually dominant and girls to be silent and submissive. If our free society is to fulfill its promise in an increasingly dangerous world, schools must be transformed into powerful agents of change, liberating both boys and girls from destructive hierarchical ways of learning and of devaluing other people. The connectedness girls cherish in human relations, the sense of caretaking that they bring to a classroom environment are prized in such superb schools as the Emma Willard School and the Madeira School. When a girl claims ownership of an idea she is asserting power and confidence in her intellect. When a girl goes to the aid of a troubled classmate, as Lydia did in Paul Lamar's class at the Emma Willard School, she showed what can and should be done to help a person who is in distress. Instead of averting her gaze, she looked anguish in the eye and moved to soothe it. When we create classrooms and schools in which the hand of learning bears this human touch, we bring about a society that values kindness. The best girls' schools produce high achievers because girls are constantly and consistently at the center of all the different considerations that go into running a school. Their needs are paramount; their values prevail.

In coeducational schools, however, the needs of boys are paramount and their values, their style of learning, and their noisy mode of communicating dominate. Academically demanding girls' schools can teach us a great deal about how to redress gender imbalance in public education, to find a new blend of styles that will benefit both boys and girls.

The goal of the best academic girls' schools is one all schools should strive for. That is to produce students—boys and girls—who emerge from the educational process as leaders and as smart, confident, and kind people who will go on to create a vastly improved society over what we have now.

And finally, isn't it time someone took a, yes, hard-headed look at that icon so cherished in male-dominated boardrooms, the bottom line? Can any society that dooms half of its pool of talent and energy to second-rate status hope to compete with truly progressive nations? Can a country whose public schools are obsessed with perpetuating unequal gender roles in classrooms truly survive and prosper in a new century so full of peril and promise?

PART THREE

The Most Dangerous
Years

CHAPTER ELEVEN

Danger—Patriarchy at Work

"I think women are just the greatest creatures. They instinctively understand everything. They know their role, they know what the planet means, they're not careless. They're the best creatures and all the way up until high school they're smarter than the boys. So what I want to know is, what happens when they're twelve that the guys suddenly take over?"

—**Actress Bette Midler,**
in an interview with *Washington Post* movie critic
Rita Kempley, November 27, 1991

Good question. We have seen how girls' schools can help change the educational system so that girls are not systematically undermined, but there is still the enormous task of overhauling the way girls and boys are socialized to behave toward each other. This is critical to helping them move through the most difficult years of adolescence. For too many girls, adolescence is a disaster—psychologically and often physically as well.

It may happen when a girl is ten or it may happen when she is thirteen, but it happens to almost every girl: Her space is invaded, her body is threatened, and she is exposed and shamed and made to feel vulnerable and dirty. She stops being a friend to boys and becomes an object. She may undergo a brutal physical lesson that will stay with her all of her life. This attack on her space metastasizes out of patriarchy's compulsion to devalue women. It shows up in behavior that has malignant effects on relations between boys and girls and men and women. Often it presents itself in behavior we view with benign neglect: the unwelcome touching of girls by boys that we see in the seventh grade, the snapping of the bra straps, the sexually explicit comments that boys make to girls—and that teachers and administrators routinely ignore. It shows up in the school gossip mill, the reputation-trashing Monday morning scuttlebutt. In its most tragic form, it shows up in the sexual payoff that is extorted from girls as the price of popularity.

None of this behavior is benign. While we have traditionally dismissed it as "boys will be boys" behavior, it is, in fact, one of the most damaging experiences inflicted on girls in order to teach them a lesson about their place in society. If you were to try to isolate one experience that makes girls feel like they are second best, the physical lesson of devaluation that is inflicted on them on the cusp of adolescence would be the single moment in which a girl's sense of herself as an independent self is shattered. A boy, or several boys, will teach her a lesson about who she is in their eyes and what her function in a patriarchal culture is supposed to be: She will be put in her place, and they will lay claim to all of the rights of superiority and entitlement that they have been trained to claim. Somewhere on the edge, just as a girl is trying to negotiate the precipice between childhood and puberty, an incident happens that will send her reeling toward disaster.

Psychologist Jean Symmes, the founder of PsychoEducational Resources in McLean, Virginia, offers this scenario: "Imagine you're a ten-year-old, saucy as the dickens, and wanting to play the boys' games. Suddenly one of them grabs you and pulls you behind the stands, and with sort of a smirk at the other guys, he throws you down on the ground and starts feeling you up. He's bigger than you. He's fourteen or fifteen. He uses physical force and you feel humiliated and dirty as if you've done something wrong. You don't want that to happen again. You don't want to be ridiculed and ashamed. You get a little more careful. You start watching where he is, and where you are. And you sit with the other girls."

Symmes counsels children as well as adults. She says that these incidents are anything but harmless. "We estimate that thirty percent of girls have had some kind of sexually invasive experience. Almost every woman I see can remember some experience like this. Typically it happens when they are coming out of chubby babyhood and just into adolescence. They are very vulnerable to fathers, brothers, cousins, the boy down the street, the janitor at school, anyone from priests to baby-sitters. I think it is part of the patriarchal teaching of women's place."

Symmes has spent many years counseling families who have children who are having difficulty in school. She sees how boys and girls are socialized. "An awful lot of male socialization is very, very destructive," she says—starting with the sexist teasing of girls and the pulling up of their skirts in elementary school that goes uncorrected by teachers. When boys misbehave, she says, teachers should call them on it, shame them if necessary, to make the point. "What's wrong with a little use of shame in the elementary school?" she wonders. She envisions a teacher taking this firm approach with a boy who has behaved badly: "We'd like you to stand up in the class and tell us why you did that." She faults female teachers for accepting what boys do, as though somehow it's not right for them to control it.

Like many other feminists, Symmes is looking at the imbalance of power between men and women in a new way. She is focusing less on women's shortcomings and more on their strengths, less on men's strengths and more on their shortcomings. "For so long, it was 'How do we get what they've got?' It's not that we are inferior. We represent the values that are coming to be needed—the values of nurturance and preservation and respect and partnership. We're not going to survive without these. The control of aggression and the teaching of this to boys is something that has to happen if we are going to survive."

THE MOST DANGEROUS YEAR

But this is not happening in our schools. By age twelve, female children have been so conditioned to pursue the grail of popularity in our sex-obsessed society that the deadly progression from too-soon maturity to too-early sex seems not only natural but required as the price of social acceptance. Girls are succumbing to sexual extortion at an earlier age than at any time in our nation's history. The teenage sexual agenda emerges with gale-force fury in the seventh grade, and it is a major factor in making the seventh grade the most dangerous year in a girl's life.

For most parents, it is alarming to think of our twelve-year-old sons and daughters as sexually active. But sexual activity is in the atmosphere, and girls, especially, are forced to confront sexual pressures in schools at a shockingly young age. Sexual harassment is seeping from junior high school down to the earliest years of elementary school. A truly low point in our cultural evolution was achieved in the spring of 1993 when the Office of Civil Rights of the U.S. Department of Education found that a six-year-old-girl in Eden Prairie, Minnesota, had been sexually harassed on her school bus by first- and third-grade boys who called her a bitch and told her in graphic terms to perform sex with her father.

The complaint by the girl's mother touched off a federal investigation that spread to the whole Eden Prairie system. The probe unearthed other incidents. A girl in first grade and a girl in fourth grade were teased by boys about their anatomy, and "shoved, touched, and called obscene, sexually derogatory names while riding the school bus," according to the report issued by the Office of Civil Rights. One parent resorted to driving her daughter to school. A sixth-grade girl at an intermediate school was tripped, spit on, and "subjected to hurtful, lewd remarks about her anatomy by five male sixth-graders," according to the report. The principal, typically, handled the incident as a case of boys using inappropriate language, instead of handling it as a case of sexual harassment.

Eden Prairie is by no means an anomaly. These incidents are part of an epidemic of sexual harassment that has engulfed our schools. Bernice Sandler, who pioneered research into sexual harassment and has been monitoring the phenomenon for more than a decade, has found that it is getting much worse. Not only is it happening to girls at younger and younger ages, it is also becoming more widespread and more visible, partly because parents and children are more aware of sexual harassment and there is a growing mood on the part of parents and children that they are not going to tolerate it. Parents, educators, and the children themselves—people who might once have dismissed this behavior as a harmless and inevitable manifestation of boys' struggle to attain manhood—are now labeling some of this behavior as sexual harassment and taking action to prevent it.

Two important studies released in 1993 documented how widespread sexual harassment in the schools actually is. The first was sponsored by the NOW Legal Defense and Education Fund and the Wellesley College Center for Research on Women. Findings were based on more than 4,200 responses from girls to a survey that was published in *Seventeen* magazine. It found that sexual harassment was rampant in elementary and secondary schools, most commonly taking the form of sexual comments, gestures, or looks, or being touched, pinched, or grabbed. Almost 40 percent of the girls who answered the *Seventeen* survey said they were harassed on a daily basis. Wrote one thirteen-year-old from Utah: "I was always scared to go to school, or at least the one class it happened in, but it still happened in the halls. I got scareder and scareder every day."

A twelve-year-old girl of Chinese heritage who lives in New York told of how the harassment had silenced her: "I grow angry, sad and I had wanted to get back at him. Nevertheless, I was very speechless, and very quiet for some time. I felt like crying but I kept it inside and didn't say anything to anyone."

A fourteen-year-old who attends a private school in Alabama gave this poignant account of being harassed since the fifth grade. "I have no pride, no self-confidence and still no way out of the hell I am put through in my school. I have been depressingly desperate for something to make me feel like I actually am not a slutty bitchy whore."

The American Association of University Women commissioned a

study of harassment in the schools that was conducted by Louis Harris and Associates. In a survey of 1,600 boys and girls, the study found that 62 percent of girls in grades eight through twelve had been harassed and 42 percent of the boys had. Five times as many girls as boys said the incidents had caused them to "feel afraid or scared," and three times as many girls said it was likely to affect their grades and class participation. One out of three girls said the harassment made them feel they did not want to go to school or talk as much in class. While a significant percentage of boys reported being harassed by girls, such conduct clearly had a much more negative impact on girls who were harassed by boys. Boys let it roll off their backs. Girls, with their intense investment in relationships, took it personally.

The effect is brutal and brutalizing. Schools become training grounds for sexual harassment.

When girls enter seventh grade, they are plunged into a world steaming with sexual awareness. Previous rules don't apply; relationships that were reliable in elementary school are betrayed. Precious secrets entrusted to new friends met during the first weeks of junior high school are blabbed about the cafeteria with calculated cruelty. Everything is shifting. Like a mountain lake, junior high looked good from a distance, but once girls plunge in they discover that the rocks at the bottom of the water are jagged, the sand is muddy, and the guys who looked neat from the other side of the lake turn out not to be, but are instead demeaning, menacing, and predatory. For many girls, the seventh grade is a very, very bad trip.

TOO MUCH, TOO SOON

Courtship rituals between boys and girls have not changed in thirty years. They are still male-driven, as evidenced by the staying power of the baseball metaphor for sexual experiences. "Scoring" is still the boy's manifest destiny. "Third base" remains the compromise of choice for seriously intimate girls who are trying to preserve their virginity and don't mind oral sex—a way of balancing their own futures with the immediate ambition of remaining popular. None of these are new ways of mediating between the competing goals of boys and girls. What I find so tragic, however, is that as confusing and difficult all of this was to us at sixteen and seventeen, girls and boys today are forced to cope with these decisions while they are literally still children. Girls and boys are being pushed to make decisions about sex today at twelve, thirteen, and fourteen that boys and girls used to sort out at sixteen, seventeen, and eighteen.

The lowering of the age for the onset of sexual activity has led most experts on adolescent sex to agree on at least one point: Children are doing too much, too soon. One of the biggest mistakes that parents can make—whether they have sons or daughters, or both—is to use their own experiences as benchmarks to help them figure out when their own children will start experimenting with sex, drugs and alcohol, skipping school, driving cars without licenses, and sneaking into R-rated movies and out at night. Our own memories grow furtive, but more important is this hard-to-face but inescapable fact: Most young people are starting to experiment with dangerous behavior much, much earlier than most of us realize.

In December 1992, the Carnegie Council on Adolescent Behavior released a sobering report on the state of America's twenty million adolescents. Entitled *A Matter of Time*, it catalogued how youngsters aged ten to fifteen years old are spending their discretionary hours in pursuits that range from the boring and nonproductive to the dangerous and self-destructive.[1] But perhaps its most important message for parents was this: "Many young adolescents first experiment with tobacco, alcohol, illicit drugs, and sexual activity during early adolescence, several years earlier than their predecessors. Many drugs that tempt them are far more hazardous and addictive than those available just a generation ago. The number of young adolescents who use alcohol, either on an experimental or abuse basis, is at least equally significant: 77 percent of eighth graders (most of them aged fourteen and fifteen) report having used alcohol, and 26 percent say they have had five or more drinks on at least one occasion within the past two weeks." If that is not hair-raising enough, consider this: Twenty-seven percent of the girls and 33 percent of the boys have had intercourse by the age of fifteen, and six out of ten did not use contraception the first time. One-fourth of these sexually active adolescents will contract a sexually transmitted disease before they graduate from high school. The most dangerous time of day for these youngsters is the block of time after school when they are unsupervised. The most dangerous place is a boy's home while his parents are away, for this is the most common locale in which adolescent sexual intercourse takes place.

Everyone tends to turn statistics into abstractions, and to fit a hypothetical "somebody else's child" into doomsday data. Thus, one-quarter of the girls may have sex by the time they are fifteen—but not my daughter or her friends. It's always other people's children. But the intense sexual pressure on young adolescent girls is not happening to other people's children. It is happening to my daughter and her friends. A year before the two national studies documented the pervasive harassment of girls in junior high, I heard about it from these girls. They knew what was happening to them. They bitterly resented the sexual stress that surrounded them. During the seventh grade, they became enraged at the high-handedness they saw among boys who were forcing an intense sexual agenda on them, and who felt free to comment on their looks and tell them what to wear.

AN EARFUL FROM THE GIRLS

One evening, midway through their seventh-grade year, a group of my daughter's friends descended on the kitchen like a tornado touching down. They were heatedly debating a parental notification bill for teenage abortions that was awaiting the governor's signature. We ended up sitting on the floor of the kitchen with a tape recorder running. The more I listened to what they were saying, the more I realized that other parents needed to hear it as well. The girls all knew what this book was about and they agreed to be recorded. I got an earful about what it's like for girls. They got a chance to ventilate their feelings, and they did. Sometimes they spoke in conversational tones, but more often they would speak in tones of anger or frustration. I listened with a growing sense of dismay. There were five girls— Lisa, Eileen, Jenny, Julia, and my daughter. Jenny and Julia began by complaining about boys who make comments about the clothes they wear or who talk about girls' bodies. As I listened, I heard a recurring theme: These boys have an inappropriate sense of entitlement. They feel they have a right to discuss how girls look and to make observations about their bodies. The girls understand the intrusion, and they resent it. My daughter was the first to use the term sexual harassment.

"It's like happened to me," she said. "I don't know what to say. I know it—like when you are sexually harassed—it makes you feel mad, but you're also embarrassed. . . . I don't know what to say. I know it happened. They know it, too, and you don't know what to do. It's like *there*."

"When I was at the locker they kept on talking about what I looked like, and my butt, and I didn't know what to do," said Julia. "I just walked away."

Jenny: "It started this year. Even this year, you would expect them to be a bit more mature, but I know guys who go out with girls just because of their chest size. Guys don't have any respect for the fact that maybe girls don't want to be treated like that—and then you go out with a guy and you don't do anything and you'll never get a boyfriend again. Never."

Julia: "Suppose you have a reputation as a slut. You never know whether a guy is going with you because you're you, or because of your reputation as a slut, and they know they can get somewhere."

I ask whether these are the same young men they attended elementary school with—boys who have in some cases been their friends since kindergarten. Julia tells me that some of the boys will "treat you the same" as they did in the sixth grade, but they will treat girls they have just met in the seventh grade differently.

"Why?" I ask.

"They knew me before they started thinking about all this stuff," she responds. "Now they won't push it, but a lot of their friends will."

I discover that the boys "rate" the girls, beginning in the first few weeks of school, based on their looks and their bodies. Jenny, who was following in the tracks of sisters who were then in high school, volunteers that her sisters "think it's disgusting that our class is already into all of these things. My parents didn't understand that any of this was going on. If my parents did they would probably ground me for the rest of my life because they don't trust that I would be able to handle it." Jenny identifies the more sexually experienced eighth-grade boys as a major influence on the seventh-grade boys—a point researchers have also made. "These guys, they look up to the eighth-graders so much because they've done all this stuff. That's what they want to do, and they start treating you differently." She disagrees with Julia: "The guys I knew last year treat me the same way all the other guys do: like dirt. Except for maybe a couple of guys who aren't very popular."

SOCIAL PIONEERS: LOOKING FOR ROLE MODELS

The popular culture, along with older high school kids, serve as guides to youngsters exploring new territory. Proof of the popular culture's impact came from events at Wheaton College in Newton, Massachusetts, which first admitted men in 1988. The men brought to dormitory life much more rowdy behavior than the women cared to endure. At one meeting to try to resolve the conflict, the men were asked where they had gotten the idea of how they should behave in college. Their answer: *Animal House*, a movie that documented lowest-common-denominator behavior in a fraternity house. If the popular culture reinforces the notion that adolescent girls are supposed to be boy crazy, we can expect that to be a dominant theme in girls' teenage years. We can expect the same result if the popular culture glamorizes girls who are helpless at math. If the culture rules that academic ineptitude is a staple of popularity, it is likely to make an impression on youngsters who are trying to figure out how teenagers act. Viewed in this light, hoary bromides such as "Boys don't make passes at girls who wear glasses" are far from harmless.

My daughter's friend Jenny is pretty, and as we were sitting around on the kitchen floor, I discovered that this is what it's gotten her: "A good friend of mine was on her bus," Jenny said, "and the guys said we want you to know you and Jenny are the best-looking girls in the seventh grade because you have the best looks and the best bodies."

"How does that make you feel?" I asked.

"Like dirt, because then I'll walk around and I'll be so self-conscious, so uncomfortable because then I realize all these people are looking at me. Our whole school is based on how much a girl will do." Later my daughter told about another girl who was considered to be a slut simply because she was pretty.

Julia describes this no-win scenario: "Once you do something, or say he exaggerates, you'll always have that reputation of being a girl who would. . . . And then all the guys think of you like that. And if you did it with the guy and you really liked him, and you don't like anyone else and they think you're going to do something, then they'll start badmouthing you because you're a tease."

These girls were acutely conscious of receiving little or no support from teachers. Several had seen a video on sexual harassment and were troubled by the fact that their male classmates said things like, "What do you expect us to do?" by way of justifying their actions. "And there was no correction!" said an outraged Jenny. Teachers see boys touching girls in the hallways and don't do anything, they complained. Says Jenny of her seventh-grade male classmates: "They look up to the popular guys in the eighth grade and they see how they treat the women, girls, whatever. They start treating them the exact same way, and next year, you know what's going to happen? The same thing, except the guys in our grade are going start trying to act like the eighth graders did. It's so sickening to sit there, to have to walk through a hall. The teachers realize it." She was particularly incensed that a small group of Hispanic boys who brought an overdose of machismo into the hallways were allowed to get away with it. "They'll walk up in the hall and touch you."

Lisa interjects an interesting piece of information: "They are fifteen and sixteen."

Jenny nods in accord and resumes: "They are so gross, and they have no respect, and teachers realize it and don't stop it."

Lisa: "That's because they are scared."

I tell them about the U.S. Supreme Court ruling that victims of sexual harassment in elementary and secondary schools could collect money damages from the school system if it failed to protect them. I suggested that this decision could produce an about-face at schools that have been tolerating the behavior they had described. The girls were not optimistic, and again I could hear the peer pressure in their voices.

"Girls my age are not going to come up to a counselor and say 'these men are harassing me,' " says Jenny. I tell her this is something parents ought to bring to the school's attention.

Julia cuts me off: "If somebody finds out that your parents called the school, then everyone will be looking at you or laughing and calling you a prude."

"I don't want people to think I'm a prude," adds Jenny. "That's not that bad, but I'd become an outcast. You know I will," she says to the other girls. "I'd be the biggest dork."

GIRLS BETRAYING GIRLS

Eileen informs me that a girl who attends her church "is notorious for classifying people as prudes or sluts. She says she'll go to third with almost any guy, (but) wouldn't go all the way because it's against our religion." "Third," the girls tell me, is "a blow job." And I realize that these girls who are twelve and thirteen are being forced to use the crudest locker-room language in order to express themselves—

language that I did not even know existed until I was in college. I know enough about interviewing not to express the shock and sorrow that I feel as I listen to the girls talk, but I feel a tightening in my gut. These girls are being robbed of their childhood, they are being forced to deal with the sexual agenda of late adolescence before some of them even enter early adolescence.

Julia says the girl polled the girls in gym class to find out whether they would rather be known as a slut or a prude. Julia called her on it and said, "Do you honestly think people want to give you that answer? What would you say? And she said, 'Well, I want to be considered a slut. Nobody is going to go around calling me a prude.' " This is a choice that a lot of her classmates would make, said Julia, "because of the way guys treat us."

Jenny interjects: "The hot popular guys will go out with you if you are a slut."

Julia: "Exactly. The girls would rather be a slut and go out with guys."

APPEARANCE AS ENFORCER

Girls have pecking orders and use each other's appearance to enforce it. My daughter told of being criticized by another girl whenever she wears a particular skirt. The first time this happened, the girl told my unsuspecting daughter to turn around and, after inspecting her, this girl announced that my daughter's "butt" was "sticking out." "It really made me mad, and she says this every time I wear this skirt."

I'm getting mad, too. "Why is she even commenting on your physical appearance? What business is it of hers?" I want to know.

"I think maybe she wants to point it out because she's jealous or something."

Eileen observes that this is a form of putting down other people. "Say you're both equal. If you put her down, then you are on top."

"Guys think they have the right to tell you what to wear and stuff," said Julia. "The other day I forgot my glasses and this guy came up and said, 'You look better with your glasses. Wear them tomorrow.' I said, 'Excuse me? Maybe I don't like 'em.' They are telling me what to do."

This is another departure from the way boys behaved in the fifth and sixth grades. "They might say you look good with your glasses on," Julia said, "but they wouldn't say, 'Wear your glasses, you don't look good without them.'"

It occurs to me as I'm listening to the girls that they understand the invasions of space, of privacy, the denigration of their appearance, the objectifying of their bodies, the betrayals of friendships and violations of trust that occur when their peers share with the whole school mortifying revelations about their romantic interests. But the girls don't have the tools to deal with any of it. They know terms such as sexual harassment, for example, but they don't know procedures for handling it, either directly by confronting the offending boy or by going to school authorities or enlisting their parents' help.

They agree with my observation. "We walk away," said Julia in a poignant moment. "That's our tool." If the girls take action, she says, "guys will say, oh, it's stupid or she's overreacting." I hear this and wince: How many times have adult women been accused of "overreacting" when they object to a sexist joke? When men attack, we are overreacting, no matter what our age, and such accusations can take crude forms: Jenny told of being in a bad mood at a party because of the way boys were acting—whereupon a boy asked her if she needed a tampon. "That's just not their business," she said vehemently.

Girls see and feel the difference between how boys and girls are treated in classrooms. "When girls make a mistake and they say something stupid in class or do something, it's held against them for a long time," said Julia. "This has happened to me. And then when a guy does something really stupid in class, it's forgotten the next day." She takes on the voice of a chorus of girls in the class: "We're not going to bring it up because he's too macho, and we're not going to bring it up and embarrass him." She returned to her normal voice and offered this scorching conclusion: "The girls don't want to embarrass the guys that way, but the guys see nothing wrong with embarrassing the girls."

Added Katherine: "If a girl is accused of being a lesbian, it sticks. If a guy is accused of being a homosexual, it's funny—grabbing another guy or fake-kissing him. Guys can do that and they just laugh it off."

"If you go into school and you look like a slut, then all the guys will like you," said Jenny. "There are guys that won't even come near you unless they know you'll do something with them."

"Okay," I said. "What if you went out with one of these guys and gave them a blow job. How would you feel?" Julia says she wouldn't do it. Jenny says she'd feel gross. But she made her point very clear: "You'd go out with a lot better-looking guys and a lot more popular guys." Would the word be out that you deliver? The girls answer in unison: Yes.

"It just gets around the whole school," said Julia, "because the guy has to blab it out. People who don't even know the girl say, oh yes, she's a slut. They don't even know how she feels about it. When I was walking home the first day of school behind some eighth-graders they were talking about who had done what."

And the girls know who the loser is: the girl. Jenny said she read an article in which a boy was talking about a couple who went together for a year and a half during seventh and eighth grades. "And the guy says, 'If I'd been going out with someone that long I'd have been to home so many times I'd have lost count.' That's what we are talking about," Jenny said heatedly. "They can't understand why people can't just have a relationship without having gone all the way. That's the way it is in junior high," she said. "Junior high!"

CHANGING SCHOOL ATTITUDES

Both the NOW Legal Defense and Education Fund and the AAUW developed blueprints for action and for sexual harassment workshops in the schools. Both strongly urged schools to develop policies that make it clear what harassment is and that it is against the law. As part of the effort to stop harassment of students, both organizations recommended that schools have workshops in which they can discuss harassment, how it feels, what the difference is between harassment and flirting. The AAUW urges workshop leaders to draw attention to differences in boys' perceptions of harassment and that of girls. And leaders were urged to remind students that sexual harassment is "in the eye of the beholder," usually a girl. What boys may try to write off as teasing is offensive to many girls. The critical concepts in distinguishing between harassment and flirting are that flirting is welcomed and wanted and makes the recipient feel good, attractive, and in power. Sexual harassment does exactly the opposite: It makes a girl feel dirty, ashamed, and vulnerable. One is legal and the other is illegal. Both organizations have taken steps to provide materials for schools so they can educate administrators and teachers as well as students about how to maintain an environment that is free from harassment. Both organizations are recommending assemblies with speakers to teach students what is appropriate and what is inappropriate behavior toward each other. Girls repeatedly told stories about their schools failing to take action to curb harassment and not believing them when they complained. The upshot is that boys got away with the behavior and kept repeating it. Girls were left to feel unimportant and unprotected. These girls are pleading for help, for they know what the harassment is doing to them. "I think schools need to pay more attention to what's going on around them," wrote a fourteen-year-old from Florida, "because girls like me are just dying inside because no one will believe us."

"Last year, we weren't inferior," explained Eileen. "Last year, we were their friends. This year we're just girls. This year it's about spreading rumors about how you went all the way with a girl. Some guys I've been friends with since kindergarten, and seeing these guys change for the worst. . . ." her voice trails off as she shakes her head.

CHANGING SCHOOLS, CHANGING BODIES

The average age at the onset of menstruation has been dropping steadily since the Industrial Revolution, due, most experts believe, to the improved health of adolescents as a result of better nutrition and an increase in body fat.

The average age of puberty is now 12.5 years for American girls, which means that many of them go through puberty at the same time they are trying to adjust to seventh grade. Most boys, however, go through puberty on an average of two years later. The exception are those who mature early and begin forcing the sexual agenda. Therefore, the majority of boys are not coping with a new school and the onset of puberty at the same time. Moreover, puberty produces far more visible physical changes in girls than it does in boys—so visible, in fact, that teachers give better grades to those who mature early.[2]

A LITTLE HELP FROM HER FRIENDS

Julie Graber, who is affiliated with the Center for the Study of Young Children and Families at Teachers College of Columbia University, emphasizes that girls can ease into menstruation far more easily if they are armed with good information about what is happening to them. Also helpful is a supportive network of friends who are going through the rite of passage at about the same time they are. A sense of normalcy is critical to how well they handle the transition. She also found that girls who start early have a tougher time. "They don't have that peer network to talk about it with, and their parents may not be anticipating it and giving them the information that eases them through it."

Anne Petersen, of the University of Minnesota and one of the nation's leading researchers on adolescent development, has concluded that puberty is not the cataclysmic biological event that earlier researchers had assured us it was. What does have more impact than is generally understood, however, is the timing of puberty on the child's mood and school achievement. Children who matured early tended to get better grades, perhaps because teachers tend to give better evaluations to physically larger pupils. Those who matured later reported having better moods. Girls who were among the first in their group to mature consistently expressed feelings of shame and embarrassment sometimes so acute that they tried to hide what was happening to them. They were less satisfied with their appearance and weight than their smaller and less mature friends. Boys, by contrast, were happy when they matured earlier and felt superior to their classmates. Seventh- and eighth-grade boys who had reached puberty reported being in better moods than their laggard classmates—presumably because they had already accomplished their primary goal of reaching manhood, while their classmates were still anxiously waiting for their own development to begin.

Petersen and her colleagues reached the overall conclusion that puberty is usually a positive experience for boys, but negative for girls.

FITTING IN

Petersen has found that the seventh-grade girls who are most likely to say that they had a poor self-image and had symptoms of depression were the girls who were academically successful. Moreover, when these girls lowered their academic achievement by eighth grade, their depression and their self-image improved. This was particularly evident in stereotypically "masculine" courses such as mathematics and science. The pattern of trading grades for popularity and a sense of personal well-being persisted into the twelfth grade. Girls, she concluded, sacrifice the long-term benefits of achievement on the altar of short-term popularity.

LISTENING TO THE OTHER SEX

Connie Flanagan, an expert on adolescence at the University of Michigan, believes we could ease the trauma for both boys and girls if we shifted the teaching atmosphere away from the didactic instruction used in junior high to the approach in which kids talk to each other, learn to listen to each other, and develop empathy and respect for what each is going through. She suggests classroom discussions in which boys would have to listen and learn about what it is like to grow up as an adolescent girl, and girls would have to listen to boys describe what they are experiencing.

She points to the effectiveness of programs in which wife beaters have had to listen to women who have been beaten describe what they felt. It is one of the few successful approaches in rehabilitating wife beaters. At the same time, men must learn to take responsibility for what they did. "Being confronted with a different point of view can make them face up to what they did."

Julie Dodge, executive director of the Sexual Assault Crisis Center in Long Beach, California, thinks discussions about gender domination can at least get youngsters thinking about the impact of their words and actions. Her center runs five-week-long programs for girls in junior high schools that focus on preventing them from being assaulted or coerced emotionally into having sex. "We teach them decision making so they can be better prepared to take care of themselves, not just in sexual assault, but also in their dating life." Counselors emphasize issues of self-respect and self-esteem. They talk to the girls about doing what is best for them and taking care of themselves. Dodge wants to begin similar groups for boys that will be led by men who will be positive role models, but she said, in a revealing moment, "they just don't have a lot of those."

Small groups in which youngsters can participate allow them to develop a better understanding of what the other adolescents are feeling, said Dodge.

There is a seductive logic in all this, but is there as much realism? Would it really make a difference if the boys in her class had to listen to Katherine and her friends describe how it felt to be treated like meat? Katherine, with her great gift for penetrating the fog of happy talk that so often surrounds proposals of this sort, was not optimistic.

"I don't know," she said. "Probably not, because the girls wouldn't say what they really feel with the guys there."

CHAPTER TWELVE

Into the Eye of the Hurricane

It was the spring of the girls' eighth-grade year. Jenny was at our dining room table with Julia and Katherine. We had fallen into another conversation, and they had agreed that I could tape it. I had listened to the girls a lot during the past year and I sensed that they were maintaining a strong feeling of their own worth and that they continued to value what and how they thought. All three continued to be outspoken, articulate, and well-informed. They placed high value on school but did not seem preoccupied with being popular. They went to an occasional party, but none of them were "dating." They rarely used makeup. My daughter subscribed to *Sassy* and *Seventeen* magazines that year and often remarked about the stories in *Sassy* that she found provocative and informative. She did parodies of stories in *Seventeen*, a magazine that continues to be a teenage reader's guide to Barbieism—and which outsells *Sassy*. By the end of the eighth grade, critical messages of the women's movement had gotten through to these girls. They were intensely aware of the imbalance of power between boys and girls and women and men.

They understood with surprising clarity the pressures bearing down on them to conform to patriarchal expectations, to submit to the myth of male superiority, and to join the sometimes deadly cult of divine thinness. They knew the role the media plays in promoting distorted body images of women. The knew about the gap between wages men and women earn. At thirteen and fourteen, they had information about the terrain that many women don't recognize until they are somewhere between middle management and the glass ceiling. These girls are savvy. If they can sustain that knowledge, it can bulletproof them against the ambushes that trap women who attempt to survive by collaborating. These girls are not interested in collaborating. They see the truth. They know it. I learned that by talking with them, listening to them.

"I have a sense of the importance of life," Jenny was saying. "I know that I could be responsible and create a life. Men don't think of it as that. Some women, if you're pregnant, a man says: 'Get rid of it. It's not my problem.' It's fifty percent their genes, and yet I have to deal with the pain. I have to carry that child for nine months and (deal with) the agony of labor. A man would never let a woman choose for him what to do with a baby."

"A lot of people think women are so gentle, more than men, more patience and stuff," my daughter offered. "I think it's because women have to put up with so much more shit that in a way they've gotten used to it and they are more patient. Now there is so much coming back that women aren't so gentle anymore. They're really becoming aware of what's going on."

I tell them of the findings of archaeologists and anthropologists that women have traditionally done the hard work of maintaining their communities. Sometimes this has meant committing infanticide when there have been shortages of resources. My daughter responds with a story she had recently read in the newspaper in which an Indian woman murdered an infant by forcing poisonous seeds down her throat. The infant was killed solely because she was female, a fact that outraged my daughter when she first read the story and continued to outrage her as she repeated it months later. "They make them kill the baby because they don't want a girl," she says. "These men are so stupid. They don't realize what a woman can do. They are in total ignorance. Men want to be awesome and they think they are. They are just wrong."

"What I don't understand is where they get this incredibly ridiculous idea that they are so great," said Jenny. "The other men lead them on," and here she struggled to express herself, something she usually has no trouble doing. "I can't say what I'm trying to say. I don't understand where it comes from. I feel a lot of women will say, 'I think I'm better than men, men are scum.' But when it comes down to it, for some reason they just feel so attached to men. They back down to any man who challenges them. If there's a man who's my peer I wouldn't back down to a mental challenge. A lot of women would back down."

Katherine became analytical. "Back when this patriarchy stuff started, all there was to get ideas and concepts from was nature. They didn't have the media or anything. But in nature a lot of animals, like male cardinals, are colored much more brightly than females. They might think the male is better than the female?"

Jenny was more hard-nosed. She focused on the fact that women carry a child for nine months, breast-feed the child, and care for it until it is toilet-trained and can articulate its desires by talking instead of crying. At that point, she said, men decide they can be fathers. "I know guys who think it is so ridiculous that women are treated the way they are. They see it as I do." She says they raise the point without any prompting from her. "I won't even talk to them and they will say women carry children for nine months, what went wrong?"

"Maybe men got sick of matriarchal societies and said, 'We've had enough,' and they revolted like women are doing now," Katherine suggested.

"There are guys who support us in the movement," said Julia. "We can't say men, the majority of men, are like this for now, but we have to remember that there are men who aren't."

I found myself being unexpectedly moved by what Julia said when she talked of being "in the movement." Nobody around that table held up a cautionary hand and said, "I'm not a feminist, but . . ." And they were willing to give credit to men who shared their belief that they were getting a bad deal.

"I don't want to dominate men," said Jenny. "I just want equality." She turned to the wage gap between men and women. "Women who have graduated from high school get paid less than a man who is a dropout. Proven facts. A woman who has graduated from college will get less money than a man who has only graduated from high school." Jenny is armed with healthy anger, not unhealthy submission.

"I am outraged that women will go all the way through college, get a Ph.D., and get stuck doing I don't know what kind of work," she said.

Julia's mother runs an international family-planning organization that works closely with the U.S. foreign-aid program. "I will commend Julia's mom," said Jenny. "We're talking a multicultural, totally horizontally done company."

"Everyone is equal," added Julia.

I was surprised by how much the girls knew about the wage gap between men and women and about how companies are run. Jenny's knowledge about Julia's mother's workplace amazed me. It occurred to me that these girls at thirteen and fourteen were already digesting important facts about what they would have to deal with when they started work, and they already had critical pieces of information: There are workplaces and industries that discriminate against women, and others that do not. These girls, who are among the brightest of their generation, are not going into job interviews with the same blinders on that their mothers did. These are the girls most likely to have their pick of employers, and if they can continue resisting, they can force change and push boundaries much further than their mothers and older sisters did. Each of these girls has at least one woman in her life who is validating her observations. The mothers of these girls are not telling them to buckle under and pretend women's lives are easy. The mothers are trying to raise strong, well-informed, opinionated, and tough-minded women who are self-confident and who can protect themselves.

These girls are grappling with the same questions that my generation raised. But there is a critical difference: Women of my generation wrestled with these questions as part of a recovery from an addiction to or, at the very least, a dependency, on patriarchy. Many of us had no idea of what happened to us during our adolescent socialization, but we knew that survival meant you had to have a man to complete your identity and assure your economic well-being. The top item on our adolescent agenda was "learn how to get a man" and you did that by practicing on boys. If you could get a boyfriend in high school, chances are you would be able to get a husband. The best way to accomplish this mission, we knew very well, was to be beautiful, and if we couldn't manage that, we'd undertake whatever remedial efforts we could to look pretty. What I was hearing from these girls was very different from the discussions my generation of women had: These girls are planning on careers and they are planning on being independent. Their voices were loud, and their observations about men and the imbalance of power in patriarchy were as clear-eyed as the observations of any adult woman I know. The girls understood that females in this culture have problems, that life for women in Western cultures is not fair. They know this, and this knowledge is extraordinarily powerful for them. They are not in denial. Moreover, in the eighth grade, they did not view themselves as dependent on the patriarchy, nor did they intend to bow to its pressures and to submerge themselves and their identities into a set of submissive expectations of what women are supposed to be.

SEX, LOOKS, AND TEENAGE GIRLS

When you listen to young girls, you discover remarkable insights. That spring evening, when Katherine, Julia, and Jenny were talking, the conversation shifted at one point to the Riot Grrls, a counterculture phenomenon of women musicians and their followers who trash patriarchy in their music and push feminism to its outer cultural limits.

"They became stereotypes of 'the feminist,' " said Julia, "and harmed the movement. You butcher your hair, and they don't realize it, but they are slowly becoming men. I don't see what's wrong with being feminine. I have a sense of femininity. There's nothing wrong with being beautiful. I have my hair long. They live to be ugly and to make theselves non-beautiful.''

"I don't do my hair or my makeup for some guy or the popular guys," said Katherine. "I do it just to look good."

Jenny offered this insight: "If I look really bad some days, I'll be totally quiet. I'd feel really quiet like I can't talk because people won't listen." She understood at the most basic level that she was valued for how good she looked, not her brain, and when she felt herself deficient in her looks, she silenced her voice. "If you look at how our school worked out," she continued, "all the people who are ugly sit together, and all the people who are pretty sit together, and all the people who are prudes sit together, and all the sluts sit together. Unfortunately, that's the way it is."

At this point, my daughter launched into a story about a girl at her bus stop whom she chose to call Suzy Q. To understand the full implications of this anecdote, it is necessary to know the meaning of the word "bop." A bop is an airhead whose driving ambition is to be popular. The previous Wednesday, it had been raining in the morning, and the girls waited inside a carport for the bus. Said Katherine: "This girl's hair curled up and she had these little curls—frizzy hair—where her straight bangs should be. She comes over, 'My hair, my hair,' whining about her hair and I'm like, 'Suzy Q, your hair looks fine,' and she goes, 'No, it doesn't.' " Here Katherine paused for dramatic effect. "Know what she did? Know what Suzy Q did? She pulled a curling iron out of her backpack!" At this news, the girls shrieked. "We're standing under the carport, she had the cord in her backpack. She started curling her hair! I go, 'Suzy Q, you are acting like such a bop,' and she said, 'Katherine, I can't believe you said that to me.' I'm like, 'Well, look at you. All you ever do is worry about your hair and how you look.' She's like, 'Well, I hate it when it frizzes. You don't have curly hair.''

"Bop" is a loaded term. Jenny says: "Being a bop and the problem of being popular is that you have to put out for guys, and, frankly, it's not worth it. The guys at our school are so . . ."—her voice drifts off briefly as she searches for the right term, which she finds with her usual dead aim. "Everytime I look at one of them I think of a weasel. Every time. They are so whiny."

Julia then told about reading an article on the kind of girls boys liked. "They were saying, 'I don't want these kinds of girls for a serious relationship, but just for a sexual relationship.' "

Jenny jumped on that point, and you could hear the triumph in her voice. "Here's a perfect example." She launched into the story of John Doe and the girl he's been dating since the seventh grade. "They were having sex. They just broke up," in their junior year in high school. "That's how long they were going out. The girl is gorgeous. She can't get a boyfriend now because she's 'worn out,' as they say. She's had sex too many times. They know they can get her. She's not a challenge. Why go out with her? She's been 'run,' as I've heard from one of my better friends. I could hit him."

Julia wanted to know the answer to an old, old question: "Why is it a macho thing for guys to have sex, but it's not supposed to be for women in guys' minds? Where are the virgins coming from?"

"They're the ones who are taking the virginity away from us," answered Jenny. "They try to put so much pressure on us. Me, frankly, if I have sex, it's going to be my decision. No man is ever going to pressure me. There are certain things about me I am going to fight for and that is one."

I observe that the pressure seems to have gotten a lot worse for them than it was for their mothers. The boys seem very predatory. I start to say, "They feel their manhood . . ."

". . . depends on sex," interjects Julia. "They have this whole idea about trying to get it as fast as they can. . . . In a culture where there are sexually transmitted diseases that will kill you, you would think people would be a little more responsible about these things. People are so stupid. It is so frustrating that a girl who is twelve years old will have sex with a guy just to keep him even though she knows he is sleeping with other people. She is not protecting herself, she can't tell her parents, she can't have them take her to a doctor. It is so frustrating to me to see someone ruining her life, especially with a guy who is only fourteen."

Jenny shares a scenario that is a mix of touching traditionalism and reality. "My first time, I want it to be special," she says. "I certainly don't want a guy who's saying, 'Oh, sorry, got to go home, my mom, curfew.' Know what I'm saying? I would imagine at that point you have this feeling even if it's false, but you have this false feeling, and all of a sudden you've got this guy saying, 'Mom's going to come home now, we've got to get out. Better get dressed.' And all of a sudden you are, 'Oh, my god, what am I doing here?' "

THE DEADLY CULT OF DIVINE THINNESS

The girls were keenly aware of how girls' images are distorted on television and in the rest of the media—in terms of both how they look and how they behave. Experts on adolescent girls' eating disorders have been warning for more than a decade that media images of women set unrealistic and even dangerous standards of beauty and thinness that teenage girls feel they must aspire to. While most psychologists who are studying eating disorders see them as behavioral manifestations of complex family dysfunctions, many believe the media images contribute to the problem.

"In every country in which a thinner body ideal is held for women, they have more eating disorders, and girls and women have more negative feelings about their bodies and how they look," says Anne Petersen. She, as have many others, pointed to the distorted figure of the Barbie doll. "That is a powerful message."

Just how distorted Barbie's figure is was established by Elaine Pedersen, an associate professor at Oregon State University, who calculated that if Barbie were five feet, five inches tall, her measurements would be 31-17-28—thinner than fashion models. When she and research colleague Nancy Markee, of the University of Nevada at Reno, looked at fifteen other fashion dolls, they found a similar pattern of extreme thinness. "Barbie is reinforcing all the other images out there in the media of the young, slim woman you see in fashion magazines and the cartoon women. Sometimes they are even worse," said Pedersen. "She's definitely part of that whole set of nonreality images and in some cases nonachievable body shapes."

Pedersen and Markee studied a group of nine four-year-olds and how they played with a variety of dolls, and they came up with an even more startling finding about the impact of Barbies on girls. "They did not seem in play activities to be affected by her shape. They enjoyed putting the clothes on. They loved weddings. These are four-year-olds. They liked doing glamorous events like fairy tales." When Barbie didn't have her accessories such as combs and clothes, the girls lost interest. This has left Pedersen wondering whether the more serious problem Barbie may present is that the doll encourages children to "play with a very materialistic part of our world." Pedersen says it is unrealistic to expect a daughter not to want a Barbie when all of her friends have them. But she says parents can counteract these images by spending time talking with their daughters about the reality of human figures and what constitutes a healthy figure. As the child gets older, she advises talking to her about what ideals of beauty are, and what models eat and don't eat in order to maintain artificially thin bodies.

The pressure to be thin extends across generations, says Anne Petersen, citing this shocking finding: "In studies in the suburbs of Chicago, researchers on eating disorders found that these girls weren't learning this all by themselves. Their mothers were doing it. Mothers were vomiting and teaching their daughters. There's been some trend toward getting a little better, but there are studies that look at these things a decade later. It has not changed that much."

Indeed, some of the messages that are being sent to our daughters seem to have gotten worse. A team of researchers led by James Gray of American University examined the body measurements of *Playboy* magazine centerfolds and Miss America contestants between 1979 and 1988. They found a significant decrease in the expected weight of the Miss America contestants over the decade. *Playboy* centerfolds remained at the low levels of body weight previous researchers had measured. In findings published in the *International Journal of Eating Disorders*,[1] researchers concluded that 69 percent of the *Playboy* centerfolds and

60 percent of the Miss America contestants weighed at least 15 percent less than they should. The America Psychiatric Association has determined that maintaining a weight 15 percent below normal is one criterion for anorexia nervosa, the obsession with weight loss that has resulted in young women starving themselves to death. Thus, the researchers wrote, "a majority of these 'ideals' of our society may be classified as having one of the major symptoms of an eating disorder."

Researchers also found a dramatic increase in the number of diet and excercise articles in women's magazines since 1959. Magazines are now pushing both diet and excercise as ways to achieve the cultural ideal of female thinness. The researchers concluded that both Miss America contestants and *Playboy* centerfolds had plateaued at a very low level of body weight, possibly because they have reached a floor and any further decrease would be impossible and dangerously unhealthy.

"Parents need to do whatever they can to combat that idea that girls are valued for looks and not for other things," says Jacquelynne Eccles of the University of Michigan. That includes giving girls alternative ways of feeling good about themselves, such as entering the science programs run by Girls, Inc., where girls can learn to do mechanical things and to create support groups within the community that emphasize the message that girls are valued for their achievements, not their appearance. She mentioned a television ad that talked about how young girls' "biggest dream" was to be in the Miss World beauty contest. It is not every girl's dream, yet media messages stressing looks as opposed to accomplishment are pervasive, whether you are turning on the television or picking up a magazine that targets a female audience. We give no such messages to boys. Research has shown that if parents combat these messages at every opportunity, if they emphasize to their daughters that appearance is not what makes a person valuable, their daughters will believe that. But Eccles doesn't think many families consistently tell their daughters that. "They don't believe it themselves. You can listen to families make comments when they see a woman walking down the street." Adults comment when a woman is overweight and when she is very thin. Instead of commenting favorably when they see a super-thin model or person, parents can point out to their daughters that the person is probably anorexic. I have done this with Katherine, and she has subsequently pointed out pictures of models who look anorexic to her.

Parents can also be vigilant about the messages they give about girls' breast size, which, as any adult women can tell you, is one of the most traumatizing aspects of an adolescent girl's life. It is a development that all of her schoolmates witness—and there is no public parallel in boys' maturation process.

Men's life-long obsession with the size of their penises, which also starts in adolescence, is a much more private event and, while doubtless sometimes damaging, is nowhere near as traumatic as our culture's preoccupation with breast size is for girls. The distorted fixation on breasts as sexual toys for boys, as opposed to their primary purpose, which is lactation of babies, makes this public development of breasts even more highly charged. And boys seize upon girls' development with deadly cruelty, teasing both girls who are "flat-chested" and those who are buxom. A girl's identity, her sense of worth, is suddenly wrapped up in her bra size—something she has no control over.

GIRLS ON TELEVISION

Katherine and her friends understand the impact of distorted female characters not only on themselves, but on boys. Jenny delivered the first shot to the show *Beverly Hills, 90210*. "It's real realistic," she says, her voice dripping sarcasm, and then she describes a high school girl who is portrayed by an actress who is "twenty-four years old. So girls who are in high school look at this twenty-four-year-old. She's a woman. Seniors, juniors, they don't look like that. They look at these girls who are drop-dead gorgeous, and they say, 'Why can't I look like that? Why isn't my body like that? Why aren't I making a million dollars acting on television?' It is so ridiculous.

"These girls who are on television who are supposed to be telling guys what we're supposed to be doing and how easy we're supposed to be, these guys do watch it and say, 'Oh, is that really how girls are?' And they've got these short skirts on skin-tight. They don't have any cellulite because that's why they got the job. They don't have problems with anything. They've got these huge chests because they probably got breast implants. I'm pissed off because I know when I'm a senior in high school I'm not going to look like her because she's twenty-four. But other people don't know that. They think of her as a senior in high school." Jenny feels betrayed by television characters who are supposed to be teenagers, who look like glamorous movie stars and go off to San Francisco and have sex for a week. To her, these plot lines amplify the sexual drumbeat. "Our whole generationship is based on sex," she exclaimed, inadvertently connecting generation and relationship into a new word. "Why should people have to have sex? Why is that all there is to a relationship?

"Why should I have to watch a television show and look at these people who are either drop-dead gorgeous or drop-dead ugly and say to myself, 'This is how I should look?' This is exactly what girls do.

"The only reason she's on the show is because of her appearance," Jenny stated flatly. "I think it's sick—women making money out of their appearance." She decided to drive her point home to Julia, who seemed on the verge of disagreeing. "It's not acting. People are like commercials." And she offers this example of a hypothetical perfume commercial. "There is a girl and she's butt-ugly and the guy she's with is butt-ugly and he's saying, 'I like this girl because of her perfume.' Would you go out and get the perfume so you can get a butt-ugly boyfriend?"

The girls found a vacuum of values and meaning in the privileged, consumption-driven environment in which they are growing up. They did not feel that parents had done a good job of raising their peers to be respectful, responsible, and thoughtful people, and the girls felt they were bearing the brunt of the results. They thought many of their peers were spoiled, superficial, easily manipulated by media images of what girls are supposed to be. They know that girls are judged by their clothes and appearance, and they know this is an empty standard. They feel the female role of childbearing, which they know is central to the perpetuation of humankind, is undervalued, and that angers them. They feel intense pressure to buckle under to a beauty and sex agenda they find shallow, and potentially dangerous. They feel used, and they resent the oppressive pressure from boys that puts so little value on precisely what girls value the most: the emotional aspects of a relationship. Teenagers are judged by such empty and materialistic criteria as what shoes they wear—are they originals or copies?—and the pressure to conform within a group is intense. "You have to do exactly what they do, be just like them, to be accepted," my daughter said. And she delivered this final analysis of what it felt like for her toward the end of her eighth-grade year. "McLean," she said, "is like poisoned powdered sugar."

PUTTING GIRLS IN THEIR PLACE

One rainy winter night during her eighth-grade year, my daughter and I were riding in the car when with no preamble she burst out angrily. She was indignant about what had happened that day in health class. The class, composed of about thirty youngsters, is divided about equally between boys and girls. The unit they had been studying was called "self under construction." The students had done two work-sheets, one on dating and another one on sexism. That day the teacher had divided the class into four groups, two groups of boys and two groups of girls. The girls in each group were asked to write down what they liked and disliked about being a girl, and the boys were told to do the same excercise.

"We wrote down stuff like having kids," said my daughter. "We put that for both like and dislike, because there's obviously the pain, but it's good to be able to do that. For dislikes we put down that we can't wear whatever we want, we have to look good, and guys don't always have to do that. For dislikes we put down things like shaving and wearing pantyhose.

"The guys didn't know what they were doing. What the guys did instead of writing down stuff about being guys, they wrote down what they liked or disliked. For likes, they wrote down stuff like beer, hot women." Also on their list of "likes" these girls put down friends. "Guys do, but not as much as girls. And one of the funny things was, instead of putting down 'boys' at the top, the boys put down 'men.' It was really funny. Like, yeah, right. They have to be all manly, and it's so dumb. They're not. It just shows how immature they are. We put 'girls.' "

The children had been assigned to do the worksheet on sexism with one of their parents. A few nights before that, Katherine had questioned me and written down my answers on the worksheet (and I am happy to report that our views coincided—prompting my husband to remark that the acorn doesn't fall far from the tree.) The children had then gone over the worksheets in class. "You know the question about whether the victim is responsible for her own abuse?" said Katherine, still steaming about some of the attitudes she had seen in her class. "One kid in my class said it was the woman's fault for making the guy mad!" I heard this and shut my eyes. "Blaming the victim" is still around, still polluting the environment between boys and girls, still enabling boys to rationalize intolerable behavior by telling themselves that girls and women asked for it. Boys as young as thirteen and fourteen had this in their heads.

"What did you say?" I asked Katherine.

"I said it wasn't the woman's fault, because it was his fault for choosing to react that way."

She said they had also discussed questions on the worksheet about gender roles. "There was one statement that said men are more intelligent than women. The girls in both groups, we both said we strongly disagreed. Tim said, 'Me and my father we really disagreed on that one. He strongly disagreed and I strongly agreed.' " Tim and Katherine are friends most of the time, but she was not impressed by him telling the class that he thought men were more intelligent than women. "He is so sexist," she said. "I think he does it mostly for show, to act macho, but sometimes I think he really is."

RECOVERING FROM ADOLESCENCE

When I talked to adult women about this book, many of them described their adolescence with painful recollections that invariably had to do with a sense of lost self, a silencing of their voice, a loss of self-confidence and of identity. One woman who is close to thirty and has successfully swum with the sharks in New York publishing circles told me of going back into her diary and reading a passage she wrote when she was seventeen: "I have no personality," she wrote. "Ruth has a personality, but I don't have any." And what shocked her when she read that passage was that when she was a teenager she had a very good personality. But at the time she felt she had none. She described her twenties as the decade she spent recovering from her adolescence.

"I can remember having to wait for a boy to open the car door and feeling like a cripple," recalls media analyst Junior Bridge. "Or having to stop when I reached a door first and having to step aside and wait for a boy to open it for me, or else go ahead and do it myself and feel like some brazen hussy." She remembers other admonitions: "Never let a boy know how smart you are. Don't talk about the things that interest you. Talk about the things that interest him. Never turn a boy down for a date. Somewhere along the way I began to feel emotionally and physically crippled, and it took me a long time to realize I was not. It colored my working and emotional relationships, and it took me a long time to sort out where that came from. The message I was getting at church, at school and at home was that in order for me to succeed I had to not have a name, not have a body, not have strength emotionally or physically. It took quite a while and the help of a therapist for me to realize I wasn't crippled, that I was quite healthy and strong, that I was a whole human being, that I had an identity and a personality and that it was okay not only to have those things but to exhibit them. All my life I had been forced to hide, not overtly, but in very subtle ways, all of who I was. Every girl is expected to give up her name. That says in a subtle way there is something wrong with you, something wrong with that name."

Junior Bridge's fight for her name began at her baptism, when the priest would not baptize her with the name her parents had chosen, which was Maxine Dister Junior (after her mother) Bridge. When she got into Catholic schools, the nuns refused to call her Junior and at her graduation from eighth grade, the presiding priest called her by her mother's name, rather than Junior. "I was so hurt that I almost didn't go up. I cried all the way up the aisle and all the way down.

"Then it occurred to me I was going to have to drop my last name. It's like people are trying to take bits and pieces of me. A finger here, an ear there, and then pop my eyes out. I'm not allowed to have a personality, I'm not entitled to a name, a face. I have a body I was taught to be ashamed of. In sex ed, I was taught it was the girls' fault, never the boys' fault. We were the harbingers of sin.

"I think about how I was taught to be passive. I had been taught to be powerless, which added to my feeling of being crippled. At first I thought I was just mad at the priest, but what I found out much later is that there was this additional rage over the powerlessness that had been imbued in me as a female in this society. I was thirteen, and it had already happened."

My generation spent its thirties recovering from our adolescence and the mistakes we made in our twenties. These mistakes showed up in bad marriages, poor career choices, too many children too soon, not enough education to get the jobs that were opening up to women. We believed that a woman could not achieve genuine and lifelong happiness unless we had a man in our lives. What no one told us is that there is no such thing as lifelong happiness and even if you fall in love with someone and have a successful marriage, you and he will invariably have to contend with periods of deep unhappiness occasioned by loss of loved ones, loss of jobs, illness. We were raised with myths, and the process of growing up became one of untangling the myths, sorting out reality from fantasy, and regaining our footing in the adult world of men and other recovering women. The awakening came slowly for some of us, overnight for others—particularly when we encountered something as spectacularly enlightening as job discrimination or rape. But no matter how the awakening comes, the recovery takes years and people talk of an entire decade in their lives in recovery—their twenties for younger women, their thirties for women in their forties or older. There is a certain symmetry in this, for it takes the decade of adolescence to do the damage, to hook women into psychological dependence on patriarchy.

In an adolescence that is male-centered, in which learning to get a man is the chief function of a girl and learning to be a macho parody of a man is the chief job of a boy, a girl will learn that she must conform to a set of patriarchal assumptions about women in order to get a man. These patriarchal assumptions are rooted in notions that men are superior, that they know everything, that they are entitled to what they want. To survive in that kind of unhealthy climate, an adolescent girl must go through a process of assimilating these notions and setting aside her other beliefs that don't conform to this worldview, particularly beliefs she might have harbored about the superiority of women. These are the beliefs that Jenny articulated so clearly when she was discussing woman's infinitely more complicated role as the childbearer and child nurturer. At fourteen, Jenny understood with every fiber of her being that this was the role that ensured the continuation of the human group and that it was women who fulfilled this role, not men. When she asked, "What went wrong?" she asked it almost in a personal way, but it is a question with ballistic implications that shakes the patriarchal system to its foundations.

At fourteen Jenny was asking the same question that emerged as I researched this book. The question presents the most profound challenge that can be leveled at the system, for it assumes that something went terribly wrong. And certainly something did go wrong. Jenny put her finger on an enormous and enduring mystery—a mystery that patriarchally skewed history has done its best to keep unsolved.

PART FOUR

*Where It All
Went Wrong*

CHAPTER THIRTEEN

A Journey Back in Time

What happened? Why and how did women become so devalued? Jenny's question intrudes into any serious inquiry into why we raise boys and girls the way we do. It took a year of research before I learned this: If I really wanted to know why girls come out feeling second best, if I really wanted to know what makes it possible for rock musicians to make fortunes writing songs about dismembering women, for girls to be ignored in classrooms, in churches, in medical schools, in governments, I had to go backward in time to the dim memories that lurk on the borders of human beginnings. As I kept going further back into history, into antiquity, and finally into prehistory, I began to find out how things once were between men and women, and where and how men rose to dominance over women.

I kept bumping into religion, and into men who early on learned how to manipulate religion to achieve gender supremacy.

We trace our religious heritage to the Judeo-Christian tradition, and our cultural and government traditions derive from the city-states of ancient Greece. But men and women had been around for a long time before that. We know that communities of men and women were creating works of art 25,000 years ago in Europe. These men and women are part of our heritage, too. They shared our instincts, and felt fear and aggression, hunger, love, grief, and a need to capture spiritual truth. They, too, sought religious explanations for the human condition. "Our deepest images of men and women come from religion," says feminist theologian Mary Hunt, director of the Women's Alliance for Theology, Ethics and Ritual in Silver Spring, Maryland. "It is one of the deepest places where people get their images of what it is like to be human."

Childhood religious experiences gave me small clues as to what females in our culture grow up with. I remember abandoning the Catholic Church, at the age of seventeen, after discovering the ruinous effects of its anti-birth-control teachings on the rural workers of Latin America. Where were these priests coming from? I wondered. Who gave them their authority over the lives of so many millions of women? What has transformed the rule of God into the rule of men who don't even have wives and children?

The power of monotheism in our culture seems so absolute as to be beyond question. But when you do question its authority and its legitimacy you discover that the Rock of Peter was built out of the schemes of early, power-hungry churchmen who stole the historical Jesus in the name of male orthodoxy and proclaimed that the creator was a he-god. You discover that unquestioning faith hides an ugly history. While some early Christians treated women as the equals of men, and revered Mary Magdalene as the preeminent disciple, masculinist Christian bishops and priests prevailed during the fierce doctrinal disputes that shook the early church. These theologian-hucksters had a surefire formula for closing a sale: the promise of life everlasting. The early Christians were told to go forth and win converts to Jesus, and they did. The result was a triumph of Christianity—and patriarchy—throughout Western culture.

At the end of a long quest, I have come to understand how it is that girls and boys grow up in America in a system predicated on the premise that males are superior. Christian churches have dominated spiritual life on our continent since the Spaniards invaded. The European conquerors brought their patriarchal systems with them, and as they drove out and destroyed the Native Americans, matrilineal systems common to many tribes also vanished. The New World became a patriarchal echo of the Old.

CHARACTERISTICS OF PATRIARCHY

Patriarchies share certain characteristics: Genealogy is traced through the male name, and property is passed from father to son. Patriarchies favor hierarchical systems of control within all of their institutions. Men run the community's public affairs and control its resources. Men have more access to education than do females. Men run the community's religion, and they use government, religion, and education to control females. Patriarchal religions use male symbols and worship masculine deities. Women are ranked below the men in religious worship—thus Mary, the mother of Jesus, is a clear notch below the Father and the Son in the Christian tradition; women are physically separated from men in the Orthodox Jewish synagogues; Muslim women are veiled and segregated. The hierarchies of nearly all Christian, Jewish, and Muslim religions—as well as the governments that they intersect with—are almost always controlled by men. And these religions work with the state to control women and their sexuality.

In the United States, for example, the Protestant and Catholic churches formed an unlikely alliance near the end of the nineteenth century to make birth control illegal. It was a transparent backlash to the first wave of the women's liberation movement that crested in the mid- to late-nineteenth century. A hundred years later, the Catholic Church, still preaching against birth control, formed another unlikely alliance—this time with the fundamentalist evangelicals—to try to outlaw abortion. By forbidding the use of birth control and outlawing abortion, the Catholic Church strove to give men an unlimited ability to control women through childbearing. Psychological control over adolescent girls' sexuality is subtly exerted through the artful use of the Virgin Mary, whose blessedness is deeply imprinted in the spirituality of young Catholic girls. Mary's chastity serves as a role model of virginity until marriage. At another extreme, Muslims use religion to justify brutal, and often deadly, female genital mutilation. The real purpose of female circumcision, of course, is to control female sexuality.

Patriarchies favor hierarchical patterns of control in families: Parents control their children, and husbands control their wives. "The rule remains with the husband and the wife is compelled to obey him by God's command," wrote Martin Luther, the great reformer who stopped short of reforming Christianity's most egregious wrong. Mothers believe they must mold their daughters to submit to the patriarchy, repeating the models of domination and submission they were brought up with. Since men control the resources—access to jobs, food, and shelter—mothers know that for their daughters to survive they must become what men want them to be. It is the women, the mothers, of Somalia and Sudan who hold the young girls down while they are circumcized and infibulated—literally sewn up vaginally so that their virginity is guaranteed until marriage.

Patriarchies are also marked by separatism between men and women. Men and women do different kinds of work, and in some communities they may even have separate living quarters. In many African communities, men own the land, but the women do virtually all of the farming and procuring of water and firewood. Peggy Reeves Sanday, a professor of anthropology at the University of Pennsylvania, has found that a pattern of shared work has important ramifications for the way the two sexes treat each other: The societies she has identified as rape-free are societies in which men and women do the same work together.

Patriarchies share a final common denominator that is of a piece with the violence they do to women. When they are challenged, when a dispute arises over territory, resources, and power, patriarchal governments, tribes, or clans resort to violence. War is seen as a legitimate means of conflict resolution, with the slaughtering of the enemy's sons and the rape of his daughters an appropriate way of destroying him, his tribe, and his culture. The folly of patriarchy, of course, is that the system requires it to sacrifice its own sons in war and to expose its own mothers and daughters to rape and murder. But since this is the way patriarchies resolve conflicts, and have for thousands of years, they must train mothers to be willing to give up their sons to war, and they must train little boys from childhood on to be tough, warrior-like, fearless in the presence of danger, and unemotional in the face of death. To ensure a pool of warriors, patriarchies have to drive feelings underground in the warrior class. This starts at a very young age—with all of the admonitions against crying, for example, and in favor of "toughing it out." An empathetic killer—who could look at the dead soldier at his feet and weep over the loss of another man's son—is unlikely to do his job very well.

IT JUST AIN'T SO

The rule of men, which has gone hand in hand with the rule of masculine religions, has succeeded by promoting the myth not only that male domination is sanctified by God but also that it is the natural order of things and has been so since the dawn of time.

It just ain't so.

Patriarchies, and the religions that fortify them, are recent developments in human history. Today they are being challenged with varying degrees of vigor and success throughout the world. The rise of the women's movement in the United States is the strongest challenge ever to a major patriarchal system. For this challenge to succeed, it is critically important for women and girls—and the men who stand shoulder to shoulder with them—to understand that patriarchies are recent, man-made social contrivances that draw their legitimacy from might, not divine or natural right. "What is crucial," writes the philosopher Maxine Greene, "is the recognition that women's relegation to private life is neither biologically based nor given in the nature of things."[1]

Modern religions, which have always dreaded science and its abilities to uncover inconvenient secrets about the universe—Galileo is the best known of the Church of Rome's science heretics—have every reason to be alarmed that scientific and historical breakthroughs are posing imminent danger to the patriarchy's health. The great store of knowledge about the ancient world that science has uncovered since World War II is mounting an unprecedented assault on the most fundamental underpinnings of the male-dominated churches and the patriarchies they are upholding. Archaeologists, art historians, linguists, and anthropologists are making convincing cases for the proposition that male domination is neither a universal truth nor part of a natural order—for it was not the principle of social order in Paleolithic and Neolithic times. It is a relatively recent development in the history of humankind. The importance of these revelations cannot be overstated: It means that patriarchies are neither immutable nor inevitable. They can be challenged, changed, and replaced.

Piecing together clues from prehistoric cave art, excavations of ancient cities, and burial sites, scientists, armed with an arsenal of new tools, have been able to reconstruct a richly detailed picture of how ancient peoples lived, hunted, farmed, traded, and worshiped. Many experts now agree that the artificial division that places a greater value on one gender over the other came about through relatively recent power grabs that dethroned the goddess religions and the matriarchal societies that worshiped the goddess, gradually replacing them with patriarchal societies that worshiped male gods and, most recently, a monotheistic male god.

In his introduction to *The Greek Myths*, first published in 1955, Robert Graves wrote: "The whole of neolithic Europe, to judge from surviving artifacts and myths, had a remarkably homogeneous system of religious ideas, based on worship of the many-titled Mother-goddess, who was also known in Syria and Libya."[2] In Greece she was known as Gaia, the earth mother, from whom all life and all earth's elements flowed, and who slew her mate every year in order to produce fertile fields. Experts now believe that goddess-worship existed in the earliest known Paleolithic communities of Europe, for goddess representations are present in cave art and figures that have been preserved for 20,000 years. Works of art, along with burial rites, attest to the earliest beliefs in the life-giving power of woman and her central role in birth, death, and regeneration. It is a theme that weaves throughout ancient religions all the way down to the modern Catholic vision of Mary, Mother of God.

THE GREAT GODDESS

These new interpreters of ancient art and more recent archaeological finds are posing provocative questions about the social organization of prehistoric communities. Citing the absence of evidence of sexual inequality in the way people were buried and in the religious and social rituals preserved in prehistoric art, as well as the absence of war imagery in art and weapons at burial sites, they are disputing the conventional beliefs that our earliest known ancestors were warriors and hunters who dominated a male-centered belief system and social order.

Domestication of wild plants and of animals, the critical components of the agricultural revolution that allowed primitive peoples to settle territories and develop stockpiles of food, occurred more than 10,000 years ago; these events marked the beginning of the Neolithic Age. Towns evolved, people began to specialize in various crafts, and extensive trade routes developed for the exchange of goods. Cultures capable of brilliant artwork flourished about 6000 B.C. at Catal Huyuk and at Hacilar, in what is now Turkey. Excavated between 1961 and 1965 by James Mellaart, who directed the work for the British Institute of Archaeology at Ankara, the discoveries at Catal Huyuk and Hacilar revealed the existence of highly developed civilizations that worshiped the goddess. Catal Huyuk contains mud-and-brick houses that have been dated to 6500–5800 B.C. Many of the houses were shrines with enormous figures of goddesses, posed as if giving birth, painted on their walls.

The idea that matriarchies may have prevailed throughout the known world at some earlier time surfaced more than 100 years ago, and it has been gaining respectability in academic scholarship ever since, albeit in the face of fierce resistance.

Johann Jakob Bachofen, a Swiss anthropologist and cultural historian, was among the first scholars to question the notion of patriarchy and monogamy as the natural foundation of human groupings with the publication of *Das Mutterrecht* (*The Right of a Mother*) in 1861. Ten years earlier, in America, Lewis H. Morgan had published a study of the matrilineal Iroquois and argued that this was the pre-patriarchal order of community life throughout the world.

Patriarchy, as the natural law—the way things have always been and always will be, as the earthly reflection of a monotheistic God who has ruled since creation—was about to come in for a rude shock. Gestalt and Jungian psychologists Jennifer and Roger Woolger, in *The Goddess Within*, credit Bachofen with being "enormously influential, seeding investigation in ethnography, anthropology, and sociology for several generations to come."[3] Among his legatees were Friedrich Engels, whose book *The Origins of the Family, Private Property and the State*, was published in 1884, and Carl G. Jung, whose *Symbols of Transformation* was published in 1912. In his book, Jung developed the idea of a psychological archetype mother who reflects the mythology of the Great Mother Goddess.

Much of the recent exploration into this theory has been inspired by the work of Marija Gimbutas, a professor of archaeology at the University of California, who along with Mellaart, helped provide scientific underpinnings for Robert Graves's statement that worship of the Goddess/Mother was the prevailing social and religious system for most of history. Gimbutas led five excavations in Europe and wrote *The Bronze Age Cultures in Central and Eastern Europe*, a study of Indo-Europeans who rode out of the Russian steppes about 4400 B.C. That work established her as a world-class archaeologist. She set forth her findings about the Great Goddess in *The Goddesses and Gods of Old Europe*, published in 1982, and *The Language of the Goddess*, published in 1990, in which she classified and interpreted more than 2,000 artifacts from Old Europe.

In *The Language of the Goddess*, Gimbutas argues that the Goddess religion was a "cohesive and persistent ideological system" that extended throughout the Near East, southeastern Europe, the Mediterranean area, and central, western, and northern Europe for thousands of years in the Neolithic period. With a working knowledge of two dozen European languages, Gimbutas leaned heavily, as she put it, on "comparative mythology, early historical sources, and linguistics, as well as on folklore and historical ethnography."[4] This broader, more interpretive interdisciplinary approach has aroused criticism in some scientific circles, with some archaeologists arguing that Gimbutas's interpretations of the symbols on goddess figures cannot be proven. She has not only stuck to her guns but has interpreted her finds and those of others as evidence of thriving communities in which the Great Goddess was worshiped as the giver of life, death, and regeneration— communities in which men and women lived side by side, at peace with each other and nature. In a 1989 interview with the *Los Angeles Times*, she predicted that it would take archaeology ten years to accept the Goddess, but that eventually she would be proven correct.

Gimbutas focused her work on the Neolithic cultures of Europe, following their symbols and artistic imagery forward into historic times, and then backward, to linkages she found in Paleolithic art. The ceramics, stones, clay figurines, and ivory and bone pieces she catalogued and analyzed date principally from 6500 to 3500 B.C. in southeastern Europe and from about 4500 to 2500 B.C. in western Europe. Among the richest sites for preserved temples and art of this period were Catal Huyuk, and her own excavations at Achilleion in Thessaly, which she worked in 1973 and 1974, uncovering some of the earliest European temples, from around 6000 B.C. She found an "amazing longevity of certain images and designs."

"The Goddess-centered religion existed for a very long time," she wrote, "much longer than the Indo-European and the Christian (which represent a relatively short period of human history), leaving an indelible imprint on the Western psyche."[5]

Traditional archaeologists had cavalierly tossed off the figurines— with their exaggerated breasts and buttocks—as early erotica or Venus figurines. To Gimbutas, looking at these through the female lens, the exaggerated sexual parts celebrated the powers of birth and reproduction ancient people worshiped in the goddess. Neolithic burial sites from this period provide additional compelling evidence about how women and men lived together in these times. Unlike more recent graves of males, which also held the skeletal remains of servants, children, and wives who were killed after their master's death and entombed with him, these ancient digs gave silent testimony to a far more egalitarian way of life. Men were buried alone, as were women. Men and women carried similar implements with them on their journey into the next world. Men and women were buried the same way.

WOMEN AS PROVIDERS

Michael and Kathleen Gear, archaeologists and writers,[6] make the point that women's status in early societies was very much linked to the roles they played as providers, storers, and distributors of food—and hence owners of the land—and they draw a sharp and important distinction between woman's anthropological role as provider and our current view of woman as caretaker. Woman's role as provider is deeply intertwined with the history of the horse. The horse became extinct in North America about 7,000 years ago. It was reintroduced to the continent by the Spanish explorers, settlers, and missionaries. Techniques of communal hunting evolved in which women would take children with them and hunt together on foot, providing about 80 percent of the food. They would surround and shoot deer or run buffalo into an enclosed area or run them off a cliff. "Women could not get far from their village," says Michael Gear, because of the need to be near their young children. However, when Native-American men domesticated horses, stolen originally from Spanish settlers, they began to hunt individually, and hunt larger territories. "Women were shoved out of the hunting scenario. The horse allowed men to become raiders."

"It means that suddenly men have the key to the economic survival of the group," says Kathleen Gear, "whereas before it was shared." When civilizations overcultivated the land, however, and began cycles of environmental degradation that led to erosion and starvation-level agricultural yields, the role of woman as provider was further undermined. "It appears to the people that Mother Earth is dying or denying them the right to live," says Kathleen Gear. "And I think even when you look cross-culturally, you find that suddenly when Mother Earth no longer provides there is a shift in the society from women to men. When earth no longer provides, women lose their status as providers. Then it falls on men, and physical strength becomes very important in securing the survival of your people. When physical strength becomes important, the decline in the status of women follows automatically."

Ancient hunting patterns in which men traveled great distances may have fostered differences in spatial skills between men and women, the Gears suggest, and may have something to do with little boys' preference for toys that move through space—cars, fire engines, airplanes. The ability to move through space translates into power: The ability to travel great distances and find your way home gives you the ability to gather precious goods that are rare, and gives you the ability to exploit a broader hunting base with more animals. Moreover, men were the expendable sex. They could be sent on long journeys since one man could impregnate numerous women, while a woman could have a baby only once a year.

These sexual distinctions, going back perhaps a million years or more, are probably related to hunting and gathering adaptations, and have important implications for how we look at differences between men and women today. "What the feminist movement began to do was say there are no differences between men and women; therefore we deserve equality," says Michael Gear. "It was the wrong argument. We are good at different things. Without the complementariness of male and female talents, human beings cannot survive."

Another critical error that women's advocates have made, according to the Gears, is to exaggerate the concept of women as nurturers. This has led to a political framework in which women are assigned a "natural" role as caretaker, peacemaker, the gentle sex.

Taking issue with this whole idea, Kathleen Gear says it arose out of Judeo-Christian perceptions, heavily influenced by the Victorians, of what women should be. And those perceptions were anthropologically wrong. "Throughout history women have been providers, and that involved killing animals. In matrilineal societies, women were the fundamental lawmakers and law enforcers. If someone committed murder, it was women who said, 'Take him out.' And women were responsible for killing the children when resources were rare. Even if you go back to the Minoan concept of Gaia, she is not some fruitcake. This is the goddess who killed her husband every year to make the fields fertile."

The thirty-year struggle of the modern feminist movement for equality has largely ignored the complementary anthropological destiny of women, which is to do whatever a culture needs to allow it to survive. This includes being physically strong so that they could provide for their communities as men did. This tradition remains strong today among Tuareg women. Writing in the November, 1992, issue of *Natural History,* Barbara A. Worley describes the women of the Kel Fadey tribe of pastoral Tuaregs of south-central Sahara, who trace their beginnings to two sisters. The tribe is matrilineal, and the women pride themselves on their strength, so much so that they are the fighters and wrestlers who uphold family prestige by their physical exploits. Tuareg men, wrote Worley, "fear the loss of honor that would ensue from beating or raping a woman." Women view their assertiveness as a desirable feminine trait. "One of the most valued roles in Tuareg society, according to both men and women, is motherhood."

The significance that prehistoric communities place on the complementary qualities of males and females shows up in religious symbolism. "The vision quest was always around themes of touching power, which was neither male nor female, but a combination of the two, and that was spiritual power," says Kathleen Gear. The literature on religions of indigenous people, including Native Americans, is replete with stories of men becoming women in order to wield spirit power. Creation stories involve male and female.

"The role for women cross-culturally until the suppression by male dominant societies was always the provider and the culture maintainer," says Kathleen Gear. But in Old Europe the matriarchal societies proved to be no match for men with horses.

THE INDO-EUROPEAN INVASION
AND THE FALL OF THE GODDESS

Gimbutas believes that by the sixth millennium an aggressive, well-armed, patriarchal culture that worshiped male sky gods had risen in the Volga basin of south Russia and domesticated the horse. She calls these Indo-Europeans "Kurgans," using the Russian word for the burial mounds of important dead men that were common in the central Russian steppes. Mounted on horseback, armed with spears, daggers, and bows and arrows, they began a series of three major incursions against the peaceful, unarmed peoples of Old Europe beginning in 4300 B.C. and ending about 2800, bringing hybridization of the Old European cultures as far west as the Rhine and spreading through the regions south and east of the Baltic Sea and to the southern tip of Scandinavia. Her theory recently received support from a research effort led by Luigi L. Cavalli-Sforza, a Stanford University geneticist, who has mapped the expansion of groups of people by using evidence from mitochondrial DNA.

The goddess-centered cultures survived the longest on the isle of Crete, where archaeological remains of an ancient high civilization were first discovered at the turn of the twentieth century. Women enjoyed high status, as priestesses, athletes, and possibly queens—a theory buttressed by the absence of evidence that dominant male gods were worshiped. Men and women participated in sports together. The most famous were the bull games, in which teams of young boys and girls would grasp the horns of a charging bull and vault over its back.[7]

In 1350 B.C. a volcanic eruption and tsunami appears to have wiped out the Minoan civilization. Crete was finally overrun about 1200 B.C. by the Dorians, who swept in on horseback from the northwest, driving the Achaeans described by Homer as occupying Greece, Crete and Rhodes, to the Ionian islands. The Dorians dominated Greece as well, and the matrilineal tradition of passing name and land from mother to child, already weakened by the Greek-speaking Achaeans, was firmly replaced by the Dorian system of patriarchal lineage. The fall of Crete, about 3,200 years ago, marked the end of the last known goddess-worshiping ancient civilization.

Religion historian E. O. James writes in *The Ancient Gods* that the Indo-Europeans brought with them their own traditions, which they incorporated under Zeus. In the cultural fusion that ensued, the matriarchal beliefs of the Goddess religions began to fold into the patriarchal divinity systems of the Aryans. Gaia—the one goddess who encompassed all of life, death, wisdom, and regeneration—disappeared. In the Olympian myths, Zeus appeared and married Hera, which, Jennifer and Roger Woolger suggest in *The Goddess Within*, may have "symbolized the humiliating capitulation of the early Mother Goddess to the sky god intruder."[8] Then, it seems, the goddesses were split up and departmentalized, and a pantheon of male gods appeared: Zeus, Apollo, Perseus, along with the departmentalized descendants of Gaia who took on parts of the goddess but never again her totality. Thus Athena—who appears in statues holding a spear and wearing a helmet, and who was athletic, resourceful, and the patroness of military might and warrior heroes—was childless.

Agriculture, which was critical to the survival of the city-states of Greece, was the special province of the goddess Demeter, and she probably represents the goddess who comes closest in heritage to archetypal Gaia. Demeter was the goddess of fecundity and the mother of Persephone. Her worship had taken hold by 1300 B.C., and she survived as a goddess well into the Middle Ages, a testament to her enduring importance, given the harshness that marked the assaults by Christians on pagan believers. Demeter's temple at Eleusis, fourteen miles from Athens, was for more than 1,500 years the center of an annual religious festival celebrating regeneration, until it was destroyed by monks in A.D. 396.

THE DAY ZEUS BLINKED

What was the appeal of Demeter that allowed her to endure so long? Why are stories of goddesses so important? If god is male, then males are god, as theologian Mary Daly has argued. But if the goddess is female, then females are goddesses. And Demeter was a powerful female goddess—an archetype for powerful females. Her story resonates to the deepest meaning of woman—not only as the generator of life, but as a powerful mother. The event that triggers the myth is the separation of Demeter from her beloved daughter, Persephone, who is kidnapped into the underworld by Hades, brother of Zeus, thus setting off yet another power play between male gods and female goddesses. A grieving Demeter wanders the world for nine days, searching for her daughter, and no one will tell her what has become of her. At last Helios tells her what Zeus has done. Enraged, Demeter leaves Mount Olympus and, disguised as an old crone, goes to Eleusis and sets up vigil at the Well of the Maidens. Eventually she reveals herself in all her splendor to the mortals and orders them to build her a temple. She takes up residence, in solitary mourning. She refuses all communication with the gods and sends forth a drought on earth. This is a major standoff. Zeus finally persuades Hades to let Persephone return to her mother at least part of each year, and the two are reunited at the temple. Before returning to Olympus, Demeter shares her rites and rituals with the Eleusians—and the mysteries and annual celebration of these rites are born.

Perhaps the most remarkable aspect of the myth of Demeter is the paramount importance given to the mother-daughter bond, which is so powerful that it brings both the gods of the underworld and of Mount Olympus to their knees. To put what happened in modern terms, Demeter and Persephone won because Demeter was tough enough to play hardball with Zeus. In effect, she threatened to shut off food and thus all of life on earth, and Zeus blinked. She who gives can also take away.

This is a tremendously powerful female story. The Eleusian mysteries celebrated the female cycle and its power to cross into the underworld and return. Priestesses officiated. To young Greek children, these must have been forceful statements of how important the female goddesses were and, by identification, the female human and her power to generate and nourish life. Fast-forwarding to today, one can see the

stark contrast between the powerful female stories and images that
flourished in the Greek psyche and the virtual absence of any such
women—women who successfully challenge the gods—in the Judeo-
Christian cultures that have taken root in modern times. A world that
so proudly traces its cultural and civic heritage back to the heyday of
Athens has marginalized the Greek gods and goddesses to historical
curiosities. We do not think of them as archetypes of powerful women
whose experiences resonate deeply into the psyches of women and
connect us to our foremothers, the women who ran communities from
the dawn of time. Few of us even think of goddesses and the Great
Mother at all.

"It is hard for us today to imagine what it must have been like to
have a goddess and her earth mysteries at the center of cultural and
spiritual life," write the Woolgers. "More than two thousand years of
Judeo-Christian culture have accustomed us to thinking of everything
divine as masculine and somehow belonging 'up there' in the heavens.
As a result we have almost forgotten what it is to regard the earth we
walk upon as sacred, as truly our mother, and as the dwelling place
of both goddesses and gods."[9]

Even Athena, patroness of Athens in its most glorious period, has
been swept underground and lost. If Athena's sway over the religious
life of Athens is mentioned at all, it is relegated to the margins of an
occasional mention of Greek mythology in the modern classroom. If
she lives for us at all, it is as a remote sculpture of stone, not as a
powerful female symbol, a powerhouse of possibilities for what women
and girls can be. Approaching Athena, embracing her as an essential
female archetype, became impossible for modern girls and women once
she was turned from a goddess into a statue, her personal qualities
frozen in another time, her own biography mostly forgotten—save
that she sprang from the head of Zeus, who had first gobbled down
her mother because he feared she might become more powerful than
he. A set piece of a lesson for women and girls is that one: Challenge
the male gods and they will eat you up.

THE POWER OF THE PAST

My daughter followed my research for this book with a lively interest and understood, as I did, that the answers about what happens to girls lay in the cultural hinterland of our past. My job was to find them— and in a very personal way I was finding them for her. I will never forget the expression that crossed her face when I began telling her about the early goddess-worshiping societies and the partnership theories advanced by Gimbutas. We were sitting in the living room of our farmhouse in the Shenandoah Valley, a place where we can feel closely connected to the earth, to a large meadow, mountains, and a creek that has run through the land for centuries. Indians hunted the property and probably farmed the vegetable garden. One day while we were cultivating it, I picked up an odd-shaped rock, covered with mud, and started to throw it into the woods. Something made me stop. I scraped the mud off on a fence post and an odd and ancient shape emerged. I showed it to my husband. We both knew it was an Indian artifact, although we were wrong in thinking it a tomahawk head. Michael Gear told me later that it was the head of a hoe used by Indians in farming.

We are closer to the cycles of nature on the farm than at any other place. We have cows and a bull, and in the spring we count on calves. We are at the mercy of nature for rain, grass, and hay, and we are at her mercy when it comes to diseases and weather. We have lost a calf to tetanus. We have had roaring floods in our creek. In the country it is easier to envision and accept the knowledge of goddess-worshiping ancient societies, where men and women were partners and fought elemental battles for survival shoulder to shoulder. When you are doing the same things that your ancestors did centuries before you, it becomes easier to imagine how people in ancient times would have worshiped female deities, and why. When I began talking to my daughter about where my research was taking me, she listened intently. When I told her how the god-worshiping warrior clans had overrun the peaceful farming communities, and when I outlined the rise of monotheism, she was engaged with a curiosity I'd rarely seen.

When I told her that the worship of a single male god was a relatively recent event, say 2,000 years in the making, compared to perhaps 10,000 years or more of female worship, she had one of those moments of revelation that women of my generation called a "click." In a single moment, she understood that the dominant male culture we are living in today did not always hold sway. It didn't used to be that way; that means it doesn't always have to be that way. "That makes sense," she said, as it began to sink in. "If you think about it, women are the ones who have the children, and without us there wouldn't be any more people, so it makes sense that they would worship goddesses."

"No matter by which culture a woman is influenced, she understands the words *wild* and *woman* intuitively," writes Clarissa Pinkola Estes.

"When women hear those words, an old, old memory is stirred and brought back to life. The memory is of our absolute, undeniable, and irrevocable kinship with the wild feminine, a relationship which may have become ghosty from neglect, buried by overdomestication, out-lawed by the surrounding culture, or no longer understood anymore. We may have forgotten her names, we may not answer when she calls ours, but in our bones we know her, we yearn toward her; we know she belongs to us and we to her."[10]

In her bones, my daughter knew that the past held promise for the future.

CHAPTER FOURTEEN

The Greeks, God, and Women

We proudly trace our cultural heritage to the Greeks. "It is our yesterday," wrote I. F. Stone in *The Trial of Socrates*, "and we cannot understand ourselves without it." Even with Athena as a patron, and a pantheon that included powerful goddesses, the religious and secular reduction of women was well under way in classical Greece. Athens, our political ancestor, was a testosterone-poisoned patriarchy by the time it reached its apex as the cultural center of ancient Greece. For the Greeks, man was the center of the universe. If Athens was the birthplace of democracy, it was also the wellspring of patriarchal assumptions that continue to plague us today. Yet even in ancient Athens there was lively debate about the role of women, and women continued to play important roles as priestesses and teachers. The religious annihilation of women would come about 200 years after the life of the historical Jesus.

From the sixth century B.C. to the rise of the Sophists 200 years later, the Greeks challenged the most deeply held beliefs of their ancestors about the relationship of man to nature. Sophists questioned the difference between what is man-made and what is made by nature, challenging the prevailing pagan religions that gave gods and goddesses credit for creating everything. Teachers and philosophers questioned man's relationship to government, who should rule, and who should be educated—and what is the appropriate role of women.

We become highly selective in our citations when we debate the appropriate roles for men and women. Overlooked is the fact that at least two of the most influential Greek philosophers—Socrates and his pupil, Plato—believed in the equality of women and argued that they should have access to the formal forms of education that were afforded boys. Although government was the exclusive province of men, priestesses were influential figures in the religious life. Religious oracles, for instance, frequently overlapped into secular matters. By classical times the oracle at Delphi had been taken over by Apollo, but the oracles were spoken through the lips of a priestess called the Pythoness.

Priestesses played important roles in the education of the Greek philosophers to whom our intellectual life is so deeply indebted. But the contributions of women have remained hidden from history until recently. We have learned a great deal about Socrates, who left not one written word behind, but we don't learn that he was taught by Diotema, a priestess and celebrated Pythagorean philosopher. Pythagoras himself was taught ethics by Themistoclea, a priestess at Delphi. Neither of these teachers merits an entry in the *Encyclopedia Brittannica*, although the entry under Themis, the goddess who personified justice and wisdom, contains an ironic note: "Themis was a giver of oracles, and one legend relates that she once owned the oracle at Delphi but later gave it to Apollo."

It's enough to make one entertain the notion that both Themis and her priestess got ripped off—one shorn of her oracle and the other of her place in history.

Socrates was a teacher of philosophy and a sophist. Unlike Aristotle, who was interested in science, Socrates was concerned with ethics and morality, the relationship of people to government, and concepts of justice. In his essay "On Liberty," published in 1859, John Stuart

Mill provided this measure of Socrates' importance to Western thought: "Born in an age and country abounding in individual greatness, this man has been handed down to us . . . as the most virtuous man in it; while we know him as the head and prototype of all subsequent teachers of virtue, the source equally of the lofty inspiration of Plato and the judicious utilitarianism of Aristotle . . . ."

Mill, Socrates, and Plato all believed in the equality of women. Mill was keenly aware of how social mores had been even more effective in subjugating women than structured political tyrannies. Social tyranny, he wrote, "leaves fewer means of escape, penetrating much more deeply into the details of life, and enslaving the soul itself."

Plato's argument on behalf of female equality rings as if it were being advanced by feminists today: "Can you employ any creature for the same work as another, if you do not give them both the same upbringing and education?" he asked in *The Republic*.

"No."

"Then, if we are to set women to the same tasks as men, we must teach them the same things. They must have the same two branches of training for mind and body and also be taught the art of war, and they must receive the same treatment."

In a passage that resonates in modern debates over gender, he argued that questions of sameness and difference ought to be measured in relation to occupations, not reproductive functions. "We meant, for instance, that a man and a woman have the same nature if both have a talent for medicine; whereas two men have different natures if one is a born physician, the other a born carpenter." If the only difference between the two "appears that the male begets and the female brings forth, we shall conclude that no difference between man and woman has yet been produced that is relevant to our purpose. We shall continue to think it proper for our Guardian and their wives to share in the same pursuits."

Plato's eerily modern feminist manifesto included war, and he wanted to give the same training in mind and body to the best of all citizens—the Guardians—and their wives as well. This, he argued, was "in accordance with nature. Rather, the contrary practice which now prevails turns out to be unnatural." The Guardians, he wrote, "will be the best of all the citizens," and "these women the best of all the women."

"Can anything be better for a commonwealth than to produce in it men and women of the best possible type?"

Once again, Plato's answer was a resounding "No."

This is precisely the same argument that feminist organizations have been making to advance the careers of women in the military and to admit women to the fast tracks of education in math and science.

THE BACKLASH

The backlash started with Aristotle.

Aristotle took all knowledge to be his own: Nothing was beyond the reach of his philosophical and scientific inquiries. His posture today would be looked upon as the ultimate display of academic egomania, but throughout most of Western educational history it has been revered. Few children in Western cultures get through school without making a passing acquaintance with Aristotle and his contributions to the structure of Western thought.

What they are not taught is that Aristotle was a chauvinist and a bigot—an overweening, macho egghead whose posture toward all creatures who were not Greek males would land him in a holding pen for the terminally non-politically correct today. Aristotle perceived nature, as well as political enterprises, in the hierarchical terms that mold our own thinking to this day. He catalogued nature as a series of dualisms that pitted superior men against inferior animals, superior Greeks against inferior slaves. The soul was superior to the body, reason was superior to passion, and males were superior to females.

His teachings have been a 2,000-year-long disaster for women. Admit women to the Guardians? Encourage them to practice medicine, statecraft, and the art of war as urged by Plato? Not a chance. Aristotle's teachings obliterated female equality from Western culture for more than two millennia.

The consequences of Aristotle's teachings were summed up by Charles Van Doren in his *History of Knowledge*: "His greatness as a philosopher and protoscientist is undeniable. Yet his errors have had enduring harmful effects. His doctrines of natural inferiority and female inferiority, respectively, justified, or helped to justify, slavery and the inequality of the sexes until our own time. His great authority also helped to defend tyranny, in the name of 'benevolent' despotism, and his doctrine of ethnic inferiority helped to justify racism."[1]

THE RELIGIOUS ANNIHILATION OF WOMEN

With the teachings of Socrates and Plato, and later of Jesus, there were opportunities for women to become liberated, emancipated, and educated. But within a period of a few hundred years, these windows of opportunity were slammed shut. Within the historic twinkling of an eye, women as leaders, as priests, and as deities were wiped out. Ancient religious texts that portrayed women as equals of men were banned or rewritten. Greek and Roman men by that time had cemented their hold on a culture that was completely patrilineal. Before the Romans sacked Jerusalem in A.D. 70, they allowed a group of rabbis to remove sacred books that they took with them in the Hebrew diaspora. They censored references to women as deities, priests, and powerful secular figures. These censored texts became the Old Testament.

The importance of this religious annihilation of powerful women figures cannot be overestimated. "Religion is the heart and soul upon which the culture is built," says Kathleen Gear. "Which is why it is so important when they delete women from the religion." The effect is to delete women from important roles in the whole social structure and to devalue the complementary qualities that they bring to the community's health and survival.

CLEOPATRA: THE LAST POLYTHEIST QUEEN

Women—at least upper-class women—played powerful roles in antiquity. Cleopatra, born in 69 B.C., was the only person other than Hannibal to pose a serious threat to Rome. Twice she tried to conquer Rome by manipulating its most successful generals. She was one of the most powerful players during a crucial era of Roman expansion. Had Cleopatra and Mark Antony's forces prevailed in the naval battle at Actium, their plan—Cleopatra's, really—was to move the seat of the Roman Empire from Rome to Alexandria. Had she succeeded, she would have changed the course of history. In Cleopatra, we find the last important fusion of polytheistic religion that worshiped both a male (Re) and female deity (Isis) as principal gods in a country that was ruled by a woman. Popular history, however, trivializes her as a femme fatale.

The pagan religions were characterized by a degree of tolerance that is remarkable in light of the religious wars that have dominated the last 2,000 years of history. As the Romans solidified their hold over the Western world, they spread the Latin language into Africa, Spain, Gaul, and Britain. Greek was the language of science and Latin the language of political administration. Educated people knew both. A common form of government, administrative laws, systems of social justice, customs of commerce, and transportation united the known world. But the Romans forced no such communality of religion.

Edward Gibbon, in *The Decline and Fall of the Roman Empire*, estimated that the Roman Empire was populated by 120 million people at the time of Claudius. Pagan beliefs held by the multitudes went back thousands of years. The pattern of tolerance, however, was being sorely tested. The Jews in Palestine, who were preparing for the arrival of the Messiah, refused to pay tribute to the Roman emperors, claiming that the creation of earth and man was the product of a single almighty god. The Jews, and later the Christians, ran afoul of the Roman Empire because they refused to put their monotheistic god side by side with the various pagan gods and goddesses in the popular pantheon. They also refused to attend games and ceremonies that required homage to the gods and goddesses. With the arrival of Jesus of Nazareth, thirty-one years after Cleopatra's death, the stage was set for the 2,000-year ascent of Christianity and Judaism, and the religious worship of one god who created man in his image. From the last admonition by Jesus to his disciples—"Go therefore and make disciples of all nations, baptizing them in the name of the Father and of the Son and of the Holy Spirit, teaching them to observe all that I have commanded you"—to today, the Christian faith has been grounded in the ideals of expansionism and eternal salvation for all who embrace it. The concept of eternal salvation was entirely new. Polytheist religions had never advanced such a proposition—and it was enormously appealing.

During the first 500 years after the birth of Christ, Christianity struggled for survival and finally for dominance as the state religion of the Roman world. During this period, it underwent a fusion of Hebraic and pagan traditions and beliefs, all the while maintaining the core teaching of one all-powerful god. Jesus, a Jew, had fulfilled the predictions of eternal salvation in the Old Testament. The teachings and writings of his apostles would be incorporated over the next several hundred years into what would become known as the New Testament.

Gibbon noted the distance from Jesus that characterizes the textual underpinnings for Christianity. "The authentic histories of the actions of Christ were composed in the Greek language, at a considerable distance from Jerusalem, and after the Gentile converts were grown extremely numerous." Put in modern terms, the legitimacy of the teachings as coming firsthand from the apostles is highly suspect. In a court of law, these teachings would be disallowed as hearsay. They are so poorly sourced that no reputable American newspaper would print them. Yet these so-called apostolic teachings have been the foundations for Christian dogma that has subjugated women for nearly 2,000 years.

By the time Jesus arrived, women had been relegated to low status in many of the Jewish sects. They sat in separate quarters from men, veiled, forbidden to participate in worship services. But Jesus viewed women as the equals of men: He included women as full participants in the Christian communities and forbade divorce, which instantly raised the status of women in their families. Jesus frequently used the wedding ceremony as a parable in his sermons, particularly when describing the eucharistic meal, which bestowed even more importance to marriage and elevated it to the status of an unbreakable sacrament. This, too, strengthened the position of women. Women were active as prophets and as charismatic voices in religious assemblies. They received the Holy Spirit alongside men. Said Paul: "There is neither male nor female; for you are all one in Christ Jesus."

Yet the tension these new teachings were provoking among the rabbinical and patriarchal traditions was evident in Paul's other admonition that women "should keep silence in the churches." This bow to synagogic mores has provided the basis for the exclusion of women from church hierarchies from the time male bishops and priests seized control of the Christian churches around A.D. 200 until today. It remains the theological foundation for the Roman Catholic Church's refusal to admit women to the priesthood.

Among the Christian sects that sprang up immediately after Jesus Christ's death were the gnostics, who welcomed women into their community meetings and gave them prominent priestly roles. Gnostic texts discovered recently in Egypt establish that some gnostics believed that Mary Magdalene was Christ's chief disciple. The role of women in the early church appears to have been highly divisive, setting up a major series of confrontations between orthodox teachings and what the early bishops called "heresy." From the beginning, orthodox Christianity was marked by a lack of tolerance for other religions and other Christian and Jewish sects. Unlike paganism, it insisted on strict adherence to dogma and doctrine. While Jesus did not establish a hierarchy of priests within his community, his circle of apostles created a prototype of a hierarchy of men who had special knowledge of his teaching. It was the beginning of a distinction between clergy and laity that Gibbon observed did not exist in polytheistic times. It was a distinction that the gnostics eschewed; in so doing, they presented the growing ranks of orthodox clergy with their most severe challenge in the years immediately following the death of Jesus. They were eventually driven underground. For nearly 2,000 years, what we knew of the gnostic sects and their version of Christ's teaching was based on records kept by bishops who sought to discredit them. Not until a series of remarkable discoveries in the Dead Sea cave areas, beginning in the 1940s, were historians and religious scholars able to get any accurate information about these early followers of Christ, how they lived, and their accounts of what he taught. These discoveries—which show that women played a central role in the early church—are rocking the tenets of patriarchal Christianity to its foundations.

Gibbon estimated that by the middle of the third century, there were about 1 million people living in Rome, and about 50,000 of them were Christians. He wrote that the Christian clergy consisted of a bishop, forty-six presbyters, seven deacons, as many subdeacons, forty-two acolytes, and fifty readers, exorcists, and porters. His list established the fact that there was an elaborate church hierarchy by A.D. 250, although Gibbon did not report whether women occupied any of the rungs. Women were persecuted as Christian martyrs, however, an indicator of the stature they had in the early church.

CHRISTIANITY AND THE STATE

The battle between Constantine the Great and his brother-in-law Maxentius at the Milvian Bridge near Rome in A.D. 312 marked one of the great turning points in history. The night before he entered into battle, Constantine is said to have had a dream in which an angel appeared and instructed him to paint the Christian symbol, the cross, on his troops' shields. He defeated Maxentius and made a series of alliances that consolidated his hold over the Roman Empire until he died twenty-five years later. During his reign, Constantine laid the imperial foundations for the expansionistic, state-protected Christian church that dominates Western culture. In A.D. 325 he convened the Council of Nicaea (now Iznik, in eastern Anatolia) to deal with challenges to the divinity of Christ. The result was the Nicene Creed, which proclaimed that the Christian faith was grounded in the acceptance of one almighty God and his Son, who were divine equals: "I believe in one God," it begins. A Christian who thus believed would find eternal life, and those who did not were condemned to eternal death. Monotheism had received the blessing of the empire.

A strain of celibate beliefs that had marked some early Hebrew and Christian cults—who viewed women as dangerous temptresses—had gained support as the bishops and priests solidified their powers over the organized church. Not enough of them were willing to endorse celibacy in the first Council of Nicaea, however. But the right of clergy to beat their wives was affirmed in the Council of Toledo in A.D. 400, and it swiftly crept from canon into common law as men were given physical authority to punish their wives. Moral denunciation of women as evil would come later, and would reach sexual savagery during the witch hysteria of the Middle Ages.

With Constantine's conversion, Christianity became the official religion of the Roman Empire, and the churches were given the right to offer sanctuary, a privilege that had been limited to the most sacred pagan temples. The affairs of the state and the church became inexorably intertwined. Christian heretics, including the gnostics, were persecuted and driven underground. By the end of the fourth century, paganism had been outlawed, as were its assemblies, rites, and sacrifices. Gibbon concluded, however, that the pagans "were to have their subtle revenge. As vast numbers of pagan proselytes thronged the churches, the churches accommodated them by slowly adopting, in the worship of saints and relics, an equivalent to the pagan mythology."[2] The fusion had practical implications, as well. By the second and third century, Roman men of the military class practiced the worship of the warrior god Mithra, who was also the god of truth and justice, in elaborate artificial caves. A male god was central to Mithraic creation myths. So, appropriately enough, was a bull. When Christianity finally triumphed, the Mythraic sanctuaries were destroyed, and Christian churches were built on the same sacred locations. Archaeologists and church restorers have discovered ancient religious paintings of Jesus that were painted over even earlier paintings depicting pagan scenes involving Mithra with the bull calf over his shoulder.

THE TRIUMPH OF THE CENSORS

"There is a distinct change that occurs between 100 and 300 A.D.,"
says Kathleen Gear. "Most of the sacred texts about the creator deities
were written by women. You have the gospel of Mary Magdalene.
When they were codified in 325 by the church council of Nicaea,
anything written by women, anything that treats women as deities,
was thrown out. Keep in mind that the men doing this are Roman
and Greek and very much patrilineal. In A.D. 421, Pope Gregory said
anyone found copying documents from the Dead Sea Scroll libraries
would be put to death. The monks had to bury them to preserve them,
which is how they came down to us." When the Dead Sea Scrolls were
first found in the caves at Qumran in the 1940s and 1950s, they were
very different from the traditional texts. At first, the scrolls were
believed to have been the work of an Essene settlement, thought to be
a small cult of Hebrew men who lived together with principles of
community property and the shunning of women. Then cemeteries
were found containing the bodies of women. Many of the same texts
were found at Masada, where a band of Jewish fanatics (long believed
to have been Essenes) died in a last stand following the sacking of
Jerusalem in A.D. 70. Suddenly, within a period of about fifty years,
long-buried texts have returned to life to confront Christianity with a
startling revelation: Early Christians worshiped female deities and
women were equated with men. The ancient texts were quite different
from the traditional teachings in the censored Bible. The archaeological
records, the sacred texts, the cemeteries where women are buried
alongside men, the way deities are portrayed in pottery—all tell a tale
of far greater equality in mainstream Judaism and early Christianity
than previously had been believed.

THE GNOSTIC GOSPELS

Among the most important finds were the discoveries of the gnostic gospels, which were unearthed in 1945 in Nag Hammadi in Upper Egypt. Hidden in a red earthenware jar, the fifty-two texts date from the early centuries of Christianity. Elaine Pagels, Harrington Spear Paine Professor of Religion at Princeton University, is one of the world's leading experts on the texts. Scholars agree, she writes, that the texts found at Nag Hammadi are Coptic translations, made about A.D. 350 to 400, of still earlier Christian texts that have been placed by various scholars at A.D. 120 to 150 or older, perhaps A.D. 50 to 100. The New Testament Gospels are dated at about A.D. 60 to 110.[3]

The gnostic gospels range from secret gospels, to poems, to "quasi-philosophic descriptions of the origin of the universe, to myths, magic, and instructions for mystical practice," writes Pagels. The texts were banned and buried at the cliffs of Nag Hammadi as part of the early struggle within the Christian church in the middle of the second century, which pitted the orthodox Christians, led by such people as Bishop Irenaeus of Lyons, against the gnostics. The gnostic texts reveal that these sects held a variety of viewpoints on such matters as the martyrdom of Jesus, the persecution of Christians, and the organization of church institutions. While the popular version of the early Christians is one of people who shared the same beliefs and revered the teachings and authority of the apostles, the discoveries at Nag Hammadi reveal sects characterized by radically different sets of beliefs and social structures. Most treated women as equals, and celebrated the feminine forms of god as well as a masculine deity.

The resurrection of Christ and who witnessed it is a central organizing principle of Christianity. Orthodox Christianity teaches that Peter was the first to see Jesus following the resurrection, which makes him first among the disciples and the one chosen to build Christ's church. But the legitimacy of these claims has always been dubious: all four New Testament Gospels record that women were the first to find the empty tomb of Jesus, and in two of them, Jesus first appeared to Mary Magdalene after the resurrection. The Nag Hammadi find creates even more doubt about the legitimacy of Peter's position than existed previously. The gnostic texts show that Mary Magdalene, not Peter, was the preeminent disciple. The gospel of Mary, writes Pagels, finds Mary Magdalene experiencing in her visions the continuous presence of Jesus, following the crucifixion, and counseling the other apostles: "Do not weep, and do not grieve, and do not doubt; for his grace will be with you completely, and will protect you." When Peter ridicules her, Levi tells him: "Peter, you have always been hot-tempered . . . If the Savior made her worthy, who are you to reject her?" The gospels of both Mark and John taught that Mary was the first to see the resurrected Christ. "Mary lacks the proper credentials for leadership, from the orthodox viewpoint," writes Pagels. "She is not one of the twelve. But as Mary stands up to Peter, so the gnostics who take her as their prototype challenge the authority of those priests and bishops who claim to be Peter's successors."

The Nag Hammadi texts reveal that the gnostics were mounting direct challenges to the authority of the bishops. They held unauthorized meetings, and men and women participated equally in religious rites—a practice sharply criticized by the early orthodox bishops. Pagels quotes Tertullian, a Roman jurist who converted to Christianity, traveled to Africa, and became one of the most influential early Christian fathers between the late second and early third centuries: "These heretical women—how audacious they are! They have no modesty; they are bold enough to teach, to engage in argument, to enact exorcisms, to undertake cures, and, it may be, even to baptize!" He labeled a woman who led a congregation in North Africa "a viper."

There is something awfully familiar about this language.

The texts tell us that some early Christians prayed to both a divine Father and a divine Mother. Mother was revered as a "mystical, eternal Silence," as "she who is before all things, the incomprehensible and indescribable Grace." The divine Mother is also described as the Holy Spirit and as the Wisdom. The origin of the universe is traced to a "great Intelligence . . . (that) is a female which produces all things." Pagels gives example after example from the texts, including passages of exquisite poetry in which the eternal and almighty power, the originator of all things, speaks in a female voice. Every one of the texts, writes Pagels, was branded heretical, and none made it into the New Testament. "By the time the process of sorting the various writings ended—probably as late as the year 200—virtually all the feminine imagery for God had disappeared from orthodox Christian tradition."

What were the reasons behind the religious annihilation of women? Pagels notes that in the gnostic texts, time after time, god—the creator—is castigated for his arrogance by a "superior feminine power." On a more practical level, however, Pagels concludes that the gnostics' interpretation of god and of humanity in terms that includes women threatened the power of male priests. To the dismay of Bishop Irenaeus of Lyons, women, including women from his own congregation, flocked to the gnostics, who treated them very well, while orthodox churchmen were shutting them out. The influx of Hellenized Jews into the movement may also have led to the subordination of women, as this was their religious tradition.

The orthodox exclusion of women was taking place against a backdrop of multiple religions and traditions within the known world. In Greece and Asia Minor, the pagan cults were the dominant belief systems and women enjoyed high status as priestesses. Some were educated and took up professions such as medicine. By the first century A.D., writes Pagels, women in Egypt had achieved "a relatively advanced state of emancipation, socially, politically, and legally." By 200 B.C., in Rome, some of the girls born into the aristocracy were being given the same education as the boys were, and within 200 years archaic patriarchal marriage arrangements had given way to vows of mutual commitment. Women were involved in business, traveled without their husbands, took part in a range of athletics, bore arms, and fought in battles. By contrast, women in Jewish communities could not be educated or participate in public worship or politics. The move toward equality was supported by the rich, Pagels writes, and opposed by the middle class.

Advocates on both sides turned to the apostles, the original teachings, to support their arguments. The gnostic text called the gospel of Philip tells of a rivalry between Mary Magdalene and male disciples who resented Jesus kissing her on the mouth and loving her more than he did them. The gnostic Dialogue of the Savior depicts Mary Magdalene as one of the three disciples chosen for special teaching by Jesus, who praises her above the others as "a woman who knew the All." The texts suggest that Peter was jealous of Mary Magdalene's most-favored disciple position with Jesus and complained that she dominated the conversation with him. "He urges Jesus to silence her and is quickly rebuked," writes Pagels. "Later, however, Mary admits to Jesus that she hardly dares speak to him freely because, in her words, 'Peter makes me hesitate; I am afraid of him, because he hates the female race.' Jesus replies that whoever the Spirit inspires is divinely ordained to speak, whether man or woman."

WHAT IF—A WINDOW IN TIME

What would the world have been like for the last 2,000 years if these teachings had prevailed? If spiritual authority were shared by men and women? If Peter had not prevailed and silenced women? If creation were seen as an androgynous event, if Eve were the equal to Adam, rather than the betrayer of humankind? What if the steps toward emancipation that women in Egypt and Rome were taking in the decades after the birth of Christ had become leaps to equality, blessed and encouraged by an emerging church? There was a window in time for women to regain some of the stature they had had in the ancient past, but the window did not remain open for very long after the deaths of Socrates, Plato, and Jesus. By the end of the second century, orthodox Christians had come to accept the domination of men over women, in every aspect of political, family, and religious life, Pagels concludes. This view has prevailed for nearly 2,000 years, with the Church of Rome a willing servant to patriarchal systems throughout the world. To Pagels, the Nag Hammadi discoveries have come at an exciting time, in which men and women are reexamining their roles in virtually every institution we have. In her view, the discoveries challenge us to do nothing short of reinterpreting history.

Certainly these discoveries that point to enlightened egalitarianism in the early Christian churches pose a severe challenge to the legitimacy of the masculinist, apostolic dogma spread by bishops and priests for centuries. The largest of these monotheistic faiths, Christianity, was established through brutal repression of paganism and zealous suppression of the histories, traditions, practices, and knowledge base of matriarchal societies. Goddess-centered societies were relegated to the status of "cults," even though they were the dominant social order from Neolithic times to the pre-Hellenic period in the Aegean. History was rewritten to justify patriarchal societies, their religions, and their violence. Those who challenged the patriarchal religions were labeled heretics and subjected to the most savage tortures.

THE WITCH-HUNTS

The establishment of Christianity came about through unspeakable brutality, directed principally against women. While Christians sought to persuade—rather than force—pagans to join their ceremonies during the so-called Dark Ages, they unleashed a wave of religious terrorism in the Middle Ages that spanned 500 years. The Inquisition and the witch-hunt hysteria spent their greatest fury on women and may have been a final assault on vestiges of pagan practices that remained as a spiritual undercurrent threatening Church authority. The zealotry of the churchmen reached its zenith in the witch-hunt craze that lasted from the mid-fifteenth to the mid-eighteenth century. The ecclesiastical authority for the torture, burning, hanging, and drowning of tens of thousands of suspected witches came from a papal bull issued in 1484 by Innocent VIII. The bull authorized two Dominican friars to wipe out witchcraft in Germany. In 1486 the two friars published the Malleus Maleficarum—The Witches Hammer—the definitive text on demonology, which specifically linked witches to the devil and instructed witch-hunters on the various ways to identify witches and extract confessions from them. The relentless campaign against "witches" was launched by the Catholic Church; later, tens of thousands of "witches" were burned during the Protestant Reformation in the sixteenth and seventeenth centuries. Old women—revered as crones in pagan beliefs—were murdered by the millions. Midwives and women who practiced herbal cures were also vulnerable to accusations of witchcraft, as were widows who inherited their husbands' lands and businesses. Sexual sadism characterized many of the tortures of women, destroyed by sexually repressed churchmen who equated sexual expression with sinfulness. Barbara G. Walker, author of *The Encyclopedia of Women's Myths and Secrets*, describes the Inquisition as "the most elaborate extortion racket ever devised, primarily developed for profit."[4] A suspect's property was immediately confiscated and turned over to the inquisitors. Over the 500-year-reign of religious terror that saw the witch-hunts and the Inquisition, she writes, "God's servants" tortured and murdered millions of helpless people.[5]

"Unable to reconcile their concept of sin with the tenderness and affection that good sexual relatedness requires, Christians turned to perverted obsessions with pain and punishment," according to Walker. Noting that Western historians are fond of contrasting barbarian cruelties of pagans with Christian morality, she concludes that on the whole paganism might have been kinder. "At least its cruelty was never so mercilessly efficient as that of Western civilization, extending from the Inquisition to the wars and concentration camps of the 20th century."[6]

The last outbreak of witch hysteria in the United States occurred in 1692 in Salem, Massachusetts, and its victims were typical: women who did not conform. Sarah Good was a beggar who went away muttering if a person refused her; Bridget Bishop owned an inn; Sarah Osborne did not go to church. The witch-hunt was merciless: Dorcas Good, Sarah's daughter, was kept in chains for nine months; she was four years old. In the end, fourteen women and five men were hanged. Most of the women were over forty and stood to inherit property, a situation that Puritans frowned upon because it created independent women. Three people died in prison, and eighty-year-old Giles Corey was crushed to death under a pile of stone. He had refused to testify, so the court could not convict him and take away the land he had willed to his children. Times were hard in Salem, just as they were at the end of the 1400s in Europe. Hard times call for scapegoats. Witch-hunts were useful ways of keeping people in line and maintaining the Christian churches' hold over uneducated and impoverished multitudes. "Rebellion is as the sin of witchcraft," preached Cotton Mather.

THE WAR AGAINST WOMEN

Governor Kirk Fordice of Mississippi unleashed a storm of criticism following the 1992 Republican Governors Conference when he declared that America is "a Christian nation." It was not merely a slap at the Judaic tradition, which it was quickly interpreted to be; it was a statement that evokes 2,000 years of war waged by men against women.

It should not surprise us that patriarchies and patriarchal religions are awash in blood. The central metaphor for Christianity is the death of Jesus on the cross. The central metaphor of the ancient goddess religions was birth, death, and regeneration. One celebrates the redemptive suffering of a male, the sacrifice by God of his only son. The other celebrates the continuous cycles of nature. One stresses pain and child abuse; the other stresses harmony. In starkest terms, one is grounded in values we traditionally think of as masculine, and the other is grounded in values we identify with the feminine. Religions around the world and across all time have served the need of human beings to explore the spiritual side of themselves and to find a source of spiritual tranquillity. This is a powerful yearning, whether it is expressed in the worship of Gaia by an ancient or of God by a modern. At critical and profoundly moving moments in the life cycle—the birth of a baby, the death of a parent—even the most cynical antireligionists are moved to talk of miracles or to wonder if, just possibly, there is a life hereafter. Religion touches all of us in varying degrees in our lives. It can comfort us. It can also cripple us.

CHAPTER FIFTEEN

Spiritual Liberation

Two thousand years of religions that have been dominated by men have been used by men to dominate women. Churchmen have defiled women psychologically and disconnected them from their spiritual history—a history of primitive female power at one with nature, a history that is so powerful that even when it was driven underground by the most brutal repression it survived as a subconscious stream.

Today feminist theologians are challenging the authority of main-stream monotheistic religions with a voice that is louder and more provocative than anything heard since the early days of Christianity. Theology students at such prestigious universities as Harvard and Princeton are churning out papers on the goddess religions. A women's spirituality movement has spread across the country, fueled by a deep dissatisfaction with the way women have been treated in masculinist religions, and by a need to rediscover a spiritual history that is ancient and true, and not the fabric of misogynistic male imaginations. They are reclaiming a spiritual tradition that can give both our daughters and our sons a healthier and more respectful way of thinking about themselves and their sexuality. The underground stream of female spirituality is bubbling up into a river that is carrying on its current a resurgence of belief in the power of feminine values: harmony with nature; respect for the earth, the environment, and the life cycles of birth, death, and regeneration; a belief that all human beings are connected to nature, and that human beings and human creativity are sacred. The values that resonate deeply into the soul of women let us talk to each other across cultures about how we provide for our families, maintain our communities, replenish our environments, and strive for peace with our neighbors. These values bind us to our past and to our futures. They have a spiritual and religious underpinning that women are reclaiming. This female spiritual center makes us feel whole. We do not have to be persuaded that it was there at the dawn of time—for nothing else makes sense. We do not have to be persuaded that it is timeless: We feel that in our bones, in the center of our beings. Centuries of religious persecution did not dry up the stream of feminine consciousness and spirituality. It has dammed up its power, and the dam is about to burst.

THE DISCIPLESHIP OF EQUALS

The feminist critique of the Bible began when Elizabeth Cady Stanton published *The Women's Bible* in 1895, with a second volume appearing in 1898. Realizing that the Bible was being used by fundamentalists to justify continued subjugation of women, that it was a political tool of men to advance male interests, Cady Stanton struck right at the heart of the attack. By challenging the authenticity of the Bible itself, she launched an investigation into modern history's most influential androcentric texts—and quite possibly its biggest literary fraud.

The investigation has heated up in the past two decades as feminist theological scholars such as Elaine Pagels, who are learned in ancient languages, have reexamined original passages included in the Bible in light of the historical and archaeological record about the New Testament period. By investigating the nuggets of evidence about the lives of women that are sprinkled through the texts, liberation theologians and scholars have been able to establish that women were far more prominent in the Jesus movement than "The Men's Bible," so to speak, would have us believe. They are resurrecting a historically valid paradigm for a Christian faith that views women as, at the very least, the equal of men. Their work is leading the way for girls and women to reclaim their rightful place within religions and the societies they influence. Among the giant killers in this field none has more standing than Elisabeth Schüssler Fiorenza of Harvard University.[1]

She argues that androcentric translations from the original Coptic and Greek texts have distorted the role of women in the early church and that, far from being marginalized "helpers," they were among the most steadfast disciples of Jesus and played critical roles in spreading his teachings after his death. Unlike the male disciples, who fled, the Galilean women disciples witnessed the crucifixion and the vision of the resurrection. She argues that the Jesus movement was a discipleship of equals and that it was a reform and renewal ministry within the Jewish faith, a messianic table community to which Jesus invited everyone. His followers were "the scum of Palestinian society," she writes. "And many of these were women."

CAN CHRISTIANITY BE SAVED?

"Theology follows life; it does not precede it," writes the Lutheran feminist scholar Elizabeth Bettenhausen.[2]

The image of God as male and of Jesus on the cross is all around us. Children are exposed to the pictures in some of the earliest books they see. Suffering and redemption, patience and pain—father power, son power—are images that spring to mind when I think of religion. When I think of Mary, it is with a sense of overwhelming sadness and loss: This is a woman who gave up her son, who made the ultimate sacrifice that patriarchy demands. The images of Christianity are not the images that nurture our humanity. They are images of loss and suffering, of giving up mortal selves to attain some higher spiritual standing, rather than images of protecting ourselves as living, creative beings who are here as part of the earth. Christianity puts god at the center of the universe, not man, and certainly not women. Some of the larger versions of Christianity, such as the Catholic and Episcopal churches, create even further disconnections between people and their spiritual centers by inserting a caste of middlemen—the clergy—who serve as earthly conduits between the two.

I have been struck over the years of reporting on the feminist movement at how many of its leaders were raised as Catholics. Eleanor Smeal and her husband, for example, were both raised as Catholics, but they did not raise their children in any faith. "We didn't raise our kids with any of the mythology," she says today. It was a hard decision for them, she told me, but it was a decision they are content with.

MYTHOLOGY

We are coming full circle. I left the Catholic Church more than thirty years ago, yet I still feel a tug. I find it hard to think of its stories as myths, even after all the research I have done for this book, which tells me that Christianity is based on myth at best and fraud at worst. I have known since college that organized Christian religions have scant credit intellectually, but I still find it hard to discredit them to my children. I find it hard—frightening even—to tell them that the mainstream religions are destructive and violent and that they institutionalize evil. Christianity's psychic hold on me is still very powerful, even though I know intellectually that it is empty, at least for me. So I write this passage with the understanding that it challenges beliefs that are deeply ingrained in many of us, as deeply ingrained perhaps as anything that shapes our understanding about who we are as men and women, as boys and girls, and finally as human beings.

But I understand now that we will never create a society in which boys and girls are equal until we challenge the image of god as male, for it is within this image that Christianity legitimizes patriarchy.

"Rationally, we know God is not male, but 'He' still provides the security and order that many seek, thereby justifying the use of violence to maintain that order," writes Karen L. Bloomquist, a member of the Church and Society Staff of the Evangelical Lutheran Church in America.[3] "Changing God-language and imagery is not an elitist exercise but a key step in the conversion from patriarchy." Whether it is a little boy on the playground teasing a little girl because he thinks she is the lesser human being, or a grown man beating up a woman, or a priest sexually abusing a female parishioner or a child— they all feel a sense of entitlement to control women and abuse women because men exist in the image of god, and women do not.

Think, for a moment, what it would mean to a little boy's perspective if he were raised from infancy with an image of the divine as female and powerful—a provider of the beauty he sees in his park playground, a creator and protector of the animals he meets or the food he eats. What if he were raised to think of wisdom as a form of female divinity—the wise crone, as opposed to the witchy hag— or if he read texts in the New Testament and learned that Mary Magdalene was Christ's most favored disciple? Or if his religious training traced the origin of the universe to a female intelligence that produced the All? What would it do to his perspective if he saw women celebrating religious rituals and if he learned to think of both a Father and a Mother as divine, or the Jesus movement as a discipleship of equals?

What would it do to a little girl's perspective if she were raised with such images of the female as divine, of women as sacred beings who trace their productivity and intelligence to a great female intelligence that produced the universe?

Organized religions have been in a decline during the last two decades, so it is not surprising that the work of feminist theologians laboring on the most challenging edge of religious scholarship would be in a twilight zone. Yet their work—whether they are trying to reframe Christianity so that it affirms the equality of women or are replacing Christ with the Goddess—is critical to redesigning a society that honors and respects females as much as males. Religion is a spiritual and ethical taproot that can contain poisonous liquids like the milkweed or juices of life like the desert cactus.

"Religion is an expression of people's most deeply held beliefs, and paradoxically it shapes people's most deeply held beliefs," says Mary Hunt, who trained for the Catholic priesthood in anticipation that the church would ordain female priests. "It gets you coming and going." Far from being timeless and eternal, religion is one of the most malleable and changeable and dynamic dimensions of human life, she says. It is "one of the most formative aspects of a patriarchal society and potentially one of the most helpful and economical ways of making social change."

If our beliefs are changing at the most profound levels—and not merely at the level of law—and if religions articulate our most deeply held beliefs, then it becomes strategically economical to look to religion as the place for change.

In the Catholic Church, for example, the image that a little girl gets when she goes to church, beginning at the age of two or three, is the image of a congregation made up primarily of women who are led by a male priest. The Virgin Mary is passive. "It is my judgment these images are deeply influential in our formation of our self-image and our image of community," says Hunt. If a man from Mars showed up at mass, he'd say, "Oh, the women go and stand there and the men do what needs to be done." That's the image children perceive, as well.

In the 1970s and 1980s, feminist theologians asked whether Christianity was inherently patriarchal and sexist, and the answer they came back with was a resounding yes. In the 1990s, they are asking an even more threatening question that is critical to the future well-being of women: Is Christianity inherently violent? Is the concept of atonement and god giving up his son the divine legitimization of child abuse? "That is a devastating critique," says Hunt. "It means one of the central images or stories of the Christian tradition is abuse, and what flows from that can hardly be expected not to be.

"We have worked through a lot of gender issues and said how can they be other than negative or unhelpful," says Hunt. "but maybe it is even worse than we thought. It's not that they lead to gender inequality and little girls end up second, but they may end up dead, and many, many end up abused."

Hunt is not given to simplistic solutions, but she believes that the image of god as male contributes to abuse. She points to cases of rural women pastors in Canada who have been abused by male clergy. "The only reason to so gender a society is for domination, not to explain differences. If you push that, and you have a gendered concept of the divine, that also functions to legitimize domination. A man who would abuse a woman pastor has to be at some level dealing with what he perceives to be his divine right."

God as male alienates women from the taproot of religion. We are the other. It allows men to act out some of their most ancient fears about women: the castration complex, for example, that many people believe is at the root of male paranoia about women; the fear of female dominance that springs from men's observation that women gave birth and nursed the children, while men sat on the sidelines for the most important anthropological task a community undertakes—raising the next generation. There was no question who the mother was, but who was the father? To control that, men had to control women's sexuality. Thus, female sexuality in the Christian tradition is next to sinfulness and should be reserved only for procreation in marriage. We don't talk about sex in our families; we teach it reluctantly in schools. We don't celebrate the female rite of passage as her entry into womanhood and her ability to bear children; we refer to menstruation as a curse, and in many families people simply don't refer to it at all. "Religious symbol systems focused around exclusively male images of divinity create the impression that female power can never be fully legitimate or wholly beneficent," writes Carol P. Christ, a theologist and author who teaches at San José State University. A woman "can never have the experience that is freely available to every man and boy in her culture, of having her full sexual identity affirmed as being in the image and likeness of God."[4]

BOYS AS GODS, GIRLS AS SLUTS

Or, as my daughter put it succinctly one day, "Girls who have sex are known as sluts. When boys do it, nobody says anything."

She was thirteen at the time of our conversation, and was complaining about the pressure girls felt to have sex, to be popular. The pressure wasn't just coming from boys: "It's girls, too. They say you have to have sex to be popular, and then they turn around and say you're a slut if you do."

I realized as I listened to her that the advice many mothers of my generation give daughters is literally beside the point. We adults are accused of giving mixed messages to teenagers: Wait until you're married, but if you must do it beforehand be sure to wear a condom. Surely these messages are full of contradictions, but that's because we are fashioning messages that address the ramifications of behavior— the threat of AIDS and teenage pregnancy—and overlooking the most fundamental message of all that we can give both girls and boys. As I listened to my daughter talk about sex and popularity, I realized that what she needed to hear had nothing to do with condoms, with waiting or not waiting. We were driving home from a weekend in the country, the two of us alone in the van with our animals. It was a good time to talk.

"You live in a culture that cheapens women and cheapens sex," I told her, "a culture in which boys are raised to think that scoring is a sign of manhood, and the earlier they do it, the more manly they are. It sets them up to prey on girls, and other girls go along with it because they are being raised in a culture where boys and men have power and they know this. They go along to get along. You live in a culture where god is male and boys are raised to believe they are little gods and can do anything they want. Everything around you is about sex—the music, the magazines you read; even the ads in the magazines are about how you can look to appeal to boys. That's not what female sexuality is about: It is about love and birth and creating life. It's connected to what women did at the dawn of time;

it is part of the most ancient and authentic human behavior. It is an expression of the greatest female power. Nobody tells you girls about your sacredness, about the ancient ties you have to nature, about the importance and power you have as creators of life. You aren't taught to value your intelligence, your powers of intuition, of thinking. Girls need to get a much stronger sense of female sacredness and worth—only when they understand how good and valuable and inviolate they are will they be able to treat their sexuality with the respect that it deserves. And when boys are taught to see the goddess in women and see female sexuality in terms of sacredness, they will treat girls' sexuality with much greater care and stop being sexual predators." I stopped and thought a moment: "When you think about girls' sexuality in those terms, it makes words like 'popularity' utterly superficial."

GODDESS SYMBOLISM

In her essay "Why Women Need the Goddess," thealogist Christ writes that goddess symbolism defeats patriarchy's teachings that women's power is inferior and dangerous, and it supports women's trust in their own power. The psychological impact of the goddess is to encourage them to know their own will and to believe their will can be done. "Thus a woman is not reduced to waiting and acquiescing in the wills of others as she is in patriarchy." But that will is not egocentric: It must be excercised in harmony with the wills and energies of other human beings.

"As women struggle to create a new culture in which women's power, bodies, will, and bonds are celebrated," Christ concludes, "it seems natural that the Goddess would reemerge as symbol of the newfound beauty, strength, and power of women."

AT THE FOOT OF THE CROSS

Divine imagery is a mirror that wields formidable power. What I tried to give my daughter when we talked that afternoon was an understanding of her own power, her will, and her worth—not merely derived from her accomplishments but as reflective of a divineness, a sacred continuum that women are reclaiming. Whether women and girls use the goddess imagery or struggle within the monotheistic religions to reclaim the feminine side of the divine, they are entitled to be reconnected to the spiritual taproot, to regain a sense of purpose, of holiness as well as wholeness—what Mary Hunt describes as some relationship to the divine or transcending reality. Women are kept alienated from their bodies and from nature, from the deepest sense of who they are. The female body is debased, tortured into thinness or blondness or plumpness, depending on the fashion of the day. An overweight man talks about losing a few pounds. An overweight woman contemplates suicide. The female intellect is neither prized or revered. We have been cut off from our traditional role of provider and boxed into the dependency role of caretaker. We are alienated from a sense of wholeness of life—and yet it is women who produce that wholeness. We are left with a hole in our gut that is filled with self-doubt and alienation. For solace, we are offered a spiritual tradition that offers as its central image a father giving up his only son for our salvation. It is an image that insists that women find something praiseworthy and redemptive in child abuse—an image that is as alien to the female experience as anything could possible be. And that is what the goddess movements, the women's spirituality movements, and the liberation theologians are trying to change.

I came across many provocative insights as I was researching this book, but none has stuck in my mind more firmly that this one from Mary Hunt, which took me back 2,000 years to the women disciples from Galilea: "What would Christianity have looked like if, instead of focusing on the dead Jesus, we had looked at the women at the foot of the cross who decided to work against this ever happening to anybody's kid again?"

PART FIVE

The Machocracy
Meets Girlpower

CHAPTER SIXTEEN

The Nexus of Evil

We don't know what the world would be like if the focus had been on the women at the foot of the cross, but we do know what it has been like ever since Christianity built its creed on the celebration of the torture and death of the prophet Jesus. The ascent of males, well under way but by no means complete in the classical world at the time of Jesus' death, continued. Patriarchy solidified its grip on Western cultures. Men owned property, women became property. In the image of god, males took power and women became powerless, supplicants, dependent on males for survival.

The imbalance of power that was founded at the foot of the cross spread to every aspect of our lives, from how boys and girls were educated, to how they were expected to behave sexually. The slut/stud scenario my daughter complained of is rooted in patriarchal assumptions that lead to predation of women by men, and it is with us to this day. There is only one difference: In the age of AIDS, sexual promiscuity can kill. Pregnancy has always been potentially lethal for girls and women—particularly when back-alley abortions were the only escape for many women. But AIDS, which kills men as well as women, has brought a deadly urgency to the search for ways of bringing up girls and boys that are grounded in mutual respect.

The slut/stud scenario is played out in our high schools with a destructive intensity that few parents are aware of. We were shaken out of our complacency in spring 1993, however, when the Spur Posse, a gang of jocks and hangers-on from Lakewood High School in Lakewood, California, captured national headlines by demonstrating new lows to which teenage boys had sunk in their relationships with girls.

The Spur Posse crashed into national awareness when sheriff's deputies arrested some of the most popular athletes at Lakewood High School in the course of a sex crimes investigation. The boys, who ranged from fifteen to eighteen years of age, were alleged to have had sex with girls as young as ten as part of a competition to see which Spur could score the most "points" by "hooking up" with as many girls as possible. Within a week, all but one of the nine arrested boys were free. (A sixteen-year-old would eventually be convicted of lewd conduct with the ten-year-old.) The young men claimed the girls were willing participants, and the Los Angeles district attorney declined to prosecute them. It was, the DA's office said, a social issue better left to schools, parents, and churches, even though sex with minor females is a felony in California. "That's how they (the girls) are trying to get popular, by doing my friends," a stocky, vacant-faced fifteen-year-old Spur told the *New York Times*'s Jane Gross.[1]

Around Lakewood High School, the girls were known as sluts—the almost universal idiom in American high schools for girls who put out.

The Spur Posse forced us to confront the tragic and inevitable outcome of an ethic that glorifies male athletes and reduces girls to being prizes in the ancient game of "scoring." What happened at Lakewood High is a telling commentary on how we raise boys. It is a long overdue wake-up call telling us that we will never improve conditions for girls until we change the way we raise boys.

The Spur Posse contains all the ingredients of patriarchal culture gone haywire. Some parents even boasted of their sons' exploits. Don

Belman (Lakewood High School class of '63) described his sons to Gross as "virile specimens." Belman's eighteen-year-old son, Kristopher, was the oldest of the Spur Posse arrested in the sex investigation. On the night of his release, Belman said his son was "all man" and the girls were "giving it away." His wife, Dottie (Lakewood High class of '67) said "those girls are trash."

Both male and female students were quick to tell reporters that the girls had been willing participants, anxious to achieve status by having sex with athletes. The boys returned to school to a hero's welcome and did the rounds of the network talk shows. "Of course they were treated as heroes; they'd been wrongly accused," Don Belman told writer Joan Didion months later. In a *New Yorker* article, Didion quoted him as saying that the girls "wanted to be looked on favorably, they wanted to be part of the clique. They wanted to be, hopefully, the girlfriends of these studs on campus."[2]

The Spur Posse provides an extreme example of the entitlement that boys are raised to expect, an extreme example of what happens when parents participate in the cult of sports and machismo and raise their sons to echo their own distorted sense of values. It is also an extreme example of what happens to girls when they are brought up to believe that the path to popularity is to be found by servicing male jocks. But lest parents of girls in All-America High in Sunny Suburbia, U.S.A., comfort themselves with the soporific bromide "It can't happen here," they should heed these words from Dottie Belman: "There's a Lakewood High in every town."

MACHO MELTDOWN

Understanding, if not charity, is called for. After one's disgust and horror at the misdeeds of the Lakewood Nine has subsided, it is possible to see the swaggering, raptorial youths for what they are—not very bright, uncertain, insecure young men who are seeing the meltdown of their macho world and are appalled at what they see.

They are coming of age with none of the sense of power and assurance that their fathers took for granted. Young white men—all of the Spur Posse boys are white—no longer have the world by the balls as they did a generation ago. They are being challenged for cultural supremacy by blacks, by Hispanics, by the Asian students who routinely best them in math and science, and by girls who compete with them for a diminishing supply of good jobs. Employed, adult white males feel under siege, and so do their high school and college-age sons.

Lakewood grew with the aerospace industry and is shrinking with it. During the epoch of vandalism and hooliganism blamed on the Spur Posse and rival gangs, the town has felt the painful end of the Cold War, military downsizing, and an anemic economy. The community is beset by unemployment, and there is more to come. Don Waldie, public information officer for the city of Lakewood, said that the threat of unemployment affected families' capacities to "hang together." But, he told me, there is far more to the Spur Posse story than that. He believes that the gang evolved because of "the charismatic behavior of just a few young men whose deeply troubled families gave them license or the opportunity to lead others into very destructive behavior patterns." He pointed specifically to the two younger Belman brothers, the "centerlessness in these young men's lives, and the capacity for the Belman brothers to be an evil center. The end product of that behavior leads inevitably to the abuse of women. That evil nexus is played out historically from generation to generation across a lot of human history."

A MOTHER LEARNS THE SCORE

Like any mother, Dottie Belman's first instinct was to come to the defense of her family. But a cruel personal crisis gave her new insight. On April 17, less than three weeks after her son Kristopher's arrest, she underwent surgery for breast cancer. "I felt I was fighting for my life in more ways than one," she told me. Soon thereafter, she moved out of the immaculate three-bedroom home on Greentop Street that had represented her dreams of life with a successful husband and all-American children. She and her oldest son, Billy, twenty-three, moved in with an aunt. Less than four months after the Spur Posse intruded into the national psyche as a quintessential example of boys turning rotten, Dottie Belman's life had been transformed by cancer, and so had her attitude about her sons, her husband, her family, and the role she had played in it. There is a compelling parallel in the cancer that ravaged her body and the one that destroyed her family.

"I've separated myself," Dottie Belman told me. "I went from doing everything for my children to totally, 'I'm out of house. I'm not there. I'm taking care of mom.' I let my children have all my nutrients. I let them suck all the good stuff out of my body until I got cancer, which was my warning sign. It took that much to get me away from that dependency. It's funny what I let my family do to me."

During the course of our interview Belman said that she was definitely shocked at the lack of respect her boys apparently have toward women. "I knew they were sexually active because they are attractive and athletic and all the things that girls are attracted to," she said, "but I didn't realize they were abusing them in any way. I was really disappointed in the way they handled themselves after the media got hold of the story. They were arrogant, and they didn't feel any remorse, and they didn't realize what this had done to my reputation as a mother. They turned into heroes and I turned into trash."

In fact, Dottie Belman was an involved mother. She supported all three of her sons' athletic careers from the time they could throw a ball. She was the ultimate team mother, and her husband was the ultimate team father. Don Belman coached his sons from T-ball to Pop Warner baseball league teams. Dottie made videos of her sons' high school football games. All three of her sons were star athletes at Lakewood High. Dana, who is credited with being the evil genius behind the Spur Posse, is memorialized as Lakewood Athlete of the Year on a plaque in the town's city hall.

"I thought they were all-American kids," says Dottie, but she also acknowledged that the family had long been dysfunctional. She describes her husband, a former Marine who is a salesman in the aerospace industry, as a heavy gambler—a charge he denies. She talks about herself as someone who was "raising and caretaking and enabling." She says she overdid it, like a lot of mothers.

What drove Dottie Belman was an intense desire to make sure that her children had a wonderful childhood—unlike hers in a household dominated by an alcoholic father. "It's the wrong approach," she has concluded. "I tried to get recognition through my family by doing more and more. And they took more and more and didn't really appreciate the things I did."

SPORTS AND THE CELEBRITY FAMILY

Much of Dottie Belman's energy was funneled into an extraordinary degree of support for her sons' athletic endeavors. "Sports was our life," she says. The family put a high premium on athletic success— "You guys are going to score home runs and be macho and make us proud," is the way she put it. Athletic stardom was the ticket to stature in the community, to the popularity that had eluded both Dottie and Don in high school. "We were enjoying our life through our children," she says. Don had been in the band, not on the football team. Dottie had been a pom pom girl, not a cheerleader. But their three strapping, good-looking sons were the big men on campus and everything their parents had envied during their own high school years. At Lakewood High, the Belmans—parents and sons—were celebrities.

In Dottie's mind, the frenetic sports world that she happily accompanied her family into is unhealthy. "Coaches today emphasize too much macho and arrogance. They are not instilling good values in the boys. It's go out there and score. You can be scoring at anything. If I were to do it over again, I'd focus on the arts, music. I'd put a guitar in their hand or buy a piano, teach them about reading. As it was, you get Cs and you can play football. We have trophies, but we have nothing else. They have absolutely nothing. At the time, it seemed like the right thing to do. A lot of other parents felt the same way. At least they are not into drugs, at least they aren't alcoholics. At least sports are healthy. But what they get from it I don't think is healthy. The girls worship guys like that. It might not happen to all the children, but it seems when I look back on it, it was a big key."

She thinks fathers need to set an example for their sons of how men can be giving, caring, and emotional. "It is so important to be macho today. It's overwhelming. A man needs to be able to cry, to talk about feelings, to look at a beautiful sunset, to be a person who loves poetry and nature, and not just talk about scoring and touchdowns and home runs."

SCUM IN THE MORNING

She blames part of her sons' behavior toward girls on their lack of respect for her. "They'd tease and joke and sometimes I'd think, 'Wait. I'm your mom, here. I'm not one of the girls.' " She also faults the movies and their blatant exploitation of sex, and the daytime television talk shows that have made sex and deviant sexual behavior a staple. "There is nothing sacred and nothing left to their imagination, and they honestly believe this is normal behavior. Two parents cannot fight this," she says. Sex is so commonplace it's "like doing homework," she adds. "I don't think my kids have raped anybody. I'm sure of it. The cheerleaders they respected, but the girls who were not popular, the only reason these boys were attracted to them was because they were easy. The whole problem with these boys was the way they treated them the next day. They treated them like scum. It's been like that forever. It's not right. These girls have no self-esteem . . . The next day, they were humiliated."

Out of what Belman calls a "nightmare I can't believe ever happened," came something terribly important that had been missing in many families with teenagers at Lakewood High School. Parents are talking with their children and becoming more aware of what youngsters are involved in. "There is an awareness of what was hidden," she says. "Maybe around the dinner table parents are saying, 'Hey, we don't like what you are doing.' There has been something positive that came out of this."

THE COST

At its deepest level, the Spur Posse story epitomizes a patriarchal culture that shames women and lionizes male athletes as the ultimate symbols of masculine dominance. It is a story of a male system of privilege and power, and of hapless women who try to survive in it. Like all systems of domination, machocracy reacts with ugliness and brutality when threatened. The cost to the girls who were playthings of the Spur Posse can be measured in the abortion one girl victim had, and in the debasement and trauma inflicted on the other victims. Years from now, the sad human wreckage left in the wake of the Spur Posse episode will still be trying to live with the psychic scars.

RAISING BOYS DIFFERENTLY

If, as Dottie Belman believes, there is a Lakewood High in every community, then there is a time bomb waiting to explode in every community. But it does not have to happen. Experts who have sought ways to improve relations between the genders have developed a number of tactics for defusing tensions and altering hostile behavior. Educators, psychologists, and students of gender issues have suggested a number of things that schools, parents, and cultural tastemakers can do to bring up boys with a more civilized attitude toward girls.

One idea many experts have offered is that schools should have assemblies at the beginning of every year to discuss sexual harassment and other gender issues, and to promote a more civilized and respectful attitude between the sexes. A mother I know whose daughter attends a large public high school makes this point: When her daughter's school experienced an anti-Semitic incident, authorities promptly called an assembly—and equally promptly expelled the offenders. This mother had no problem with that reaction, but she made this comparison: "They make a big deal when that happens once every couple of years, but every week I know a girl is being verbally berated by a boy at that school and two or three times a year there's a date rape. If we have these series of talks about anti-Semitism, what ought we to be doing about the gender bias against women every day?" It is a compelling argument.

THE SLUT/STUD DICHOTOMY

Julie Dodge, the sexual assault expert who ran assemblies at Lakewood High School after the Spur Posse incident, said the girls were also deeply concerned and angry about the double standard that labeled sexually active girls as sluts and sexually active boys as studs. Dodge told them it is necessary to have the same standard for both: If it is negative behavior for girls, then it should be for boys, and if it is viewed as positive behavior, then both parties should gain status. This is an important message to give to boys: It levels the playing field between them and girls.

Questions during the assemblies revealed a dismaying lack of knowledge about the law. Girls did not know they had a right to say "no" at the very last moment before intercourse. Boys showed an unwillingness to accept responsibility when it came to forcing sex acts such as acquaintance rape. They were eager to blame girls for leading them on. The reactions the experts encountered from the boys at Lakewood, said Dodge, are typical of what they have seen in other schools. "We blame the victim, which is generally the girl, and we are not holding the perpetrator responsible." We are not raising boys so that they understand that, no matter what a girl does or wears, they are responsible for their own behavior. It is important to train girls to make clear what they want and what they don't want, and to train boys to respect that.

When schools fail to take action against boys who sexually harass girls, girls learn victim behavior. No one is standing up for them or showing them how to stand up for themselves. It sends an equally bad message to boys: They can get away with that kind of behavior. Schools need to enforce an atmosphere in which respect between the genders is as important a value as racial and religious respect. Students must be held accountable for their behavior toward the other sex. Written policies about sexual harassment, for example, should be distributed to every student from elementary school on.

Schools can take another important step by elevating the status of girls' sports to that of male sports, by being as proud of the girls' field hockey team that wins the regional playoff as they are of the football team. This automatically raises the status of women athletes in the school and forces boys to look at some girls, at least, in terms of their accomplishments, not just their bodies. Schools can also begin the long, difficult process of deglamorizing macho sports and taking some of the swagger out of the jocks and athletes. One way of doing this is to raise the academic standards for athletes. Another is to deemphasize the importance of male varsity sports events in the weekly cycle of school life by giving them a low-key treatment in public address announcements and urging teachers to refrain from making references to the athletic activities of students in their classrooms. Or, if they do, to make sure teachers give girls who are athletes the same kind of attention they give to boys. What is very clear is that boys' athletic programs still enjoy enormous preferential treatment in schools, and so do male athletes. More than two decades after Congress passed Title IX, forbidding discrimination in schools that receive federal funds, a survey done in Montgomery County, Maryland, one of the most affluent and progressive counties in the nation, found huge disparities in spending in its high school sports programs. During the 1990–1991 school year, about 75 percent of its athletic budget went to male sports and 25 percent to its female athletes. Vigorous enforcement of Title

IX would force schools to shift funds from male to female sports or to upgrade the resources given to female athletes so that they are the equal of men. In our sports-obsessed culture, that would send a powerful message about how much we value girls.

KEEP BOYS AND GIRLS TOGETHER

Raising boys differently begins in infancy and childhood, not in high school. Childhood play and work patterns can be used to foster respect in boys for girls, instead of contempt. "Have boys do things for girls more," advises Jacquelynne Eccles of the University of Michigan. Have them play together and work together, she says, instead of letting them follow their natural inclination to segregate themselves by gender at a young age.

"As long as they are segregated, all kinds of sex roles are being reinforced. Boys and girls both need a whole range of experiences to develop leadership, caring, competence, assertiveness," and they can get that by playing together instead of apart. Adults, Eccles insists, must promote integrated play, otherwise the boys will monopolize the tools and equipment they associate with action and adventure—and the girls will not have access to them, because they won't fight with boys over possession of tools, equipment, and bicycles.

PARENTS AND THE MEDIA

Parents need to be vigilant about counteracting the messages their children get through the media, which bear a heavy burden of responsibility for perpetuating ruinous gender stereotypes. From beer commercials that depict girls as prey to ads that glorify athletes, the stud/slut messages are drummed into adolescents during the average of twenty-three hours of television they watch each week. When multimillion-dollar-a-year athletes brag about sleeping with thousands of women, they legitimize promiscuity and the use of women as sex objects. When athletes, actors, and rock stars are photographed with starlets and groupies, it reinforces the message that girls are valued for their looks and sexual performance.

It has fallen to the lurid lyrics of rap and rock to represent patriarchy's most violent cultural attack on women. Rock, heavy metal, and rap reach more adolescents than any other medium. Together these are the media in which a macho world in a meltdown is asserting the patriarchal dominance of men by debasing women. From the violence of Saturday morning cartoons, to the violence against women that is a staple of films, to the pathological lyrics of popular music, the entertainment industry has become a major player in patriarchy's war against women. The lyrics are rife with sexual sadism and blaming the victim. "Body Dismemberment," by Rigor Mortis, which Capitol Records brought out in 1989, describes a scene in which a woman—described merely as "bitch"—is dismembered by an axe-wielding man as she reaches sexual climax. He wants to know why she made him do this and concludes by calling her a "stupid fuck." Women are constantly referred to as bitches who are to be beaten, punched, villified, and killed if they offend the man. Watching women bleed is another recurring theme. The music is obsessed with oral and anal sex; graphic lyrics describe these acts in the most degrading terms. At the same time, the music dwells on the idea that women are constantly available for sex and that they just can't get enough oral sex. The title of the 2 Live Crew song tells the story: "Dick Almighty." The lyrics are puerile penis worship for the truly insecure.

The *Journal of the American Medical Association* notes that headphones and transistor radios have made it possible for youngsters to be constantly exposed to rock music. According to research cited in the journal, the average teenager listens to 10,500 hours of rock music between the seventh and twelfth grades. This is only slightly less than the entire number of hours spent in the classroom from kindergarten through high school. As they reach seventh grade, teenagers begin to explore heavy metal and rap. Sexual sadism and murder throbs through the music lyrics. There is no cultural parallel preaching female domination of males.

The effects of this mindless garbage are plainly visible. On July 12, 1993, the *New York Times* carried a report about a group of teenage boys surrounding a sixteen-year-old girl at a crowded Manhattan swimming pool, ripping off her bathing suit, and fondling her—the fifth such incident that week. In a follow-up story, the *Times* painted a picture of an adolescent world that has been polluted by venomous animosity between the sexes, animosity that has become so acute that girls said they'd abandoned hope of finding a decent boy to date. Boys, in their interviews, repeatedly referred to girls as "bitches" and bragged about proving their manhood by ganging up on girls and humiliating them. A few days after that article appeared, the *Washington Post* reported an upsurge in teenage dating violence, and quoted Barrie Levy, author of the 1991 book *Dating Violence: Young Women in Danger*, as saying that 25 percent of teenage girls have experienced violence from their dates. In the Superior Court of the District of Columbia, officials started a program for male batterers who are as young as thirteen. Experts blamed rap music, but they also said that girls tolerate the violence because they wanted to hold onto their boyfriends. A boyfriend was their source of self-esteem.

In its report on violence and youth issued in the summer of 1993, the American Psychological Association found that film and television portrayals of women in victim roles exacerbates violence against them. "Male youth who view sexualized violence or depictions of rape on television or in film are more likely to display callousness toward female victims of violence, especially rape," the APA reported. It noted that such violence is found on X-rated and R-rated videos that are widely available to teenagers.

Violent behavior, the APA reported, is a learned behavior. Parents need to carefully and honestly look at the levels of violence in their own homes, and how they talk and act out negative gender stereotypes with each other. Parents can watch television with their children and discuss the negative impact of gender violence or stereotypes. The APA describes these as critical viewing skills that help children to distinguish between fiction and fact and to recognize unrealistic violence that is portrayed without negative consequences—such as pain. Children can also be encouraged by their parents to think of alternative ways of solving a problem, other than violence. Parents can express disapproval of violence and restrict viewing of violent shows. They can—and should—pay attention to the lyrics of the music their children are listening to. It was not until I sat down and read transcripts of dozens of songs that I had a full appreciation of just how awful— and how pervasive—these ghastly lyrics are. Parents need to discuss this with their sons, and to help both their sons and their daughters understand that these are messages of hate and domination that poison the well of human affection and respect.

Parents should also present countervailing messages in their own relationships. My husband, for example, frequently compliments me on my column after he has read it in the newspaper. When my children hear this, they hear him appreciating my work, not my appearance. When children hear their father complimenting their mother on her cooking or on her looks, but not on her work, it sends a message that he values her principally for her work in the domestic realm. Think about the fathers who said, "We didn't keep points like the Spurs did, but we talked about scoring." What they are saying is that this behavior is acceptable. When fathers wink at their sons about the sexual exploits of male athletes, they send a powerful message across the generations that women are souvenir sex objects, nothing more. Women in these conversations are always referred to more negatively than are promiscuous men, and this gives boys the idea that it is appropriate to trash women who have sex.

When stories about promiscuous male icons appear in the media, parents should turn them into teaching opportunities by talking with their sons about healthy sexual relationships based on feelings of affection and mutual respect, as opposed to unhealthy relationships in which women are merely used and discarded.

Parents may always be uncomfortable discussing sex with their children. But we don't have to go directly into a clinical discussion of intercourse. We can start by talking about the early stages of sexual explorations between boys and girls, and the puzzling and scary feelings that accompany them. We can ask younger sons such questions as: "How do you know you want to kiss Suzie, and not Jane? How do you know you want to hold this girl's hand? What are you feeling?" Instead of coming out with an absolute do or don't, we can help the child find a reason behind an action he wants to take—and help him explore the impact of his action on a girl.

Like my daughter and her friends, all teenage girls are aware that they have been left with the options of being sluts or prudes, while boys who have sex attain power. Girls are angry over this—and they should be. The unfairness is blinding. But they see it far more clearly than boys do. Boys need to become much more aware of this double standard and the bind it puts girls in. This is a conversation that mothers are especially competent to have with their sons—for they can recall what it was like to be a girl.

MOTHERS AND SONS

My oldest son came into the kitchen one night while I was standing at the kitchen sink. He was thirteen, and he leaned against the table behind me and said, "Mom, what is a diaphragm?"

I did what any mother would do: I gulped. Then I answered. In the years that followed we had several conversations about sex, birth control, and the feelings that are associated with sex and loving relationships. The experience convinced me that this is not a conversation that should be left exclusively to fathers. As a mother, I was concerned about my son's physical and emotional health, and I wanted to make very sure he did not get some girl pregnant. Not just for his sake, but for hers as well, I wanted to make very sure that my son understood that sex is not a male rite of passage to be undertaken at the expense of girls. I talked about sex in terms of a loving relationship that is based on a serious commitment between people. I know now from the way he has conducted his life in the fourteen years that have passed since his first startling question that this is what he believes. It is possible to inoculate sons against the overpowering messages of sadism, lust, and exploitation that surround them. When we raise our sons to be respectful of girls and women and their sexuality, we take a giant stride in our journey toward a world in which girls can be anything they want to be. But for that dream to become reality, we must also develop new ways of raising girls.

CHAPTER SEVENTEEN

Girlpower

Peel away the bar graphs, the academic cant and the psychobabble that has obscured the subject, and a number of truths emerge about how we can raise girls to be self-confident, self-directed, independent women.

• The most important lesson we can teach our daughters is that they must expect to support themselves. They should never expect anyone else to support them.

• They must also understand that they have the power to make their own life choices and that they must learn to exercise that power.

Choice and economic independence are the foundations of woman-power, hence they are the first crucial lessons in teaching our daughters girlpower. These lessons can be reinforced throughout our daughters' upbringing by strategies that enable girls to recognize themselves as competent people who have bright futures ahead of them.

This vision of an independent future is critical in teaching our daughters how to achieve—and how to use—girlpower. Adolescent girls who see bright futures ahead for themselves are far less likely to become pregnant than those who have lower aspirations. This research finding has inspired a number of efforts by girls' advocacy organizations to link teenage girls with the exciting world of careers. The Ms. Foundation, Girls, Inc., the Girl Scouts of America, An Income of Her Own, to name just a few, are offering examples to girls about how they can become economically autonomous. The message is that there is another path to girlpower than through the eyes of boys.

Parents play a critical role in helping girls maintain their vision and their power. We can talk to our daughters about our own work. We can encourage them to explore a wide range of careers and interests. We can share with them the truth about the choices we make as women and mothers, and the successes and ambiguities of women's lives. For parents to do this effectively, however, we have to work on our own vision of what girls' lives can be, the goals we set for them—and whether they are attainable.

Even someone as conscious about gender issues as Jacquelynne Eccles admits to having two very different reactions when her daughter started having trouble in high school, as had her son. "She did much better than he did and when she started having trouble it wasn't as big a deal to me." She intervened with tutors and other measures to help her son, but reacted to her daughter's trouble by feeling she would be fine. "Why did I react so strongly when it happened to Chris and not to my daughter?" It was, she said, because she had the expectation that "he'll have to support a family in the back of my mind." Even today, after two decades of change brought on by the women's movement, Eccles and other researchers still find that when they ask parents what they want their junior high school student to be, those who have daughters express the hope that she will be happy, and those who have sons answer with an occupation. Eccles speculates that this may have some impact on girls' greater tendency to suffer from depression. "It may be easier to become a doctor than to become happy. We may be setting up something more unrealistic and unobtainable for girls than what we expect for boys."

One way to strike a better balance is to talk more to boys about being happy and their role in relationships, and more to girls about what they can be.

Teenage girls report being depressed not only more frequently than boys, but for longer periods of time. Given the fact that adult women are three times more likely to be depressed than men, it appears the pattern begins in adolescence. Why this is remains open to debate, but one theory is that the different coping mechanisms girls and boys have may contribute to girls' greater rates of depression. Adolescent boys and girls are equally interested in each other, but boys seem to be able to cope with love's losses better than girls do. They put it behind them and move on, while girls focus on the breakup and keep talking about it, stirring the emotional pot. This theory suggests that one way for parents to help girls deal with depression more effectively would be to encourage them to use the boys' mechanism, and to put the setback behind them. If a girl has a picture in her mind of a bright future in which she will be an independent person—the same vision boys have—she will be able to use that coping mechanism to good effect.

THE POWER TO CHOOSE

As long as girls live in a world that defines them by their desirability to men, popularity will be important, and it is important for mothers not to deny it. To say it doesn't matter is unrealistic—and will cause a rift between mothers and daughters. Far better, says therapist and author Marianne Walters, is to help girls figure out how to deal with the pressure—where to make compromises, and where not to. This is a first lesson in the excercise of girlpower. Walters is the mother of three grown daughters, and she is the is one of the authors of *The Invisible Web*, a landmark study by feminist psychologists of the role of gender in family systems therapy. Her advice on the popularity issue was unequivocal: Discuss our own ambivalance about it with our daughters, for they feel it, too.

Parents can provide guidance by what they praise, and what they deem important. If we stress the importance of boys and being popular, that establishes the social agenda as a priority. If we praise our daughters' school efforts instead, that helps establish a different priority. "These messages are very important," says Walters. "That's really how value systems are developed."

Teenagers are not all sex-crazed. In fact, it's more likely that the culture is sex-crazed and teenagers are trying to resist it. Almost universally they tell researchers that they wish they had waited until they were older to have sex. In one study, nearly a quarter said they believed in abstinence before marriage.[1]

But the emphasis we place on feelings in girls, on their interpersonal skills, and on their well-developed ability to care for others is precisely what sets them up to succumb to sexual overtures of boys—and they usually regret it.

Proof of this is found in a study by Marion Howard and Judith McCabe, who asked more than 1,000 sexually active girls sixteen years of age or younger what topic they most wanted to have more information about: A whopping 84 percent of the girls checked the item "how to say no without hurting the other person's feelings."[2]

Parents can help girls by teaching them to set boundaries. This means coaching them on how to ask questions and how to frame social situations in the context of choices. It means teaching them to constantly question boys' behavior with them and get them to feel comfortable saying: "Why do you think it's all right to do that?" and "How do you think it makes me feel?" Or to teach them to say, "No, stop, it's not all right." The goal is nothing short of changing the image in boys' minds of what is appropriate behavior toward girls and women and to make them more reflective about their sexual desires. At the same time, parents will be teaching their daughters that they have the power to make choices about the social and sexual agenda— that they can say no. If the boy chooses to end the relationship, they know precisely what he was in the relationship for. Girls who are raised with a vision of independence and financial autonomy, who are self-centered rather than man-centered, will have the confidence to make choices that will promote their own well-being. If the choice comes down to hurting themselves or hurting someone else's feelings, girls who have practiced these skills and have a clear eye about what is at stake will place their own welfare first. They will feel entitled to do that.

PROTECTING GIRLS

Parents' very realistic fear that their daughters will be molested creates a critical difference in the way girls are brought up. Parents fear that their girls can be hurt because of their sex, and this creates ambivalence about what girls ought to be doing, how much to protect them, how to let them go. One of the best ways to protect girls is to educate them about the dangers and the steps they can take to avoid perilous situations.

Peggy Reeves Sanday, the University of Pennsylvania anthropologist who wrote *Fraternity Gang Rape*, says that it is vital for parents to warn their daughters about the dangers of being alone or with just another girl in a group of males. Whether they are at an unchaperoned drinking party in the home of someone's parents or in a fraternity house, they are in danger of being isolated and jumped by several boys. When several boys have sex with the same girl, it is called a "train." The usual defense is that the girls were willing participants. Sanday has talked to many victims of these "trains," and all of them, she told me, "have either been comatose or in some other way unable to consent or they were simply terrified." Clearly girls who are alone with a group of boys and who are drinking and using drugs are putting themselves at enormous peril. And even though they think the boys are their friends, a dynamic occurs in these situations that causes boys to turn into predatory exhibitionists, a dynamic that is driven in part by a strong period of bisexual desire in adolescent boys.

Sanday speaks from personal as well as professional experience. When she was fourteen years old, she passed by a church gym where a boy she had dated was playing basketball with some other boys. They invited her inside, and she joined their game. Suddenly they jumped her. She was able to escape and run home. "My very presence there seemed to be leading them on in some kind of odd, inexplicable sexual game they were playing with each other."

I asked her what parents can tell daughters. "Make it clear that when you are with a group of guys, if you are a teenage girl, you have to be very, very careful. You have to be aware that something like this can happen. Unfortunately you are torn between wanting to have a good time and always being on the lookout. Young women have to be educated about the double standard in the minds of guys and the importance to them of sex expressed in front of each other."

Parents need to discuss with their daughters what the dangers are and what they can do to protect themselves—whether it is dating in groups, or not going out with boys who are older than they are, or not going to isolated places, or taking a self-defense course. Girls need to know that while they have authority over their choices, there are dangers that they may face, simply because they are female. We need to talk with our daughters about the misbehavior of males—ranging from the construction workers who stare and make "body parts" comments at women to the acquaintance or stranger who attacks in the night. As long as male violence against women remains pervasive in the culture, daughters need to know the dangers and have their eyes open.

NEW OPPORTUNITIES AND NEW CHALLENGES FOR GIRLS

Anne Doucette-Gates, associate director of the Center for Young Children and Families at Columbia University's Teachers College, thinks the struggle to find a livable balance between intellectual accomplishment and personal popularity may produce even more aftershocks today than in previous times. This is because the expanded opportunities young girls and women now have still collide with traditional roles society has set for women, roles that manifest themselves in adolescence. As a result, she said, young women will often "play down" their untraditional accomplishment and aspirations. "It's not easy for them to figure out how to be liked by the opposite sex and still enjoy a coherent, assertive identity themselves. So much of self-esteem and self-concept is not only built on how one feels internally, but also on the assessments other people have of you." In my generation, girls felt they had to hide good grades— but most of us did not feel we had to hide career aspirations since we did not have them. Today's girls who want to be engineers or lawyers may find it even more painful to reconcile their ambition and their desire to remain popular, particularly if the boys they associate with harbor traditional views of women and put down girls who violate gender rules.

There are costs to violating these rules, there are rewards, and girls need to know what the score is so they can make choices that are right for them. Many girls see themselves as being forced into unacceptable either/or choices, and the effects are lasting. Many mothers are being rejected by adult daughters who blame them for encouraging them to make feminist choices about having professional careers but who failed to tell them that there are consequences, such as that it may be harder to find a mate once you are out of college or that when you delay childbearing into your thirties you run a higher risk of being infertile. These women enter therapy in their late twenties and thirties, having failed to grasp the idea that it is up to them to choose how they are going to construct their lives. Girls have to know that they can make decisions and create results. At the same time, mothers need to be very clear about what the repercussions of female power can be. There is a price to pay for refusing to conform to patriarchal expectations. "To entitle a daughter," says Walters, "means she may not get a man."

BACKPATS FOR POWER

President Clinton did something Jacquelynne Eccles would have approved of when he appointed his wife to head the health care reform task force. He said he had never seen anyone as good as she was at forging consensus. He bragged about his wife and sent a powerful message to today's adolescent girls and boys. The most highly visible woman in the country was being valued for what she could accomplish—not her appearance.

Eccles says we need to get away from "this tremendous ethic of modesty" and let girls shine by bragging about their talents, their intelligence, and their accomplishments. We should pat our daughters on the back more.

This is advice I took to heart after our interview, and when Katherine brought home good grades, for example, I made sure that one of us told my husband so that he could compliment her. I told my sister when we talked long-distance, and she would praise her and encourage her. As Katherine headed toward geometry in ninth grade, my husband told her that she was going to have a lot of fun in the course, an expression of his confidence in her abilities. Six weeks after school started, I took her with me to the 1993 installation ceremonies for the National Women's Hall of Fame in Seneca Falls, New York. "Come Stand Among Great Women," the invitation read, and we did. Katherine met some of the honorees, as well as people I know who are supporters of the Hall. On the plane ride up, she had told me she was averaging a 98 in geometry. Several times over the weekend, when there were opportunities to brag about Katherine, I told friends about her geometry grade. This was a crowd that knew all about the importance of math for women. She was duly congratulated. And every time, she beamed.

Cinda-Sue Davis, a biochemist who runs the University of Michigan's summer science program for girls, believes that the key to helping girls be all they can be is to give them constant encouragement and to set high goals. "I knew no scientists when I was growing up.

But I remember going to Disneyland and seeing a rocket and saying I wanted to grow up to be the stewardess on the rocket to the moon. And I remember my mother saying: 'Wouldn't it be more fun to be the pilot on the rocket to the moon?' "

GIRLS AND SPORTS: LEARNING TO LOSE

In 1987 Paul R. Ray & Co. surveyed seventy-five people at the executive-vice-president level and higher at seventy-five Fortune 500 companies. Ninety-five percent of them had participated in a high school sport. Carol Hollenshead, who directs Michigan's Center for the Education of Women, is a firm believer in the benefits of team sports for girls, but she emphasizes that she is talking about team sports that are well coached, where girls learn to take risks and to lose, as well as to win.

Out of her own history, she could see how this played out. After she and her husband married, they fell into conversation about their experiences in the S.A.T.s, and she was shocked at the difference. "I felt when I sat down to take those tests that my whole life was in front of me, that my whole future was hanging in the balance. It panicked me. My husband viewed it as a game."

Tammi Reiss is testament to the impact sports can have on girls' self-confidence. When she graduated from high school in Eldred, New York, she held the New York state scoring record for the number of points made by a high school basketball player—male or female: 2,871. She is only five feet, six inches tall. She was also valedictorian of her high school class. She attended the University of Virginia on a full scholarship and played point guard on the top-ranked women's basketball team.

"I had a positive self-concept," she says of her high school years, and it was constantly being reinforced because of her accomplishments in basketball. Unlike her friends, she did not feel the need to chase the grail of personal popularity. She had found another way to feel good about herself.

FATHERS AND DAUGHTERS

Oddly, given the nature of our patriarchal system, fathers are more important than many of them realize. They play a critical role in how high their daughters aspire and in the girls' future relationships with boys and men. Fathers can enable their daughters to soar or they can cripple them into dependency. The psychological and educational research is replete with information that points to the role fathers play in influencing girls' career choices, their sense of competence and worth, and their willingness to take risks. Time and again, when I interviewed women who have succeeded in nontraditional fields, they spoke of their fathers' influence. One housewife I know, who can fix just about anything in a house, told me that she had been an only child, so her father taught her everything he would have taught a son. I heard this refrain many times: "My father raised me like he would have raised a son." Or "My parents raised me the same way they raised my brothers."

In the summer of 1983, the Women in Science Program at the University of Michigan gave brief questionnaires to about 1,500 incoming freshmen women who had indicated an interest in science or math or who had scored a 550 or higher on their math S.A.T.s. Five hundred and thirty women responded to the questionnaire.[3] The study found that fathers were particularly important as a source of encouragement for women going into science, math, and engineering.

"The self-esteem literature shows it is the other parent who has more to do with how children feel than the same-sex parent," says Eleanor Linn of the Center for Sex Equity in Schools at the University of Michigan's School of Education. "We need to have fathers who are telling girls how smart and capable they are."

The father-daughter relationship is fraught with ambivalence, writes Walters's coauthor Betty Carter in *The Invisible Web*. And it is more so today than before. The new possibilities that girls and women have for designing their lives create tensions and anxieties within fathers who were raised to believe that a girl's path to happiness lies in finding a good husband, while they also know that the divorce rate makes this an uncertain option.

One of the most common ways in which fathers can disable girls is by overprotecting them, infantalizing them, and dooming them to a "daddy's little girl" pattern of dependency. This is a logical outcome of a patriarchal culture, but it is one that fathers and mothers need to be mindful of. There's nothing wrong with this as long as a daughter is also guided toward self-reliance, writes Carter. The "daddy's little girl" pattern so conforms to the cultural mandate to treat girls differently than boys that "father can easily be unaware of its elements of control and dominance and its negative effects on their wives and daughters." And she highlights one very important point that mothers need to be aware of in dealing with husbands, not only on behalf of themselves, but also on behalf of their daughters.

When mothers who were brought up to placate and defer to men fail to communicate forthrightly to their husbands about their own needs, their daughters notice this, and they will probably have one of two reactions: They will assimilate this pattern of communicating with men or they will challenge their mothers as to why they are behaving in such a way toward their husbands. The first response is the one that points a girl in the direction of trouble; it trains a girl to be afraid to say no, to be afraid of hurting other people's feelings. The second response is one that will prompt both mothers and daughters to reexamine the family female-to-male communication system. The core issue is one of entitlement: Girls need to be brought up so that they feel as entitled to speak forthrightly and to present their needs as boys do. Girls first learn how to do this in dealing with fathers and with brothers. To raise daughters with that sense of entitlement, mothers raised in an era that taught them to be deferential may well have to re-assess how they stand in relation to their husbands. This is the nexus at which girls first learn how to relate to men, and it can affect everything from how they maintain control sexually to how—and whether—they ask for a raise.

ENTITLED DAUGHTERS

My daughter is a close observer of how I negotiate my way across such male/female minefields as who does the housework. One Sunday afternoon, for example, I started to wash a large electric griddle. "Why are you washing that?" asked Katherine. "You didn't use it." In fact, she was right. My husband had used the griddle for his breakfast. I explained that he was feeding the cows, we were trying to get away in a half-hour, and in the interest of teamwork, I was cleaning the griddle. Also, as half-owner of the cattle, I could have been up in the barn feeding them, and my husband would then have had time to clean the griddle. Katherine semed satisfied that we'd worked things out fairly. These conversations about power relationships are critical to a girl's self-image, because they let her know her mother has choices, and so has she. What had caused my daughter to be alarmed was that I was cleaning up somebody else's mess—a female role she's not keen to take on. She wanted to know why I wasn't resisting the drudgery associated with women's lives. You could almost hear an accusatory note in her voice that said I was betraying her by caving in to ancient social expectations. At thirteen, she understood with remarkable clarity that my fights are hers, and hers are mine.

Frequently Katherine will watch a transaction (or perhaps a failure to transact) between my husband and myself, and react with this question: "Why do you let him get away with that?" Sometimes she's kidding, but sometimes I also hear a more serious note that puts me on the defensive. I am torn between a feeling that she is intruding and my desire to encourage her to observe, question, and challenge. When I posed this dilemma to therapist Walters, she suggested that rather than answering Katherine's question, I ought to ask her how she would do it differently. "Take it out of relation to you. Once children start critiquing their parents' relationship they are in territory over which they have no control. It's not productive. But it is very productive to talk to people about how they would handle these situations and to get a range of options across. So it becomes a discussion of choices, rather than an explanation."

SEPARATION OR A NEW CONNECTION?

The traditional view of mothers and daughters is a relationship in which the daughter grows up and moves away to the home of her husband. It is a relationship framed by separation, even rivalry. But the move of mothers out of the home and into the workforce has changed the dynamic between many mothers and daughters. With both of them working, often at professional jobs, they have more in common. Research by EDK Associates, a polling firm specializing in women's issues, has shown that daughters think much more highly of their mothers than they have in the past. When the National Coalition of Girls' Schools asked students from kindergarten through grade twelve to nominate their "women of the year" in 1992, invariably the girls selected their mothers. I read hundreds of their letters, and it was both reassuring and invigorating: These girls delighted in their mothers' encouragement and their accomplishments. Many wrote of how their mothers cared for them and their siblings, and were always available to them, even if they worked full-time. Many also described how much fun they had being with their mothers. They praised their mothers' charity work and highlighted their mothers' professional work. One nominated her stepmother, who works with homeless people in California. "My mother," wrote a senior in high school, "because she is the only one who has always believed in me and supported me and been able to follow her own dreams at the same time." To these girls, the woman of the year was the mother who was holding up the other end of the mother-daughter connection. These girls understood that in this connection lies their strength to resist and survive. The bond between mother and daughter is far more powerful than most of us realize, and it lasts through adolescence.

Marianne Walters views family relationships as an ongoing process within which people are renegotiating their affiliations with each other. She envisions a new relationship between mothers and daughters—a circular one that is reciprocal. This is the pattern of relationship that she has with her daughter, Suzanna Danuta Walters, who wrote *Lives Together/Worlds Apart, Mothers and Daughters in Popular Culture.* Suzanna Walters is proving what women can do when they don't spend their twenties in recovery from an adolescence that drives girls into a search for autonomy from mothers—a search that almost inevitably catapults them into dependency on men. She is deeply connected to the history of women through her mother. In her book, Suzanna was working with her mother's thinking and pushing it along into new frontiers, using it to analyze how mothers and daughters are often depicted in the popular culture as adversaries in a power struggle. It is an adversarial relationship that keeps women from joining hands across generations to change the sexist culture that is the culprit. But a reciprocal relationship that she and her mother envision empowers both mother and daughter and gives both of them the courage to bring about change. Mothers and daughters united are far more powerful than they are divided.

LISTENING TO OUR DAUGHTERS

Marianne Walters spoke about her daughter with a sense of respect and admiration—a sense that I find I have for my own daughter. Both of us are listening to our daughters in ways that are out of the ordinary: I am listening to my daughter because of the book I am writing. Marianne listens to her daughter because they are creating ways of looking at relationships together. We have given importance to our daughters' thinking that might not have occurred if our professional work had been different. I did not anticipate this result when I started work on this book, but by listening as closely as I have to my daughter and what she has to say about everything from politics, to school, to relationships, to food, religions, family members, and our various animals, I have given her standing that she might not otherwise have achieved in our family. I realize I can give her something other than love, which comes with virtually no thought, no judgment, no holding back. I can also give her admiration and respect for how she thinks and how she handles herself. This requires me to stand head to head with my daughter, and not look down upon her because she is young, and to let her stand head to head next to me; it requires me to see her as a person of accomplishment—a person who is her own agent—not as a child who is merely a receiver of my mothering. As I look at her this way, my expectations of her take on a new dimension: They are less attached to me, more attached to her; they are disentangled from my emotions and more attached to her accomplishments.

I realize that as I have been listening to her in this new way during the past year I have not only given her added stature within the family, I have also given her power. This is a discovery for me. I know now that mothers can give their daughters stature by listening to them, validating their observations, engaging them in conversations about such forbidden topics as gender issues and relationships, and that this is a way to give them power within the family.

Very often during the past year I found myself stopping family conversations so that my daughter could further explore a thought or challenge something someone else had said. Often I did it because of what I had learned in the course of researching this book. I also did it frequently because I wanted to hear what she had to say for this book. Within the family, Katherine was having an opportunity to challenge male systems and to flex the muscle of female authority. Reforming a culture so that daughters are as cherished as sons, to use Ruth Bader Ginsburg's phrase, takes time, as we have learned. But one thing mothers—and fathers—can do individually to help our daughters is to give them a foundation in our families that is grounded in respect and admiration. We can make sure they are not interrupted at home and that their voices are as listened to at the dinner table as anyone else's.

A former television producer I talked with says she coaches her daughter on how to be verbally combative, without being disrespectful of elders. "I'll tell my husband, 'This must be hard for you, because she gets in your face a lot,' and he says, 'That's okay. If she can stand up to a six-foot-five male she won't let anyone else run over her.' "

I have heard my daughter, time and again, say to both males and females, "Hey, you're interrupting me." At dinner one night in her seventh-grade year, she turned to my husband and announced: "You're stifling my life." A daughter who is heard, respected, and honored within her family as a full and complete person will stand a much better chance of demanding the same treatment from the world.

THE BIG LIE

I was raised to believe that boys and girls and men and women were equal. Like many women of my generation who went into the work-force with these blinders firmly in place, I was blindsided. I am now convinced that one of patriarchy's most effective devices for disabling girls and women is to entice us into believing the seductive lie that women and men are treated equally in this culture. Mothers who raise daughters to believe this are setting them up for a fall. We must tell them the truth, for in this truth is their power and ours.

This is why I found Julia's comments about being in the women's movement so touching. I have heard too many girls—and adult women, as well—say "I'm not a feminist, but I'm for equal pay." Women and girls resist the label, in part I think, out of denial. It's a mirror effect: If you acknowledge that a group of people is discriminating against you, and that group is the dominant group to whom you look for expertise, it follows that you would say to yourself, "Maybe they are right. Maybe there is something wrong with me. They have a reason to discriminate against me: I'm less worthy." That is a devastating thing to think. And for women and girls it is not a truth: The social structure inhibits them from achieving all they can. But how many young women have the constant reinforcement that tells them that it is society that is discriminating against them, that it is society that is out of step, not them, that it is culture and society that are deficient, not them? How much easier to deny that discrimination exists than to take on a whole culture. This is a particularly daunting task in adolescence when a girl's success within the social structure seems to depend almost completely on her relationships with males. How many girls are strong enough to risk social self-destruction by declaring themselves to be feminists—and thus direct challenges to boys?

When I began this book with the feeling that my own daughter was headed into a hurricane, I had no idea that discussions about choice, about the ambiguity of women's lives, could be as affirming to her as they are. I did not realize that coaching her to establish boundaries by talking directly to boys about how they act would build within her a sense of authority and self-directedness by validating her desire not to be forced into sexual behavior she doesn't want. But I understand now how these new patterns of communicating with girls can help keep them on course, and keep them strong and self-confident because they tell girls the truth. These new patterns encourage girls to maintain an authentic vision of their lives as self-centered, rather than to assimilate themselves into a male-centered teenage mythology. These are the secrets of girlpower. And it is truthfulness that gives them their power.

VALIDATION

A decade ago, I did an interview with an obscure Harvard professor who had just written a book that Harvard University Press was having trouble getting reviewed. They were hoping that a female columnist might give it some attention. The author came to Washington and I interviewed her at the *Post*. The interview went on much longer than we had planned. I knew I had met someone who combined a dazzling intellect with the spirit of an explorer. She was uncovering secrets about the condition of women in Western cultures. She was also talking political heresy: She was saying women were different and it was just fine to think like a woman. I ended up writing two columns back to back about her book, something I'd never done before. Looking back, I now realize that Carol Gilligan was the first person who had really told me about the value of thinking like a woman, who made me feel that it was terrific. When a paper such as the *Washington Post* devotes two columns to a book, publicists can use them to promote reviews and publicity in other newspapers. Because there are, even today, so few women columnists to take an interest in scholarly books that empower women, the public rarely learns about them—while anti-feminist rubbish decrying "political correctness" meets critical acclaim. By contrast, Gilligan's book, *In a Different Voice*, became a landmark work that sold more than 360,000 copies. Gilligan was named Woman of the Year by *Ms*. magazine, and she has gone on to achieve great fame and influence.

We did not see each other for the next decade. But ten years later, we both attended a conference sponsored by the AAUW. At one point, she was asked to talk about the work she was doing at the Laurel School in Cleveland, and she told stories of girls applauding female teachers who ignored rules the girls thought were foolish. Gilligan's work at the Laurel School was later published in *Meeting at the Cross-roads*, a book in which we hear the voices of girls "on the edge of adolescence," as she put it. At the conference, she talked about how groups of teachers and students at the Laurel School met to discuss what was on girls' minds, and to help them deal with the sexism they felt, the silencing all around them. In these gatherings, the girls had a chance to use their voices, and the teachers were rediscovering theirs. As the conference broke up for lunch, Carol came over to where I was standing talking with some people and we embraced. It was a hug that reached across a decade, and it came with a joyous spontaneity. We were both moved, and surprised by it. "You were the first one to write about my book," she said. In so doing, I had validated her work. And then I realized what she had done for me: "You were the first one who told me it was okay to think like a woman."

We had lunch together, and she told me more about the work her team was doing to maintain the connection between girls and their women teachers whose own voices had been silenced in adolescence. These were the teachers who teach that everyone is equal in democracy, when the girls knew perfectly well that they are not equal. I told her about Katherine, who was then twelve, and who saw the inequalities of the world for what they were. I sought Carol's advice about this dilemma: If I told Katherine that things were not equal for women, she would eventually begin to wonder whether there was something wrong with women. If I told her men and women had equal opportunities, I would be lying to her: I know they don't, so did she, and I would be setting her up with the same big lie women of my generation carried in our minds. I asked Carol what I should tell my daughter, and this is what she said: "Tell her that she's right, things are not all that great for women, but that together, you and she will make a difference."

CHAPTER EIGHTEEN

The Vision Quest

For American males making the perilous voyage into the new century, the future holds the promise of a scary new freedom that will replace the macho bondage in which they—like American women—have been held.

For females the journey is even more frightening, but the true social and economic equality that is seen on the distant shore makes the terror of the journey infinitely worthwhile.

For men and boys, the journey is away from dominance. For girls and women, the journey is toward empowerment. For both, the prize is the true joy that is found in relationships based on equality.

These are two different quests: For men, the journey will allow them to escape the lonely extremes of independence and autonomy that patriarchies drive them into, and the corrosive self-doubt that accompany such remoteness. For women, the journey will enable them to reassert themselves as full partners in their societies.

THE BENEFITS FOR BOYS

"I look at the way my father and brother were raised," says media analyst Junior Bridge. "They were denied the full range of their personalities, their gentility, their artistic and creative capabilities, the full range of their emotions. That wasn't manly. Although it looks like men are the privileged class, and economically they are, I look at my dad, who could have been a writer or something creative. He was good at math. He ended up being a budget officer for the Defense Department. He drank himself to death, as did his kid brother. Part of that malaise was caused by the fact that as a man he was denied the full range of expression. He had a genius I.Q. and he died twenty yards out of the gutter. My brother has done very well, but I have watched over the years how he as a white man has had a lot of doors opened—but society has forced him to close a lot of doors in himself."

If men can learn relational skills, the art of being dependent on others—skills that can be taught within families and through collaborative learning, for example—they can relinquish this illusion. A woman guiding a man on such a journey can tell him how pleasant it is to take time to make up one's mind, to be able to process a lot of information thoughtfully, to interconnect with other ideas. This is what hierarchical male systems, which stress competition and being first with an answer, usually dismiss as indecisiveness—as in, "women can't make up their minds." In fact, it is a process of working one's mind. It yields far more intricate results than the process that produces the fastest answer—often with the least information. Integrated thinking is something else that men can learn from us.

In their journey away from dominance, boys and men will have the opportunity to become more thoughtful of others and to learn to form the kinds of deep, relational networks that women have—the kinds of friendships that support and nourish us when careers are faltering, marriages are ending, and children are hovering on the brink of delinquency. For women, "a little help from my friends" is not an empty phrase: Often it is a rescuing lifeline. This is one of many things boys and men can learn from us. They do not deserve to be brought up in the arid emotional isolation that patriarchies inflict on them.

Boys don't have to be mean-spirited toward each other. All too often this translates itself into being mean-spirited toward girls. Schools that encourage aggression, that pit boys and girls against each other in a game of dodgeball are not indulging youngsters in an innocent playground game: They are deliberately promoting rivalry between the two sexes and sanctioning boys ganging up against the girls.

The locker room/Lakewood High vision of a man's relationship with a woman is an indignity and an abuse of women. But what these high school juveniles don't understand is that they are cheating themselves, too. They are setting themselves up for a life in which they can never have a real relationship with a woman, for rich, satisfying relationships can only work when they are based on equality and fairness. Girls lose out in this equation, too, of course. But in the end, the high school athlete/studs who treat girls as sex toys are left with nothing. Their emotional growth stops at the most elemental level. Their ability to comfort and care for another person, to be tender, never has a chance to develop at all. The high school stud grows into a relational cripple, doomed to a life of the chase because that is all he is capable of doing.

Boys can be raised to be far more civilized and relationally competent. We do our sons no favor when we write them off as inept in interpersonal relations because of their gender. We consign them to a life driving toward meaningless and emotionally sterile achievement, without the emphasis on personal happiness that is their right. We need to teach them how to get along with each other and how to get along with girls. Parents and teachers need to implant into the minds of boys the rigorous new social requirement that they behave with respect toward each other and toward girls. In these early years, they must be taught to listen, not to interrupt, to share, to work cooperatively, and to tone down their voices, literally and figuratively. They, too, can learn the value of being thoughtful. If schools and families and youth-serving organizations encourage and nurture these qualities in boys throughout their childhood and adolescence, we will produce adult males who are far less self-centered and more connected to others.

FEMALE AUTHORITY: RECLAIMING TURF

The journey for girls is one of reclaiming turf and reestablishing female authority. Only in so doing can they define the world, move in it, and help solve its problems. To do this effectively, women must learn their history. They must know the story of the brutal war against them that has been fostered by male-centered monotheistic religions. The history of strong women, whether they were goddesses, queens, warriors, or poets, is an inspiring chronicle that lends authority to feminine power and the female role of providing. This is the history that fills the void women feel at their center when they are raised in patriarchal systems that disconnect them from their feminine power, that force them to stifle their instincts and intuitions, to dull their intellect, to pretend that what is isn't, and what isn't is. The void can be filled only when women and girls are brought up in a culture that values what they do and who they are, not how they look or what they can do for men. Girls and women need to think of themselves in new ways—as powerful, strong, resourceful people who come from a powerful, strong, resourceful heritage in which they provided for their communities and ensured survival of their families and tribes by whatever means were necessary, whether war, statecraft, agronomy, or fiscal management.

We have reached a time in history when the sticky fog of patriarchy is being dissipated, and we can begin to rediscover who we really are and the history that has brought us to this point. Both sexes are on a journey toward self-discovery. It is a voyage that prehistoric societies thought of in terms of a vision quest, and those quests always evolved around a goal of touching spiritual power, which was neither male nor female but a combination of both.

Anthropologically, what men and women do in different environments is whatever it takes for their community to survive and for their generation to reproduce itself. And this is precisely why men and women in patriarchal cultures today have to make their two different journeys, with their two different quests. Their survival as individuals and families depends on achieving a balance of power between the genders, and our survival as a planet depends on listening to the female ethic of conservation and renewal, respect and cooperation, instead of browbeating, dominance, and war.

We can start by talking about differences—what's real and what's imagined, what is biologically produced, what is culturally imprinted. We can teach ourselves where it all came from, where it went wrong, and what we can do to restore harmony between the genders and between competing interests in our communities. This is a great strength and vision that women and girls who are empowered can bring to new societies. Words like harmony and respect are words that articulate an ethic we cherish and understand.

This is not to say that a hierarchical system that uses force and war as a means of enforcing dominance has no place. War has been used to secure peace. But it is to say that new systems that pay more attention to process than to power, to securing results for the common good rather than to feeding the egos of status-seeking men, must become the standards of acceptable behavior. We need to understand that exclusive reliance on the hierarchical style deprives us of a rich repertoire of human skills and behavior. We need also to understand that the hierarchical characteristics endemic to patriarchal systems are usually instruments of blunt force, and they have caused centuries of human misery. Hierarchy has done a lot of damage. This needs to be acknowledged.

CHANGING EXPECTATIONS

Children cannot make the transition into a gender balanced society alone; it is a journey adults have to go on, as well. For we have to learn gender history so we can change the future, and we have to learn about all the poorly defined expectations lurking in our own heads so we can understand the harm they do, the limits they set. When a sophisticated and dedicated researcher such as Jacquelynne Eccles admits to having two very different reactions when her daughter and son had trouble in school, we can safely assume that none of us are free of genderized expectations. Parents expect girls to be better readers than boys, and we read more to little girls than to little boys. When we send a girl off to first grade with the expectation that she will do better at reading than her brother, but not as well in math, we launch a chain reaction of self-fulfilling prophecies. The difference between boys and girls is a mix of biology, culture, and the personalities each of them is born with. But an awful lot of it is also in our heads.

How much impact do the stereotypes stuffed into our heads really have on children? I got an answer one day while my husband and I were visiting friends at their beach house. Our host is a partner in one of the nation's most prominent law firms. His wife is a well-educated, firmly compassionate woman. That spring, their eldest daughter had graduated second in her class at one of the nation's top law schools. This is not a couple that sets limits on girls' achievement. But one afternoon during our visit the subject of this book came up—and I told them I was looking at how we raise children, and why girls come out of this process feeling second best. With us in the room was the couple's twenty-one-year-old daughter, who has a fraternal twin who was not present. Our hosts were talking about how they had raised their twins and one of them said that they had not treated the daughter any differently than they had the son.

"That's not true!" their daughter cried out. "I remember one time at the beach when I was nine years old the surf was rough and you let (her brother) go out in the ocean and I had to stay on the sand and build sand castles."

Her mother and father both quickly explained that her brother had always been physically large and strong, and that's why he'd been allowed to go into the water while she had been restrained. They asked her what she would have done.

"I probably would have done the same thing," she admitted. "But playing in the ocean and having to stay on the beach building sand castles are not the same thing," she said. "And it sent me a very clear message. It told me that my brother could handle the ocean, and I could not."

Twelve years later that message continued to reverberate in her mind with a painful import her parents never intended. Without meaning to, they had protected her, kept her from risk, shielded her from danger while her twin was given a chance to brave the ocean. In that instant, she knew he was better than she was, and she never forgot it

These are the messages of worth and value, domination and submission, of good and not so good, of normal and "other" that fill childhood. It's the adversarial static that distorts boys' and girls' views of each other, interferes with their communications, and thrusts them each into rigid behavior patterns that are dictated by their gender rather than who they are, what they can do, and what they feel. Narrow definitions of what is masculine and what is feminine prevail, and children eagerly seek to behave in ways they believe are appropriate. Pushing and shoving is condoned for boys—but not for girls. Nurturing is raised to a high art in girls—and ruthlessly driven underground in boys. The benefits of sharing, of stressing the interconnections between little boys and little girls are dismissed, while the toughness and strength of little boys is prized. Boys quickly pick up cues that they are "better" than girls and, tragically, so do girls. The messages that men and women have about each other today are messages they got in childhood and all throughout their schooling. The lucky ones find out at some point in their adulthood that the messages they got were false, distorted, and destructive, riddling relations between the sexes with suspicion and lack of respect. One glaring example of this occurred when a father was overheard correcting his son for saying "shit." "Don't say 'shit,' " the father admonished. "Say 'stuff.' Shit is what your mother does." And with that, another mother had the bearings blasted out from under her—and the noise will resound into any relations her son has with women.

We must learn to see the blindingly clear link between the roughneck four-year-old male who is cheered on for intimidating his playmates and the abusing husband who punches out his wife. We must understand that there is a direct connection between the behavior of a six-year-old boy who pulls up a girl's skirt on the playground, and the laughter of his pals, and the fraternity boy who bonds with his brothers by offering up his date for gang rape. When adults fail to correct nasty behavior by male children they set the stage for them to be abusive to girls and women as they grow older. And when girls see disrespectful behavior by boys toward girls being condoned, they get the message that this behavior is acceptable—and it's what girls should expect.

We are still designing children based on antiquated notions of what is masculine-appropriate and what is feminine-appropriate. We see this mind-set as a shortcut for thinking about people—a system for socializing people into what we think is appropriate. But it is not a shortcut, it is a blind alley. It diminishes the potential of girls to develop themselves fully and, of course, the potential of boys as well. When we have 58 percent of eighth-grade girls telling a national survey that they have earned money babysitting and only 6 percent of the boys have, we have clearly sent two very different messages. It means we are still depriving boys of their natural interest in young children. We don't need to keep repeating this cycle of exaggerated and destructive gender roles.

PATRIARCHY: HARDWIRED

Many women who joined the modern women's movement during the past twenty-five years did not realize how difficult it would be to change the system: Whether it was reforming education or winning equality in the workforce and at home. History should have prepared us for the backlash of the Reagan-Bush era, for an equally virulent backlash occurred at the end of the nineteenth century. Many of us who embraced the principles of equality that the women's movement stood for thought we could slip some feminist software into the culture's drive, and things would change so that the true promise of democracy would be fulfilled. We did not realize how hardwired patriarchy was into the culture. We did not understand the quantity and power of the subtle and not so subtle dependency messages girls get from infancy onward, nor the impact of the domination messages boys receive. Nor did we understand the critical role that boys play in this process. After nearly three decades of fragile progress, it is clear to me that we cannot change the way we raise girls until we change the way we raise boys. We cannot make the world a better one for girls until we produce boys who are not hostile to women.

The women's movement has failed to confront the critical role religion plays in patriarchies. It is the spiritual enabler of domination. It plays a bedrock role in maintaining men's power over women.

Throughout much of the 1970s and all of the 1980s the leaders of the women's movement found themselves locked in battle with the leaders of organized religions such as the Catholic, fundamentalist, and Mormon churches over the issue of abortion. Many women and men, as well, found themselves alienated from churches and organized religions. Religion gets short shrift in the popular press. Much of the work that feminist scholars have done to resurrect the history of the early church and to mount their challenge to the historic authority of the Church of Rome has gone unnoticed by leaders of the feminist movement and the public. The intellectual revolution of the 1990s will come when the fusion occurs between the feminist critique of patriarchy and the feminist critique of monotheist religions that are centered on a male god figure. They are the last great chains binding women into slavery, for they sanctify male dominance.

A return to pantheism is one path that women have taken in order to express their spiritual and psychological lives, and while that may seem radical to some people, it reconnects mothers and daughters to our most ancient and empowering truth: the female cycle of birth and regeneration. Without us, human history would be over. The male contribution to the process, on the other hand, can be stored in sperm banks. The ancient goddess worship is one way for women to reclaim their spiritual center in a oneness with nature that authenticates wisdom as She and provides women with a feminine image of the divine.

The fight about whether we should allow prayer in the public schools is a phony fight. The real fight should be to have schools teach young people what religions do in various cultures. Adolescents ought to be informed about the feminist critique of Christianity as part of history and religion courses in schools. A tall order? Yes. But without doing this, we will not be able to change the way boys and girls are raised in this culture, or the way they view each other. Christianity, patriarchy, and abuse are all wrapped up together, and together they doom girls to second-class citizenship. To ignore this connection and its poisonous effect on male-female relations is to allow it to go on, just as ignoring child abuse within a family perpetuates it.

I did not expect religion to play as important a part in my research as it did. Intellectually I knew religions are important to social structures, and I knew that a conspiracy of patriarchs had perverted the early Christian church. It took me a solid year of research before I understood the profound impact this has had on the status of women and men in the world today. This was a revelation to me, and I hope readers, particularly those who have been disenfranchised from religions, will be persuaded as to the importance—and the promise—the feminist critique of Christianity holds for all of us.

LIBERATION AT THE CROSSROADS

We are at the next crossroads in the women's movement. In my mind I see a crowd gathering, women and men walking out of different disciplines, down the steps of their institutions and into the public consciousness, carrying with them their discoveries, breaking out of the isolation they have been working in, and empowering each other and the rest of us. Here, at this crossroads, bold thinkers from all of the different disciplines that are studying how men and women came to be as we are can mount a final assault on the patriarchy, an assault that will liberate all of us, boys and girls, men and women, from a system that destroys so many people. Only then, I am convinced, can we create a culture in which girls are raised to be all they can be—a culture in which our daughters are as valued as our sons.

The journey for boys and men away from domination and the journey of girls and women toward empowerment is a journey to a land of mutual respect. It will begin in the hearts and minds of adults—parents, teachers, ministers, leaders of boys' and girls' service organizations, and all of the purveyors of the popular culture that are currently operating to reinforce the negative and destructive images that devalue girls and entitle boys. This cultural propaganda lays the groundwork for destructive relations between the genders just as surely as government propaganda is used to whip up public fury.

If we can work on redesigning children in our own minds, developing a better fix in our own adult heads of the qualities we want to foster in people—male and female—we can lay a solid foundation for nurturing the best qualities in boys and girls, women and men, and for securing a lasting peace between the sexes. This is the vision quest we can have for the girls who stand on our shoulders—for our daughters, and our sons as well. This is the peace of the promised land.

NOTES

CHAPTER TWO

1. Humphrey, J. H., *Stress Among Women in Modern Society*, Springfield, IL: Charles C. Thomas, 1992, pp. 61–62.
2. Rubin, J. Z., F. J. Provenzano, and Z. Luria, "The Eye of the Beholder: Parents' Views on Sex of Newborns," *American Journal of Orthopsychiatry*, 1974, Vol. 44, pp. 512–519.
3. This study is reported in *The Psychology of Women*, a widely used textbook by Margaret W. Matlin. The observation as to the importance of these findings is hers.
4. This research was published in *Child Development*, 1978, Vol. 49, in an article entitled "The Influence of Sex of Child on Parental Reactions to Toddler Children."
5. This study, cited by Margaret W. Matlin in *The Psychology of Women*, was done by H. A. Moss and originally published under the title "Early Sex Differences and Mother-Infant Interaction," in a book entitled *Sex Differences in Behavior*, Friedman, R., R. Richart, and R. Vande Wiele, eds., New York: Wiley, 1974.

CHAPTER THREE

1. Fausto-Sterling, A., *Myths of Gender*, New York: Basic Books, 1985, p. 36.

CHAPTER FOUR

1. Bem called her theory "gender schema." It is discussed at length in *The Psychology of Women*, by Margaret W. Matlin, pp. 53–55.
2. Best, R. *We've All Got Scars*, Bloomington: Indiana University Press, 1983, pp. 79–80.
3. The National Center for Clinical Infant Programs is now formally known as Zero to Three, and it is located at 2000 14th Street North, Suite 380, Arlington, VA 22201. It is a national, nonprofit organization dedicated to improving the physical, emotional, and cognitive health of infants and toddlers. Among those participating in the *Heart Start* report were Ernest L. Boyer, president of the Carnegie Foundation for the Advancement of Teaching, who wrote the foreword, and T. Berry Brazelton, M.D., of the Children's Hospital Medical Center in Boston, MA, who wrote the preface.

CHAPTER FIVE

1. Rich, D., *MegaSkills*, New York: Houghton-Mifflin, 1992.
2. Nelson, M. B., *Are We Winning Yet? How Women Are Changing Sports and Sports Are Changing Women*, New York: Random House, 1991.

CHAPTER SIX

1. Cited by Myra and David Sadker in "What Girls Learn from Hidden Lessons," *Tennessee Teacher*, November–December, 1986, p. 26.
2. At the time this study was done, Sandler was the director of the association's Project on the Status and Education of Women and Hall was the associate director. The study, called *The Classroom Climate: A Chilly One for Women*, was published by the Association of American Colleges in 1982. It has since defined the terms of the discussion about how women are treated in higher education.
3. Krupnick's findings were published in an article, "Women and Men in the Classroom," in the spring, 1985, issue of *On Teaching and Learning*, a publication of the Danforth Center.
4. Lockheed and Klein's work was published in an essay entitled "Sex Equity in Classroom Organization and Climate" that was included in *Handbook for Achieving Sex Equity through Education*, S. Klein, ed., Baltimore: Johns Hopkins University Press, 1989.
5. These findings were published in an article Stevenson wrote with his colleague Max Lummis in the February, 1990, issue of *Developmental Psychology*.

CHAPTER SEVEN

1. This study of college seniors who graduated in 1988 was done by Lucy Sells of the University of California at Berkeley and the Math/Science Network. She found that the more math a person's major required, especially calculus, the better a person's chances of getting a job and the higher the salary would be.

2. This data is drawn from *Women in Mathematics and Physics: Inhibitors and Enhancers*, published by the University of Michigan in March, 1992. This report examines the impact of family and schools on girls through graduate school and includes valuable insights from campus focus groups.

3. This study was published in *Developmental Psychology*, 1983, Vol. 19, pp. 200–209.

4. Fennema and Peterson's theory is explained in "Autonomous Learning Behavior: A Possible Explanation of Gender-Related Differences in Mathematics," an essay included in the book *Gender Influences in Classroom Interaction*, Wilkinson, L., and C. Marrett, eds., Orlando: Academic Press, 1985.

5. The National Coalition of Girls' Schools is headquartered in Concord, MA. Proceedings of the symposium were published in a paperback report entitled *Math and Science for Girls*.

CHAPTER EIGHT

1. Tidball's research was first published in an article entitled ' Perspectives on Academic Women and Affirmative Action," *Educational Record*, 1973, Vol. 54, pp. 130–135. In the November–December, 1986, issue of the *Journal of Higher Education*, she published another stunning finding: Women's colleges graduated five times the national average of women who went on to earn doctorates in the natural sciences. In this article, "The Baccalaureate Origins of Recent Natural Science Doctorates," she also wrote that previously all-male institutions that had integrated were "among the poorest contributors" of women to natural science doctorates.

2. Lee, V. W., and A. S. Bryk, "Effects of Single-Sex Secondary Schools on Student Achievement and Attitudes," *Journal of Educational Psychology*, 1986, Vol. 78, pp. 381–395.

3. Lee's research made headlines when it was published in the June, 1992, issue of *Education Week*.

4. I saw an example of this in the fall of 1993 at West Potomac High School, a public school in Fairfax County, VA, when Cheryl Zimmermann, a five-foot-six star place kicker on the football team, made front-page news by being crowned homecoming queen at halftime. The school's principal, Terresa Caldwell, told me that she is determined to provide a school atmosphere that supports girls, and the people she hires think the same way.

CHAPTER TEN

1. Lamar described his experience with the Dodge Study in remarks delivered at the Emma Willard School in 1990.

2. In one of the few cases to reach the U.S. Supreme Court, a male challenged the all-women admissions policies of the nursing school at Mississippi University for Women. The court ruled in his favor, finding there was no state-supported nursing school in his part of the state. It did not strike down single-sex public education, but it did rule that states had to demonstrate a compelling interest in providing such programs.

3. Bekebrede's criteria were drawn from an article she wrote that was published in the 1987–1988 *Vincent/Curtis Educational Register*.

CHAPTER ELEVEN

1. Carnegie Council on Adolescent Development, Task Force on Youth Development and Community Programs, *A Matter of Time: Risk and Opportunities in Non-School Hours*, New York: Carnegie Corp., 1992.
2. Petersen, A., "The Gangly Years," *Psychology Today*, September, 1987, pp. 28–34. While Petersen was at Pennsylvania State University, she and her colleagues studied 335 adolescents who were randomly selected from two predominently white, middle- to upper-middle-class suburban school districts. They monitored two waves of youngsters as they moved from the sixth through the eighth grades. She found that the timing of puberty has much more of an impact on mood and school achievement than is generally understood to be the case. Children who matured early tended to get better grades than their slower-maturing classmates, perhaps because teachers tend to give better evaluations to larger pupils. Those who matured later reported having better moods.

CHAPTER TWELVE

1. Wiseman, C. V., et al., "Cultural Expectations of Thinness in Women: An Update," *International Journal of Eating Disorders*, 1992, Vol. 11, no. 1, pp. 85–89.

CHAPTER THIRTEEN

1. Greene makes this point in her essay "Sex Equity as a Philosophical Problem," included in *Handbook for Achieving Sex Equity through Education*, Klein, S., ed., Baltimore: Johns Hopkins University Press, 1989, p. 32.
2. Graves, R., *The Greek Myths, Vol. 1*, New York: Penguin, 1979, p. 13.
3. Woolger, J. B., and R. Woolger, *The Goddess Within*, New York: Ballantine Books, 1987, p. 432.
4. Gimbutas, M., *The Language of the Goddess*, San Francisco: HarperSanFrancisco, 1989, p. xv.
5. Ibid., p. xvii.
6. The Gears are the authors of a series of books about aboriginal people on the North American continent, including *People of the River* and *People of the Earth*. Their aim is to inform the public about recent archaeological discoveries and reconstructions of our heritage through popular fiction.
7. For a provocative discussion of this pre-patriarchal era and its disintegration, see Riane Eisler's *The Chalice and the Blade: Our History, Our Future*, San Francisco: Harper & Row, 1987.
8. *The Goddess Within*, p. 27.
9. Ibid., p. 15.
10. Estes, C. *Women Who Run with the Wolves*, New York: Ballantine Books, 1992, p. 7.

CHAPTER FOURTEEN

1. Van Doren, C., *History of Knowledge*, New York: Ballantine Books, 1991, pp. 47–48.
2. Gibbon, E., *The Decline and Fall of the Roman Empire*, New York: Penguin, 1985, pp. 546–547.

3. Pagels is the author of *The Gnostic Gospels*, which won the National Book Critics Circle Award and the National Book Award in 1980, and from which much of this discussion is drawn.

4. Walker, B., *The Encyclopedia of Women's Myths and Secrets*, San Francisco: Harper & Row, 1983, p. 439.

5. Ibid., p. 1088.

6. Ibid., p. 1012.

CHAPTER FIFTEEN

1. Elisabeth Schüssler Fiorenza's most celebrated work is *In Memory of Her: A Feminist Theological Reconstruction of Christian Origins*, published in 1983. At the time, she was professor of New Testament and Theology at Notre Dame University. This discussion is drawn from that work.

2. Bettenhausen's observation is contained in the foreword to *Christianity, Patriarchy and Abuse*, a collection of essays by feminist theologians who are looking at the role of Christianity in perpetuating a culture that abuses women and children. These theologians are struggling to remain within the Christian tradition, although they are grappling with the fundamental question of whether it is possible to be a feminist and a Christian.

3. Bloomquist's essay "Sexual Violence, Patriarchy's Offense and Defense" is published in *Christianity, Patriarchy and Abuse*, Cleveland: The Pilgrim Press, 1989, pp. 62–69.

4. Christ, C. P., *The Laughter of Aphrodite*, San Francisco: HarperSanFrancisco, 1987, p. 119. This observation is contained in her essay "Why Women Need the Goddess."

CHAPTER SIXTEEN

1. Gross, Jane, " 'Where Boys Will Be Boys' And Adults Are Befuddled," *New York Times*, March 29, 1993, p. Al.

2. Didion, Joan, Letter from California. "Trouble in Lakewood," *New Yorker*, July 26, Vol. 69, 1993, pp. 46–65.

CHAPTER SEVENTEEN

1. Jonathan E. Fielding, M.D., M.P.H., and Carolyn A. Williams, Ph.D., R.N., administered questionnaires to 3,500 juniors and seniors at four inner-city high schools. In an article in the July, 1991, issue of the *American Journal of Preventive Medicine*, they reported that 83 percent of sexually experienced teenagers said "that the best age to initiate intercourse is older than their age at initiation, and approximately 25 percent of both sexes who have had intercourse said they believed that sex before marriage is wrong."

2. This was reported in the January/February, 1990, issue of *Family Planning Perspectives*.

3. These students were re-surveyed in their senior year, along with a survey group of 124 men who met or exceeded the S.A.T. cutoff. The findings published by researchers Jean D. Manis, Nancy G. Thomas, Barbara F. Sloat, and Cinda-Sue Davis present one of the most comprehensive and detailed pictures ever assembled of the influences that motivate men and women to choose careers in science, mathematics, and engineering.

RESOURCES FOR GIRLS

Here are a few resource organizations that have programs that empower girls:

Girls, Inc.
National Resource Center
441 W. Michigan Street
Indianapolis, Indiana 46202

The Girl Scouts of the U.S.A.
830 Third Avenue
New York, New York 10022

An Income of Her Own
Programs on Entrepreneurship for Young Women
Joline Godfrey, co-founder
406 Lion Street
Ojai, California 93023

This organization, set up by a group of women entrepreneurs, runs conferences that expose adolescent girls to a number of women entrepreneurs who have succeeded in a diversity of businesses.

The American Association of University Women
1111 Sixteenth Street NW
Washington, D.C. 20036

Regional and local branches of AAUW run gender-equity workshops for parents and teachers. AAUW also has a summer camp for girls who are interested in math and science.

The National Coalition of Girls' Schools
Meg Milne Moulton/Whitney Ransome
Executive Directors
228 Main Street
Concord, Massachusetts 01742
508-287-4485 (phone/fax)

The coalition sponsors conferences designed to familiarize girls with technology and to help teachers teach math and science to girls.

BIBLIOGRAPHY

Arcana, J. *Our Mothers' Daughters*. London: The Women's Press, 1992.

Astin, H., and C. Leland. *Women of Influence, Women of Vision: A Cross-Generational Study of Leaders and Social Change*. San Francisco: Jossey-Bass, 1991.

Banner, L. W. *American Beauty*. Chicago: The University of Chicago Press, 1983.

Berger, P. *The Goddess Obscured: From Goddess to Saint*. Boston: Beacon Press, 1988.

Bergmann, B. *The Economic Emergence of Women*. New York: Basic Books, 1986.

Bernard, J. *The Female World*. New York: Free Press, 1981.

Bernard, J. *Women and the Public Interest: An Essay on Policy and Protest*. Chicago: Aldine-Atherton, 1971.

Best, R. *We've All Got Scars: What Boys and Girls Learn in Elementary School*. Bloomington: Indiana University Press, 1983.

Boswell, J. *The Kindness of Strangers: The Abandonment of Children in Western Europe from Late Antiquity to the Renaissance*. New York: Vintage Books, 1990.

Boyer, E. *Ready to Learn: A Mandate for the Nation*. Princeton: The Carnegie Foundation for the Advancement of Teaching, 1991.

Brown, C., and J. Pechman, eds. *Gender in the Workplace*. Washington: Brookings Institution, 1987.

Brown, J., and C. Bohn, eds. *Christianity, Patriarchy, and Abuse: A Feminist Critique*. Cleveland: Pilgrim Press, 1989.

Brown, L., and C. Gilligan. *Meeting at the Crossroads: Women's Psychology and Girls' Development*. Cambridge: Harvard University Press, 1992.

Bynum, C. W. *Fragmentation and Redemption: Essays on Gender and the Human Body in Medieval Religion.* New York: Zone Books, 1991.

Cantor, D., and T. Bernay, with J. Stoess. *Women in Power: The Secrets of Leadership.* New York: Houghton Mifflin, 1992.

Carnegie Council on Adolescent Development: Task Force on Youth Development and Community Programs. *A Matter of Time: Risk and Opportunities in Non-School Hours.* New York: Carnegie Corp., 1992.

Charlesworth, M. P. *The Roman Empire.* London: Oxford University Press, 1951.

Christ, C. P. *The Laughter of Aphrodite: Reflections on a Journey to the Goddess.* New York: HarperCollins, 1987.

Committee on Women in Science and Engineering, Office of Scientific and Engineering Personnel, National Research Council. *Women in Science and Engineering: Increasing Their Numbers in the 1990s.* Washington: National Academy Press, 1991.

Davis, F. *Moving the Mountain: The Women's Movement in America since 1960.* New York: Simon & Schuster, 1991.

Edelman, M. *The Measure of Our Success: A Letter to My Children and Yours.* Boston: Beacon Press, 1992.

Eisler, R. *The Chalice and the Blade: Our History, Our Future.* San Francisco: Harper & Row, 1987.

Elliott, W., and N. McDonald. *Western Political Heritage.* Englewood Cliffs: Prentice-Hall, 1957.

Estes, C. P. *Women Who Run with the Wolves: Myths and Stories of the Wild Woman Archetype.* New York: Ballantine Books, 1992.

Fausto-Sterling, A. *Myths of Gender: Biological Theories about Women and Men.* New York: Basic Books, 1985.

French, M. *The War Against Women.* New York: Summit Books, 1992.

Friedan, B. *The Feminine Mystique.* New York: Dell, 1964.

Gibbon, E. *The Decline and Fall of the Roman Empire.* New York: Penguin Books, 1985.

Gilligan, C. *In a Different Voice: Psychological Theory and Women's Development.* Cambridge: Harvard University Press, 1982.

Gilligan, C., N. Lyons, and T. Hanmer. *Making Connections: The Relational Worlds of Adolescent Girls at Emma Willard School.* Cambridge: Harvard University Press, 1989.

Gilligan, C., J. Ward, and J. Taylor, with B. Bardige, eds. *Mapping the Moral Domain: A Contribution of Women's Thinking to Psychological Theory and Education.* Cambridge: Harvard University Press, 1988.

Gimbutas, M. *The Language of the Goddess.* San Francisco: HarperCollins, 1989.

Ginot, H. *Between Parent and Teenager.* New York: Avon Books, 1969.

Godfrey, J. *Our Wildest Dreams: Women Entrepreneurs Making Money, Having Fun, Doing Good.* New York: HarperBusiness, 1992.

Gore, T. *Raising PG Kids in an X-Rated Society.* Nashville: Abingdon Press, 1987.

Greer, G. *Sex and Destiny: The Politics of Human Fertility.* New York: Harper & Row, 1984.

Heilbrun, C. *Toward a Recognition of Androgyny.* New York: Alfred A. Knopf, 1973.

Heilbrun, C. *Writing A Woman's Life.* New York: Ballantine Books, 1988.

Helgesen, S. *The Female Advantage: Women's Ways of Leadership.* New York: Doubleday/Currency, 1990.

Howe, F. *Myths of Coeducation.* Bloomington: Indiana University Press, 1984.

Humphrey, J. *Stress Among Women in Modern Society.* Springfield, IL: Charles C. Thomas, 1992.

Huston, A., et al. *Big World, Small Screen.* Lincoln: University of Nebraska Press, 1992.

Kaschak, E. *Engendered Lives: A New Psychology of Women's Experience.* New York: Basic Books, 1992.

Keith, S., and P. Keith, eds. *Proceedings of The National Conference on Women in Mathematics and the Sciences, St. Cloud State University, 1989.* St. Cloud: St. Cloud State University, 1990.

Kerber, L. and J. Mathews, eds. *Women's America: Refocusing the Past.* New York: Oxford University Press, 1982.

Kerr, B. A. *Smart Girls, Gifted Women.* Dayton: Ohio Psychology Press, 1985.

Klein, S., ed. *Handbook for Achieving Sex Equity through Education.* Baltimore: Johns Hopkins University Press, 1985.

Koblinsky, M., J. Timyan, and J. Gay, eds. *The Health of Women: A Global Perspective.* Boulder: Westview Press, 1993.

Lakoff, R. *Talking Power: The Politics of Language.* New York: Basic Books, 1992.

Laskin, D., and K. O'Neill. *The Little Girl Book: Everything You Need to Know to Raise a Daughter Today.* New York: Ballantine Books, 1992.

Lerner, G. *The Majority Finds Its Past: Placing Women in History.* New York: Oxford University Press, 1979.

Loden, M. *Feminine Leadership, or How to Succeed in Business Without Being One of the Boys.* New York: Times Books, 1985.

Macoby, E., and C. Jacklin. *The Psychology of Sex Differences.* Stanford: Stanford University Press, 1974.

Matlin, M. W. *The Psychology of Women.* New York: CBS College Publishing, 1987.

Matyas, M., J. Combs, and E. Ehrenfeld. *Girl Scouts, Science and Mathematics Linkages for the Future: A Workshop Manual for Adult Leaders.* Washington: American Association for the Advancement of Science, 1991.

McGrath, E., G. Keita, B. Strickland, and N. Russo, eds. *Women and Depression: Risk Factors and Treatment Issues.* Washington: The American Psychological Association, 1990.

Miedzian, M. *Boys Will Be Boys: Breaking the Link Between Masculinity and Violence.* New York: Doubleday, 1991.

Miles, R. *The Women's History of the World.* Topsfield: Salem House, 1989.

Miller, A. *The Drama of the Gifted Child: The Search for the True Self.* New York: Basic Books, 1981.

Miller, A. *Society's Betrayal of the Child.* New York: New American Library, 1986.

Millett, K. *Sexual Politics.* New York: Avon Books, 1970.

Minnich, E. *Transforming Knowledge.* Philadelphia: Temple University Press, 1990.

Mitter, S. *Dharma's Daughters: Contemporary Indian Women and Hindu Culture.* New Brunswick: Rutgers University Press, 1991.

Moss, R., with H. Dunlap. *Why Johnny Can't Concentrate: Coping with Attention Deficit Problems.* New York: Bantam Books, 1990.

Nelson, M. B. *Are We Winning Yet? How Women Are Changing Sports and Sports Are Changing Women.* New York: Random House, 1991.

O'Barr, J. and M. Wyer, eds. *Engaging Feminism: Students Speak Up and Speak Out.* Charlottesville: University of Virginia Press, 1992.

Pagels, E. *The Gnostic Gospels*. New York: Vintage Books, 1989.

Reinisch, J. M., with R. Beasley. *The Kinsey Institute New Report on Sex: What You Must Know to Be Sexually Literate*. New York: St. Martin's Press, 1990.

Rich, D. *MegaSkills*. New York: Houghton Mifflin, 1992.

Rosenberg, R. *Beyond Separate Spheres: Intellectual Roots of Modern Feminism*. New Haven: Yale University Press, 1982.

Sanday, P. R. *Fraternity Gang Rape: Sex, Brotherhood, and Privilege on Campus*. New York: New York University Press, 1990.

Scarf, M. *Intimate Partners: Patterns in Love and Marriage*. New York: Ballantine Books, 1987.

Schlissel, L. *Women's Diaries of the Westward Journey*. New York: Schocken Books, 1982.

Schüssler Fiorenza, E. *In Memory of Her: A Feminist Theological Reconstruction of Christian Origins*. New York: Crossroads, 1992.

Shaw, E., and J. Darling. *Female Strategies*. New York: Walter and Company, 1985.

Stone, I. F. *The Trial of Socrates*. Boston: Little, Brown, 1988.

Tannen, D. *You Just Don't Understand: Women and Men in Conversation*. New York: William Morrow, 1990.

Travis, C., and C. Offir. *The Longest War: Sex Differences in Perspective*. New York: Harcourt Brace Jovanovich, 1977.

Van Doren, C. *A History of Knowledge: The Pivotal Events, People, and Achievements of World History*. New York: Ballantine Books, 1991.

Walker, B. *The Woman's Encyclopedia of Myths and Secrets*. San Francisco: Harper & Row, 1983.

Walters, M., B. Carter, P. Papp, and O. Silverstein. *The Invisible Web: Gender Patterns in Family Relationships*. New York: Guilford Press, 1988.

Walters, S. D. *Lives Together/Worlds Apart: Mothers and Daughters in Popular Culture*. Berkeley: University of California Press, 1992.

Weitzman, L. J. *The Divorce Revolution: The Unexpected Social and Economic Consequences for Women and Children in America*. New York: Free Press, 1985.

Wilkinson, L. C., and C. B. Marrett, eds. *Gender Influences in Classroom Interaction*. Orlando: Academic Press, 1985.

Winspear, A. *The Genesis of Plato's Thought*. New York: S. A. Russell, 1956.

Woolger, J., and R. Woolger. *The Goddess Within: A Guide to the Eternal Myths That Shape Women's Lives*. New York: Ballantine Books, 1987.

SELECTED REFERENCES

Following are a list of publications that were used by the author that may be useful to readers who want to pursue further information.

A Capella: The Realities, Concerns, Expectations and Barriers Experienced by Adolescent Women in Canada. Canada: Canadian Teachers Federation, November 1990.

Adelman, C. *Women at Thirtysomething: Paradoxes of Attainment*. Washington, DC: U.S. Department of Education, 1991.

Carter, E., P. Papp, O. Silverstein, and M. Walters. *Mothers and Sons, Fathers and Daughters.* Monograph Series, Vol. 2, no. 1. Family Therapy Practice Center, 2153 Newport Place, NW, Washington, DC 20037.

Frazier-Kouassi, S., et al. *Women in Mathematics and Physics: Inhibitors and Enhancers.* Lansing: University of Michigan, 1992.

Gardner, A. L., C. L. Mason, and M. L. Matyas. "Equity, Excellence, and 'Just Plain Good Teaching.' " *The American Biology Teacher,* Vol. 51, no. 2, pp. 72–77.

Gilligan, C. "Joining the Resistance: Psychology, Politics, Girls and Women." *Michigan Quarterly Review,* 1990, Vol. 29, pp. 501–536.

Girls in Schools: A Bibliography of Research on Girls in U.S. Public Schools Kindergarten through Grade 12. Wellesley College Center for Research on Women, Wellesley, MA 02181–8259, 1992.

Graber, J. A., and A. C. Petersen. "Cognitive Changes at Adolescence: Biological Perspectives," in *Brain Maturation and Cognitive Development,* Gibson, K., and A. Petersen, eds. New York: Aldine de Gruyter, 1991, pp. 253–279.

Hall, R. M., and B. R. Sandler. *The Classroom Climate: A Chilly One for Women?* Project on the Status and Education of Women of the Association of American Colleges, 1818 R Street, NW, Washington, DC 20009, 1982.

Harris, L., and Associates. *Hostile Hallways: The AAUW Survey on Sexual Harassment in America's Schools.* American Association of University Women Educational Foundation, Washington, DC 1993.

I Can Be What I Want to Be. A career planning workbook for junior high school students and their parents, developed by the National Black Child Development Institute and the Women's Educational Equity Act Program, U.S. Department of Education, printed and distributed by the National Black Child Development Institute, Inc., 1463 Rhode Island Ave., NW, Washington, DC 20005.

In the National Interest: The Federal Government in the Reform of K–12 Math and Science Education. Carnegie Commission on Science, Technology, and Government, 1991.

Learning About Women: Gender, Politics, and Power. Proceedings of the American Academy of Arts and Sciences. February, 1989, Vol. 116, no. 4.

Lee, V., and A. S. Bryk, 1986. "Effects of Single-Sex Secondary Schools on Student Achievement and Attitudes." *Journal of Educational Psychology,* November 5, 1986, Vol. 78, pp. 381–395.

Lee, V., and H. M. Marks. "Sustained Effects of Single-Sex Secondary School Experience on Attitudes, Behaviors, and Values in College." *Journal of Educational Psychology,* September, 1990, Vol. 82, pp. 578–592.

Mason, C., J. B. Kahle, and A. L. Gardner. "Draw-a-Scientist Test: Future Implications." *School Science and Mathematics,* 1991, Vol. 91, pp. 193–198.

Math and Science for Girls. A Symposium Sponsored by the National Coalition of Girls' Schools, Concord, MA, 1992.

Matyas, M. L., L. Baker, and R. Goodell, eds. *Marriage, Family, and Scientific Careers: Institutional Policy Versus Research Findings,* proceeds of a symposium sponsored by the American Association for the Advancement of Science annual meeting. San Francisco, January, 1989.

Nicholson, H. J. *Gender Issues in Youth Development Programs* (1992), and Nicholson, H. J., and J. D. Frederick, *The Explorer's Pass: A Report on Case Studies of Girls and Math, Science, and Technology*, 1991. Both were published by Girls, Inc., National Resource Center, 441 West Michigan St., Indianapolis, IN 46202.

Petersen, A., and K. Hood. "The Role of Experience in Cognitive Performance and Brain Development," in *Genes and Gender: V, Women at Work: Socialization Toward Inequality*, Vroman, G. M. ed. New York: Gordian Press, 1988, pp. 52–77.

Petersen, A. C. "Adolescent Development." *Annual Review of Psychology*, 1988, Vol. 39, pp. 583–607.

Petersen, A. C. "Can Puberty Come Any Earlier?" *Psychology Today*, 1979, Vol. 12, pp. 45–47.

Petersen, A. C. "The Gangly Years." *Psychology Today*, September, 1987, pp. 28–34.

Petersen, A. C. and L. Crockett. 1987. "Biological Correlates of Spatial Ability and Mathematical Performance." *Annals of the New York Academy of Science*, 1987, Vol. 517, pp. 69–86.

Petersen, A. C., R. E. Kennedy, and P. Sullivan. "Coping with Adolescence," in *Adolescent Stress Causes and Consequences*, Colten, M.W., and S. Gore, eds. New York: Aldine de Gruyter, 1991.

Stein, N., N. L. Marshall, and L. R. Tropp. 1993. *Secrets in Public: Sexual Harassment in Our Schools*. The Center for Research on Women, Wellesley College, co-sponsored by the NOW Legal Defense and Education Fund, 1993.

Wellesley College Center for Research on Women. "How Schools Shortchange Girls." 1992. This report was commissioned by the American Association of University Women Educational Foundation and was published jointly with the National Education Association.

INDEX